DECISION-MAKING
GROUP INTERACTION

DECISION-MAKING GROUP INTERACTION

Third Edition

BOBBY R. PATTON
California State University, Los Angeles

KIM GIFFIN
Professor Emeritus, The University of Kansas

ELEANOR NYQUIST PATTON
Ph.D., The University of Kansas

HARPER & ROW, PUBLISHERS, New York
Cambridge, Philadelphia, San Francisco, London,
Mexico City, São Paulo, Singapore, Sydney

1817

Sponsoring Editor: Barbara Cinquegrani
Project Editor: Eric Newman
Cover Design: Joseph Cavalieri Graphics
Production Manager: Jeanie Berke
Production Assistant: Paula Roppolo
Composition and Text Art: ComCom Division of Haddon Craftsmen, Inc.
Printer and Binder: R. R. Donnelley & Sons Co.
Cover Printer: Lehigh Press

Decision-Making Group Interaction, Third Edition

Library of Congress Cataloging-in-Publication Data

Patton, Bobby R., 1935–
    Decision-making group interaction/Bobby R. Patton.—3rd ed.
        p.   cm.
    Includes bibliographies and index.
    ISBN 0–06–045066–5
    1. Small groups.   2. Decision-making, Group.   3. Social
interaction.   I. Title.
HM133.P37 1989
302.3′4—dc19   88–24329
                                                                CIP

88 89 90 91 9 8 7 6 5 4 3 2 1

Contents

Preface   ix

CHAPTER 1 / INTRODUCTION TO THE DECISION-MAKING GROUP   1

Definitions   2
A Short History of the Study of Small Groups   5
Premises   7
Applications   9
Notes   9

CHAPTER 2 / COMMUNICATION WITHIN THE GROUP   11

The Message   11
The Sender of the Message   14
The Receiver of the Message   16
Nonverbal Communication   21
Summary   26
Applications   26
Notes   26

CHAPTER 3 / THE ORIENTATIONS OF PEOPLE IN GROUPS   29

Motivations Toward Group Participation   30
Personality Factors of Group Members   33
Perceptions of Others   35
General Predispositions   38
Exchange Theories of Interaction   40
Summary   41
Applications   42
Notes   42

CHAPTER 4 / INTERPERSONAL BEHAVIOR IN GROUPS   45

Task, Maintenance, and Self-Oriented Behavior   45
Trust and Cooperation   48
Supportive and Defensive Behavior   49
Conformity and Independence   51
Choice Shifts—Safe or Risky?   53
Summary   54
Applications   55
Notes   55

CHAPTER 5 / LOGICAL PROCESSES AND PHASES IN DECISION MAKING   57

Group Development Theories   58
A Contingency Theory of Group Development   61
The Critical Assessment of Phases   62
Prediction from Past Experiences   63
Summary   66
Applications   66
Notes   66

CHAPTER 6 / THE PROBLEM-SOLVING FORMAT   69

Identifying a Common Problem   69
Analyzing a Problem   72
Evaluating Proposed Solutions   80
Implementing a Decision   81
Summary   85
Applications   86
Notes   86

CHAPTER 7 / LEADERSHIP   87

Characteristics of Leaders   88
Styles of Leadership   89
Situational Leadership   91
Task and Maintenance Functions   94
Group-Centered Leadership   97
Leadership Behaviors   99
Summary   100
Applications   101
Notes   101

CHAPTER 8 / GROUP CHARACTERISTICS AND THEIR EFFECTS   103

Norms   103
Cohesiveness   106
Task   109
Group Size   111
Gender Makeup of the Group   112
Summary   113
Applications   114
Notes   114

CHAPTER 9 / CONFLICT AND COOPERATION   117

Interdependence and Conflict   117
Conflict Within the Group   119
Conflict Between Groups   123
Promoting Cooperation   126
Summary   128
Applications   128
Notes   128

CHAPTER 10 / FACTORS THAT LIMIT GROUP EFFECTIVENESS   131

Procedural Problems   131
Process Problems   133
Personality Problems   138
Summary   139
Applications   140
Notes   140

CHAPTER 11 / EFFECTIVE GROUP DECISION MAKING 143

Strategies for Effective Group Decision Making 143
Lateral Thinking 146
Promoting Group Creativity 148
Summary 154
Applications 154
Notes 154

CHAPTER 12 / IMPROVING ABILITY BY OBSERVING OTHER GROUPS 157

Observing and Consulting with Task Groups 158
Interpreting Observed Group Behavior 159
A Model of Reporting 161
Applying Insights to Your Own Behavior 172
Summary 173
Applications 173
Notes 173

APPENDIXES 175

APPENDIX A / EVALUATING GROUP PERFORMANCE 177

Self-Report of Needs, Perceptions, and Orientations 177
Observational Approaches to the Study of Groups 192
Summary 209
Notes 210

APPENDIX B / A CRITICAL ANALYSIS OF FACTORS RELATED TO DECISIONAL PROCESSES INVOLVED IN THE *CHALLENGER* DISASTER 213

DENNIS S. GOURAN, RANDY Y. HIROKAWA, AND
AMY E. MARTZ

The Shuttle Launch Process 215
Failure of the Process 216
Conclusions 231
Notes 232
Works Cited 234

Index 237

Preface

The 15 years that have elapsed since the publication of the first edition of this text have provided an impressive increase in our knowledge about communication processes in group decision making. In this third edition we have attempted to sort, select, and focus on the new research that enhances our understanding of group processes.

Effective group decision making is vital to the maintenance of participative democracy. We believe it important to select for sustained analysis those communication practices, patterns, and circumstances that are likely to promote or inhibit group interaction. Our experiences in teaching about groups and in watching groups in action have provided us with a perspective that is both analytical and prescriptive.

Much of our lives, all of us are working with others, developing new ideas for our mutual benefit. Back in 1970 Alvin Toffler in his book *Future Shock* predicted an increasing emphasis on temporary groups brought together for a specific task and a decreasing emphasis on permanent states in bureaucratic administration. This prediction has been realized, and we can now envision a world with even greater opportunities for people to have a voice in decisions affecting their lives, a greater diffusion of relevant and useful information, and a greater need for all citizens in a democracy to be effective decision makers. These opportunities demand higher levels of communication training and skills.

We believe that education concerning decision making is at the heart of a liberal arts education. We agree with Dr. Jean Mayer, president of Tufts University:

> [People] need to learn to coordinate widely disparate pieces of information to form the basis of decision making, and they need to learn how to make a decision. In daily life, in every aspect of existence except for specialized scholarly research, synthesis of information plays a vital role in its analysis. The ability to arrive at complex decisions should be the hallmark of the educated person.*

We acknowledge the advice, assistance, and encouragement of our students, colleagues, and friends. Specifically, we acknowledge the contributions of Marilyn B. Heath, Michael J. Boring, Virginia L. Meserve, Heather Wukelich, and Larry Nadler in the preparation of the manuscript. Professional colleagues and students at the University of Kansas and Kuring-gai College of Advanced Education in Australia provided important support. We also wish to thank the following reviewers for offering suggestions on this revision: Teresa Barnes, Ohio State University; Rod Carveth, University of Hartford; Anthony Clark, University of Florida; Ted Gundel, Concordia College; Tom Jenness, University of Idaho; and Frank Lower, Louisiana State University, Shreveport.

Bobby R. Patton
Kim Giffin
Eleanor Nyquist Patton

*J. Mayer, "A Jeffersonian Ideal," *The Chronicle of Higher Education,* 10 (November 8, 1976), 32.

DECISION-MAKING
GROUP INTERACTION

chapter 1

Introduction to
the Decision-Making Group

In January 1986, the world was stunned by the explosion of the U.S. space shuttle *Challenger,* which resulted in the deaths of its seven crew members. After 24 successful space shuttle missions by NASA this accident was viewed initially as an inevitable cost of such pioneering efforts in space. Subsequent investigations, however, focused on NASA's "flawed" decision-making processes.[1] After public hearings on how NASA officials decided to launch *Challenger* on its doomed mission, former Secretary of State William Rogers is reported in *Time* magazine to have stated:

> "Does everybody know what everybody else is recommending?" He wondered aloud why those involved had not been required to take clear stands on life-and-death safety issues and had not had their positions recorded. And, Rogers concluded, he was certain the members of the presidential commission agreed with him that NASA's decision-making process "shows a serious deficiency" and was "clearly flawed."[2]

The decision-making processes of the NASA officials were held up to rigorous scrutiny and criticism. Since the group had obviously arrived at the wrong decision, the decision-making *process* needed to be examined to discover why things went wrong.[3]

The significance of groups in our culture is no longer subject to controversy. There are literally more groups than people in the United States, for each of us is a member of a number of groups, often diverse in their nature. These groups have immense impact on our daily lives as we invest our time, livelihood, and well-being in them. Further, groups to which we do not belong may determine our fates: a selective service board, the president's economic advisers, a university's educational policies committee, or a NASA administrative team.

Groups have long fascinated behavioral scientists. In this chapter we shall attempt to set the parameters for this text by defining key terms, examining briefly the background of group research, and previewing the premises of the book.

DEFINITIONS

Decision making in a group involves people talking together for the purpose of cooperatively resolving a mutual concern. This process is the essence of democratic action. It is cooperative in that all viewpoints need to be voiced (although a view held by several persons actually may be voiced by only one). It is purposive in that an attempt is made to identify and resolve a need felt by a number of people. In many cases the membership of a group—who is *in* the group and who is *not*—is determined by the *degree of concern mutually shared* by the group members.

A mutual concern may be the need for agreement on a policy committing group members to a selected way of behaving. The word *committee* connotes mutual commitment. A mutual concern that requires group action is one that each individual, working alone, probably could not resolve. Even if the concern is simply to *be* with other people, to share thoughts and feelings, certain ways of behaving are facilitative and desirable. If the concern is one that requires a pooling of resources—material, energy, time, and effort—it is even more important to reach a commitment that allows personal interdependence.

The decisions sought by groups cover a wide range of goals and conditions. A group of students and teachers attempts to develop a new set of required courses for a major academic program. A group of students living in a dormitory reaches an agreement on a revised set of rules for behavior in their living area. Two families share their resources and build a beach cabin. A small part of an industrial organization prepares a report defining a company problem, evaluating a proposed change in policy, or outlining a specific plan of action. Six commuters arrange a route and time for departure for a car pool. An industrial "task group" prepares a plan for reducing air pollution in a chemical fertilizer plant. People living within a city block, most of whom would hardly recognize each other on the street, meet and develop a neighborhood youth recreation center, a Scout troop, a new agreement regarding the renting of their houses, or a Saturday evening get-together.

In each of these examples are certain common factors: identifying a mutual concern, analyzing a situation, and producing a desired change in the form of a contract, a product, an event, or a procedure.

The term *group* has proved difficult to define. A history of the study of groups could be written in terms of a series of concepts—society, primary groups, reference groups, membership groups, and small groups—moving from higher to lower levels of abstraction. As the social psychologist Theodore Newcomb has observed, "The term 'group' . . . has achieved no standard meaning."[4]

Today the most common working definition of a group involves two elements: It is a small number of individuals in interdependent role relations, and it has a set of values (norms) that regulate the behavior of members in matters of concern to the group. Thus, this definition relates both to the size of the group and to an individual's behavior as it affects other individuals in the group.

A large number of experimental or laboratory studies use the definition developed by Bales: A "group [is] any number of persons engaged in a single face-to-face meeting or series of meetings in which each member receives some impression of each other member . . . as an individual person, even though it be only to recall that the other person was present."[5] This definition seems to imply a limited number of persons, but says little about their behavior.

Another definition frequently used by researchers who work with natural, "real-life" groups implies almost any collection of people. This usage specifies neither size nor behavior. For example, a study by Venable dealt with "a relatively stable group" of college students; this group consisted of 42 women taking the same academic course.[6] Homans not only used the term to refer to a primitive tribe, a street gang, a roomful of factory workers, and a New England village, but also made inferences from the study of these groups *in combination.*[7] Such treatment seems to imply that "a group is a group," regardless of size or interpersonal relationships. Studies using this loose definition are frequently valuable, since typically they deal with "real," not laboratory-created, data; however, the research results must be carefully handled when compared with the results of other studies based on more restrictive definitions of the term *communication.*

By focusing on decision-making groups, we limit our concerns to situations in which members recognize that they form a unit and are acting intentionally together. We see five conditions necessary for such a group to exist:

1. *Two or more people* joined together by a common issue or concern. We are primarily concerned with groups small enough that the presence of each person is significant to the interaction process. When group size exceeds 20 people,

some loss of individual contributions can be expected. We shall describe studies that examine the importance of group size to the optimal accomplishment of task. Typically the "small group" consists of three to eight members.

2. *Interdependence.* We all know what it means to depend on another person, but if people depend on each other in equal degrees, so that they unavoidably influence each other, they are interdependent. The behavior of each member of the group determines and is determined by that of the others. This interaction can be viewed as circular, with cause producing effect and effect turning into cause as it feeds back to the original cause. Face-to-face interaction is thus required.

3. *A common goal.* A collection of individuals may board an elevator. From our perspective this collection is not a group. However, should the elevator fail to function properly and become stuck between floors, a group will be quickly formed as all the individuals become concerned with dealing with their mutual problem. People may join together to engage in issues of personal growth, which becomes the unifying goal. Even if the goal is not perceived as a problem to be solved, decisions will likely need to be made.*

4. *Communication.* Individuals working collectively on an assembly line do not constitute a group until they are interacting. Communication is required for individuals to coordinate and act as a single unit. How well group members understand one another—how clearly they are sharing their ideas, values, and feelings—will be important determinants of the effectiveness of the group. Communication includes all verbal and nonverbal behaviors to which meaning may be attributed.

    We object to the limited definition of communication employed by such renowned social psychologists as Ivan Steiner, who restricts it to motivation and coordination of member efforts.[8] Rather than consider communication from this limited perspective, we shall treat it as synonymous with the term *interaction,* including all the behaviors that occur in the spontaneous give-and-take among group members.[9]

5. *Norms.* A common set of values is necessary to regulate the behavior of members if the group is to continue to exist. Group members articulate their values and in the process

---

*We changed the title of this text from *Problem-Solving Group Interaction* in the first edition to *Decision-Making Group Interaction* for two reasons: People may have no alternative but to deal with issues that truly have no solution, and some task groups fail to perceive a problem orientation.

establish a consensus regarding judgments to be made. Unless people ascribe to the values of a given group, they will not choose to join or continue to be a member. Such norms allow members to think of themselves as a group, to have a collective perception of unity, a conscious identity with each other.

Thus, the group that will be the focus of this book typically consists of three to eight people with a common goal and established norms, who are interdependent and engaged in face-to-face communication.

A SHORT HISTORY OF THE STUDY OF SMALL GROUPS

Although the study of groups is largely a twentieth-century phenomenon, research began in the nineteenth century. This research focused upon "the pathological crowd," the nature of social-interaction processes, two persons (dyads) as the basic social unit, and the family as the primary group. Researchers were philosophically oriented in their investigations, and they argued about the fundamental origins of people's social behavior. The argument was between the environmentalist-behaviorists and the innate-environmentalists; the latter eventually won the debate. The controversy ended in the 1920s, when attention no longer centered on philosophy, but focused on the development of a more rigorous scientific methodology.

Kurt Lewin was instrumental in applying the experimental methodologies to the study of small groups in the 1930s. One of his typical techniques was to create different groups with known characteristics and observe their operation. For example, he might set up groups under different types of leaders, observe how the leaders acted and the members responded, compare the various interactions, and draw empirically based conclusions about the dynamic effects of leadership. Through such simple yet sound procedures, theoretically relevant hypotheses were tested under experimental conditions. Lewin was thus successful in linking group theory, real-world problems, and experimentation.

Research in the 1940s expanded in two directions: Extensive methodological improvements were made, and quantities of empirical knowledge were accumulated. Valid and reliable theory, however, remained sparse.

The field of small groups was accepted as a respectable area of study. Following Lewin's leadership, Morton Deutsch tested the differential effects of cooperation and competition in groups.[10] Alex Bavelas controlled experimentally who in the group could send information to whom and tested the effects of communication networks on group satisfaction and efficiency.[11] A major theme in post-Lewinian research has been the sociopsychological question of the group's effect upon the individual member.

Paralleling research on the nature of groups was the instruction in group process and discussion developing in the college social psychology and speech communication departments. Teachers were challenged to translate the findings of the researchers into methods of improving communication within groups. Business and industry joined this move as size and organizational complexity provoked problems of decision making at all levels.

The 1950s and 1960s saw a research boom. Of special significance was the contribution of Robert Bales.[12] Bales developed an empirical technique for observing groups in action. He applied a standard method of classifying interaction to determine how decision-making groups function in different phases of meetings and how the members assume duties that contribute to the well-being of the group. His work shifted attention from the group's effect on its members to the influence of certain variables upon the effectiveness of the group. How do variables such as leadership styles, member personalities, and group size affect the interaction process? Bales's observational technique has been used widely in studying groups and the development of theory.

Another approach to the study of groups is the "laboratory method" in which a group studies itself. In 1947 the National Training Laboratories were begun in Bethel, Maine. They were "designed to try out new methods for re-educating human behavior and social relationships." In these laboratory groups, called t-groups (for "training"), the members diagnosed and experimented with their own behaviors and relationships.[13] An enduring feature of the t-group throughout its development has been its emphasis on feedback, a built-in mechanism for personal change. Research in this area has tended to emphasize the possibilities for human growth when individual members expand their awareness of their own feelings and those of others.[14]

In the 1970s, group researchers made several significant contributions. First, the gap between the study of the individual and that of the group diminished; instead of viewing the individual as being apart from the group, often pitted against it and contending with it, researchers typically saw the individual as being *within* the group. Second, there was a shift from focusing on the external effects of the group to a genuine concern with group process; instead of measuring opinions before and after a meeting, researchers now tended to concern themselves with what went on within the meeting. Third, the laboratory groups provided self-analytical data, giving researchers new insights into emotions and feelings as they affect behaviors in a group.

In the 1980s investigations of small-group behavior once again affirm the fact that any major research effort faces a dual problem. Researchers must identify certain parts of their world to understand relationships among those parts—a process that may be called *conceptualization.* They must also develop ways of measuring those parts of their world—a process that may be called *operationalization.* Inquiries into the behavior of small groups have been plagued by the fact that the parts of reality to be studied and the ways in which they should be measured are neither obvious nor static—quite the contrary. Efforts have been made and are being made to find the most useful concept and measurement combinations at any given time and to adopt new, more useful combinations readily, as they are discovered.[15]

Researchers and scholars are attempting to tie the theories of small-group behavior to actual groups in operation. Unless a theory can be validated in operation, no purpose is served. The focus has moved from experimental laboratory groups to real-life groups studied without controls or manipulation. Real behaviors are thus the focus of contemporary research, rather than artificial ones subject to limited generalization. This book will attempt to provide research findings capable of being validated by the study of actual groups.

PREMISES

We believe that theories of decision-making groups should be subject to observation, application, and verification. As we examine various research reports, we shall note what seem to be the tendencies of most similar groups. Since each group is unique, all-inclusive generalizations cannot be made. On the other hand, to include all relevant qualifiers would make valid generalizations about most groups impossible. Therefore, we have attempted to walk the thin line between overstated generalizations and overly cautious reservations.

Decision making is a province claimed by many disciplines, for example, sociology, economics, psychology, management studies, statistics, operations research, education, social work, political science, philosophy, and of course communication. Thus, scholars of decision making differ widely in their models, approaches, methods, and applications. The common core in the research is the concern for communication and effectiveness.

In examining group communication as process, we wish equally to avoid explaining the behavior of the parts as being simply a function of the group as a whole and explaining the nature of whole as a total of all individual members' actions. Our goal will be to consider both the individuals involved and the group as a unit, noting the interaction within and the relationship between process and outcome.[16]

"If we can just talk it over we can find the right answer." This is one of a number of popular myths concerning groups. We shall try to point out the error of such myths and show how they can seriously undermine the effectiveness of decision-making groups. Good communication will not assure good decisions, but a group with communicative problems will have difficulty arriving at the most desirable outcome.

We believe that the study of groups is a serious component of higher education. We base this belief upon four major premises.

1. *The small group is an individual's defense against the dehumanizing aspects of a mass society.* The progress of society poses a severe threat to our individualism. As societal complexity increases, so does the necessity that people work cooperatively to survive and attain personal goals. The basic justification for a group's activity is that it provides individuals with the opportunity to develop their capacities. The enhancement of individuals in a group may take many forms, but when the group ceases to serve individuals and minimizes their worth, its usefulness ceases. Since individuals today experience a growing dependency on groups of all descriptions, it is important that people be familiar with the dynamics of group interaction. Once people have acquired an understanding of the nature of groups, the bases of their development, and their interrelationships with individuals and other groups, they have the capacity for greater prediction and control.

2. *Small-group methods are transferable to other life situations.* Research on groups is committed to understanding the behavioral functioning of human systems. Communication principles suitable to the decision-making group are readily applicable in such dyads as husband and wife, boss and employee, and parent and child.

3. *Small-group methods can educate individuals to improve the quality of their decision making by teaching them to be aware of the presence and dynamics of manipulative pressure on their life.* Group methods are sometimes criticized as manipulative devices, but an understanding of the potentialities of groups can provide insight for balancing coercive elements in the process. Behavioral choices occurring to individuals can expedite action by the group without infringing on their "selfhood."

4. *Understanding and applying the principles of group decision making and communication can make a group func-*

tion more effectively. As members of groups we have choices available to us that can enhance the well-being of the group both in arriving at a sound decision and in improving our relationships with the group members.[17] Historically, for example, the U.S. success in the Cuban Missile Crisis of 1962 can be partially attributed to the leaders' learning from the decision-making interaction problems that led to the ill-fated Bay of Pigs invasion in 1961.[18] It is hoped that the decision-making teams in NASA will now be able to correct and avoid the decision-making problems that led to the 1986 tragedy.

5. *A process has no beginning or end; it is not a thing to be easily observed and analyzed.* In the group, all of the elements are interactive; that is, each affects the other and is in turn effected. In dealing with this holistic phenomenon we have elected to focus attention on those factors that are important if we are observing or participating in group decision making.

APPLICATIONS

1.1. Meet in a small group of four to six of your classmates. Compile a list of all of the groups to which the members of your group belong. Classify the groups and discuss differences in the communication processes.

1.2. A number of groups are formed to deal with personal problems. Discuss any experiences in such groups, for example, support groups and church groups. How do the experiences in these groups differ from those in decision-making groups?

1.3. Attend a meeting of a campus decision-making group, such as a planning group for a dormitory or house party. Form impressions about the goals of the group and the ways in which the communication either helped or hindered achievement of the goals.

NOTES

1. *Time,* March 3, 1986, pp. 18–20.
2. *Time,* March 10, 1986, p. 34.
3. A special issue of the *Central States Speech Journal,* 37, No. 3 (Fall 1986), was devoted to studies from communication scholars of the factors that allowed the tragedy to occur. One of the studies is included as Appendix B.
4. T. M. Newcomb, "Social psychological theory: Integrating individual and social approaches," in *Social Psychology at the Crossroads,* ed. by J. H. Rohrer and M. Sherif. New York: Harper & Row, 1951, pp. 37–38.
5. R. F. Bales, *Interaction Process Analysis: A Method for the Study of Small Social Groups.* Reading, Mass.: Addison-Wesley, 1950, p. 33.

6. T. C. Venable, "The relationship of selected factors to the social structure of a social group," *Sociometry,* 17 (1954), 355–357.

7. G. C. Homans, *The Human Group.* New York: Harcourt Brace Jovanovich, 1950.

8. I. D. Steiner, *Group Process and Productivity.* New York: Academic Press, 1972.

9. See the study by M. S. Poole, R. D. McPhee, and D. R. Seibold, "A comparison of normative and interactional explanations of group decision making: Social decision schemes versus valence distributions," *Communication Monographs,* 49 (1982), 1–18.

10. M. Deutsch, "An experimental study of the effects of cooperation and conflict upon group process," *Human Relations,* 2 (1949), 129–152 and 199–231. Discussed in Chapter 12.

11. A. Bavelas, "Communication patterns in task-oriented groups," *J. Acoust. Soc. Am.,* 20 (1950), 725–730. Discussed in Chapter 2.

12. Bales, *Interaction.* This work is discussed in Chapter 10.

13. L. Bradford, J. R. Gibb, and K. D. Benne, *T-Group Theory and the Laboratory Method.* New York: Wiley, 1964, p. viii.

14. J. R. Ogilvie and B. Haslett, "Communicating peer feedback in a task group," *Human Communication Research,* 12 (1985), 79–98.

15. D. E. Warnemunde, "The status of the introductory small group communication courses," *Communication Education,* 35 (1986), 389–396.

16. A. Fuhriman, S. Drescher and G. Burlingame, "Conceptualizing small group process," *Small Group Behavior,* 15 (1984), 427–440.

17. J. D. Andersen, "Working with groups: Little-known facts that challenge well-known myths," *Small Group Behavior,* 16 (1985), 267–283.

18. I. A. Janis, *Victims of Groupthink.* Boston: Houghton-Mifflin, 1972.

chapter 2

Communication Within the Group

This entire book is about communication. Interaction among people refers to communication, although some researchers refer to group communication as only the amount and types of verbal messages sent. Recognizing that communication is the essence of the small-group experience, we feel that it is appropriate to focus upon key components in the communication process: the message (what is communicated and how), the sender or speaker, and the receiver or listener. We shall then consider some of the research that has focused on communication patterns.

In this chapter we have chosen to be both theoretical and *prescriptive.* We believe that skills in communication are crucial for the effective functioning of the group and offer our suggestions as guidelines.

THE MESSAGE

The semanticist I. A. Richards has aptly observed, "What is said depends on how it is said and how it is said on what is said. What we say and how we say it are inseparable. . . ."[1] As we discuss the message, we shall consider both what is said, and how it is said.

The content of our messages can be obtained from three levels of a person's personal experience:

1. *The perceptual level.* This level refers to a report from the sense data a person receives. From touching, seeing, hearing, smelling, and tasting a person can report these phenomenal data to others in the group. This level constitutes the first-hand facts that can be verified for accuracy. Like a witness at a trial who is restricted to personal knowledge, permitted neither to draw conclusions nor to give hearsay evidence, data at this level can approximate certainty. If members of the group are not in a position to "see for themselves," they can accept the perceptions of others.
2. *The cognitive level.* With clusters of perceptions and personal constructs, one can communicate a view of reality. This personal cognition is based upon inferences and includes conclusions drawn from facts. The facts of the perceptual level can be verified more easily than those of this level where conflicting viewpoints are likely.
3. *The judgment level.* A person can also communicate values about the world. Such judgments vary greatly from person to person since our ideals, morals, and bases for judgment vary greatly.

While the first level can approach certainty using a scientific mode of validation, the other two levels lack such conclusive validation and can only approach varying degrees of probability. The social sciences constantly confront such a perspective.

Our language presents additional problems of reporting. *In the first place, people view facts, events, and ideas from different experiences, from different frames of reference.* Someone who lives in Alaska certainly has a reference for the words *winter* and *snow* different from that of someone born and raised in Texas. In other words, through associating a word to personal experiences, and to the feelings the word elicits, individuals produce particular meanings. People see the world not as it is, but *as they are.* Their opinions, interests, motives, and attitudes differ from those of their neighbors. The total of their experience, thinking, and feeling gives them unique abilities to conceive and grasp an idea. No two people witnessing the same automobile accident will give identical testimony about it. A mountain means different things to a ski enthusiast, a lumberman, a miner, and a forest ranger. Ask 20 adults to define the word *happiness* and you will get vastly different definitions. People vary widely in life experiences related to culture, religion, race, politics, morals, and family background. They also differ greatly in personality and character, which affect their mental and emotional reaction to words.

Language scholars point out that people attach denotative and connotative values to words. *Denotative* meanings are logical, objective, and extensional. A denotative meaning points beyond a person's mind to the reality of the outside world. Denotation has an explicit referent, like the section on a map that represents a definite territory. We can, for example, point to the state of Nebraska as a geographical entity. We often associate denotative meanings with concrete or *name* words, such as *chair, bar,* or *wall.* Yet the terms *denotative* and *concrete* are not the same because an individual's frame of reference will determine whether words have implications beyond the naming of a real object. Clearly, to prison inmates, *wall* and *bar* will have meanings related to their particular environment.

Words also have associative value; *connotative* meanings are emotive, subjective, and intensional. To someone from West Virginia, the mention of Nebraska probably will produce only the denotation of a western plains state. However, to a person strongly identified with Nebraska, the word *Nebraska* may evoke so many personal feelings that an outsider can have little idea what the word actually means.

How the message is communicated is likely to be related to the basic intention underlying the message. We suggest four communication intentions that can account for most human efforts to achieve a desired effect or elicit a desired response:

1. *To maintain social contact and affiliation.* Much of our communication is designed to gain social validation from others. We may speak to people for years and not even know their names, but we mutually acknowledge each other. Such conversation remains rather superficial and includes little that is controversial or disclosing. The intent here is to be liked and affirmed. Initially in a small group, people will stay on this level until a task is presented or an issue evolves. Smiling and nodding affirmation continue to signal such an intention.
2. *To elicit and gain information.* This intention grows from a genuine need to know. Rather than a "How are you?" that reflects the first intention, this type of questioning is important for a group to utilize. Such querying can open the door for the necessary sharing of information and establishment of procedures and focus.
3. *To promote relationships.* Moving beyond the first intention, much of our communication is designed to promote a particular type of relationship. Dominant behavior signals attempts at leadership and may force others into submissive roles. Interdependence can be promoted by demonstrating affiliation and caring for the group.
4. *To change the environment and others.* Much of the work of a group is geared toward problems and tasks that require

changes. We may choose to participate in a group because of this option. Issues of power and control reflect this intention.

These intentions are operationalized as communication style. Norton developed an inventory in 1983, identifying both verbal and nonverbal behaviors that combine to form an overall image of one's communication style.[2] He presented 42 statements, such as "willingness to disagree," "making accurate statements," and ten subconstructs of communication style: dominant, dramatic, contentious, animated, impression-leaving, relaxed, attentive, friendly, open, and communicator image. The two subconstructs of *dominant* and *open* were most likely to provide clusters that were predictive of a communicator's overall style.

If an individual's intention, either conscious or unconscious, is to exert power over others, certain communication behaviors will reflect this intent: speaking louder than others, interrupting others, seizing opportunities to promote pursued ideas and feelings, and steering the topics of discussion. The person who is more relationally oriented will evidence a willingness to listen and understand other people's points of view, be more relaxed and willing to be open rather than strategic with comments offered.

This topic of communication style is an appropriate transition point to our next topic.

THE SENDER OF THE MESSAGE

Before you as a member of a group attempt to work with others to reach decisions, you should carefully evaluate your qualifications. You should determine (1) your own beliefs, (2) your true motives, and (3) your credibility.

Evaluating Your Own Beliefs

The first problem that you must confront is one that originates with yourself. Why do you believe that you should influence others? Who are you to tell them what they should believe or do? You will need to compare carefully your perceptions with theirs; insofar as possible you should do this without bias or prejudice. Look at their beliefs with an open mind, seeking to *understand* what they believe; this consideration includes an objective evaluation of *why* they believe it. In effect, you should ask them to *inform* you; that is, to *help you understand* the basis for their beliefs. As they do this, you should apply the criteria for credibility that we ask you to apply to yourself in the next section. You may be surprised to find that you and others do not really see things very differently—you only thought you did.

Or you may find that their view is more credible than yours. Be careful: Do not reject their views simply on the basis of your own personal biases; also, do not accept their views as better than yours unless you really become convinced that they are based on stronger foundations.

Examining Your Motives

Suppose, however, that others' beliefs are, in your judgment, unacceptable; you have sought to understand what they believe, and why, and you have determined that it fails to meet the tests of credibility. Suppose also, that you are convinced that you should try to help them adopt a different view: yours. You will need to look at your own motives. Is it just your ego or pride that makes you want to influence others? Do you want to "straighten them out," just to show that you are "better" in some way? Or are you motivated by a sense of responsibility, a desire to help them have a more useful view? Do you believe that changing their view can make their lives, as well as yours, more satisfying? It may bother you to recognize that how they act may influence your own happiness; perhaps you should recognize that you feel more psychologically comfortable if people you care about, or people in close association with you, act as you do. This may very likely be the case, and you may need to recognize that your motives are mixed or complex, that you are (1) somewhat concerned about the group's happiness and (2) also moved somewhat by concern for your own. Few of us do things for single, simple motives; fewer still do things for the pure benefits of others.

Assessing Your Credibility

The major task before you is to gain the group's respect for your ability to perceive and to understand the situation in question. This is clearly a problem of your credibility. Does your group believe in your ability to make relevant observations and to report them honestly and accurately? If you really do not meet these criteria, can you correct your behavior? If so, do so. However, more often than not, you actually do meet the credibility requirements, but your group does not realize this. Essentially, then, your problem is to establish your credibility *in their eyes.* Your goal is to present yourself and your message so that your listeners view you as a credible source. How do you do this?

Let's begin with expertise. Perhaps through a personal illustration, you can show your familiarity with the topic. You may also state directly what experiences you have had with the subject—why you feel qualified to discuss this topic. You will also enhance your expertise through a careful examination of evidence supporting your points. After all, experts are supposed to know the "facts" of the case, so make sure that you bring out the most important facts. The way you handle your evidence also makes a difference. For example, you will appear more knowledgeable if you are careful to cite your sources. Finally, experts do not guess; they are specific. Take the time to verify information so that you can be authoritative.

If you use evidence carefully, you also will have started to demonstrate your trustworthiness and your goodwill. To increase this trust, you will do well to display character traits the group holds in high esteem. Usually this means a degree of humility and an expression of warmth, friendliness, tact, and diplomacy. A genuine regard for the group's customs and manners, as well as for the occasion, will contribute to your trustworthiness. Goodwill can be demonstrated in various ways. For example, it is helpful to keep checking with group members to see whether they understand what you are saying or whether they have questions about your information. You can do this by carefully observing nonverbal feedback, from time to time even asking them whether they understand what you have been saying, and, if not, inviting them to raise questions. You can also tell them how they can get additional information on the topic.

We recall a group member who repeatedly said, "I'll be honest with you," or "to be honest . . ." When you sit back and think about it, what do such statements imply? First, we might assume that the speaker hadn't been fully honest with us except when he prefaced his comment with that phrase. Or perhaps he'd really prefer not to be honest with us. We get the definite impression that there may be times when he isn't honest or he thinks that his story is so unbelievable that we could consider him dishonest. In any case, doubt is implanted in our minds, for why else would he have to call our attention so frequently to his intent to be "honest"?

THE RECEIVER OF THE MESSAGE

Contrary to a common assumption, the listener role is not a passive one: It requires active involvement if communication is to take place. We have all learned to "fake" listening, to appear to be interested in a classroom lecture while our minds are elsewhere, daydreaming or engaging in private planning.

In fact, we have become quite adept at *not* listening. In our society we are constantly bombarded with noise, so we learn to close our minds to distractions. Our brain selects those cues that have significance for us. This capacity to ignore insignificant noise is a genuine blessing, but it can lead to bad listening habits. The listener determines whether communication will take place.

Listening for Information

Much listening in a group has for its purpose the obtaining and retaining of some form of knowledge. Not only must you listen for the content of the message, but you must also seek to evaluate its credibility: Should you believe what is said? To what extent does it agree with your experience, the reported experience of other persons in whom you have confidence, and the general wisdom accepted by most people?

Listening for an accurate understanding of the message as well as seeking to assess its credibility are important functions to achieve whenever you're a member of a group. However, although you are critically seeking to assess the credibility of a message, you must do so in a way that does not limit (1) your ability to receive it or (2) the speaker's ability to present it. If you are judgmental or hypercritical while trying to listen to a speaker, you may not be able to listen with an open mind. In addition, if your nonverbal behavior is negative, the speaker may become inhibited and falter in his or her presentation. It is not easy to be both open-minded and sensitive to credibility at the same time. However, this is exactly your responsibility as a listener in a group.

Listening for Decisions

Critical evaluation of ideas is essential to all of us in the decision-making process. However, to achieve this, we must hear fully what the other members of the group have to say—to hear them out and to avoid giving them negative feedback that will impede the full and free expression of thought and feeling. Usually this means suspending critical judgment until we understand their message. Too frequently we let our predispositions block new ideas or ideas contrary to our beliefs from entering our minds and fail to give them consideration. We have perfected the debater's technique of refuting point-by-point controversial ideas as they are presented to us.

Let's assume that a person is authentically trying to communicate with us. What critical assessments do we make after we have given a fair hearing to his or her comments? Begin by asking yourself four questions: (1) What is the speaker really saying? (2) Does the speaker make sense? (3) Why should I believe this? (4) Why is this so important?

1. *What is the speaker really saying?* In this first question our search is for the true meaning of the speaker's ideas. Are there hidden meanings? Are there double meanings? If the speaker's meaning appears to be obscure, we may search for

probable reasons for his or her not being more explicit. Deliberate ambiguity is a common tactic of people who feign good intentions in order to deceive listeners. Irresponsible speakers are frequently vague; they fail to use names, numbers, dates, and places, but rely on generalities of all sorts. Terms that mean vastly different things to different people, such as *truth, freedom, progress,* and *the people's will,* may be used. If the speaker's meaning is not clear, ask clarifying questions.

2. *Does the speaker make sense?* There are four common flaws in reasoning that you should watch for when you evaluate ideas: non sequitur, false causes, hasty generalizations, and the bandwagon appeal.

A *non sequitur* is an instance in which one statement does not follow from another. If someone were to say, "Enrollment in American colleges is declining; I guess I don't need to go to college," that person would be guilty of using a non sequitur. The mere fact that enrollments are declining says nothing about the value of a college education. This particular non sequitur is obvious to most of us, but some of them are much more subtle and much more difficult to detect. Unless a listener carefully reflects upon the sequencing of a speaker's statements, such errors in reasoning often go unnoticed.

A speaker commits a *false cause* fallacy when he or she ascribes something as the cause of an effect when in reality it is not the cause at all. When someone tells the group that we have to curb labor unions because the growth of labor unions has brought with it considerable unemployment, we can quite legitimately ask whether a causal relationship actually exists between labor unions and unemployment. Doesn't a general business recession often cause rising unemployment? We should always test assumptions of causal relationships. The following three questions are especially pertinent: (a) Is the ascribed cause the real cause? (b) Is it the only cause? (c) Is it an important cause?

We are all given to *hasty generalizations.* "I once had a German shepherd dog that was lazy. I just couldn't get it to do anything. I guess German shepherds just can't be counted on for much." Frequently we hear such statements in conversation. Similar statements find their way into group meetings. A hasty generalization occurs every time we generalize about something from too few instances. In the above statement the "expert" on dogs generalized from a sample of one. It is important that a critical listener ask whether the speaker's conclusions are drawn from sufficient examples. In others words, does it make sense to generalize from the data base the speaker is using?

The *bandwagon appeal* suggests that we should believe something because "everybody believes it," or it suggests that we do something because "everybody is doing it." People may be convinced by this "follow the crowd" form of reasoning. In such cases people surrender individuality and bow to conformity. Whenever a speaker is trying to ground an argument in the thought that "it is commonly held" or "everybody seems to be doing it," the listener should be wary. Does it make sense to do something merely because there are others doing it? A number of college students each year commit suicide. Does it follow, therefore, that you should commit suicide?

3. *Why should I believe this?* Before making a decision on an issue we should become thoroughly acquainted with the available supporting data. If the primary reason for listening is to find important information about a topic and its corroborating evidence, you should raise the question, "Why should I believe this?" If the speaker fails to answer the question, it is highly appropriate to ask questions about supporting evidence. We suggest that you ask: (a) What is the source of the speaker's claims? Do they stem from the speaker's personal experience? Statistical data? The testimony of authorities? Specific examples? Direct observation? (b) Is the source of the speaker's evidence reliable? Is the source competent to observe? Is the source prejudiced or biased?

4. *Why is this so important?* Debaters have for years used a device known as the "so what" technique. It consists of questioning the importance of the opponent's arguments. The "so what" technique is equally useful in evaluating the ideas of a group member. A speaker may develop a point with meticulous care but fail to demonstrate that it has significance. If so, you should rightly ask, "So what? Why is this important?" Certainly most commercial testimonials should receive the "so what" treatment. A prominent Hollywood star drinks a certain wine cooler. So what? A baseball superstar eats a particular breakfast cereal. So what? If a member of the group were to argue that you should oppose capital punishment because it was opposed by the greatest criminal lawyer of all time, Clarence Darrow, you should say, "So what?" What you should be interested in is Darrow's *arguments* against capital punishment.

This section on listening for decisions can be summed up with four words: *meaning, reasoning, support, significance.*

Listening with Empathy

As you listen both for information and to make effective decisions, you also need to be able to empathize with the speaker, that is, identify with the speaker's feelings and point of view. Gary Cronkhite has offered the following analysis:

> Empathy—the ability to feel and understand what another person is feeling and thinking—is probably the most valuable asset a communicator can acquire. Empathy is both a cause and an effect of successful communication. In fact, cause and effect in this case blend so completely that in a broad sense we can say that empathy is communication.[3]

Empathic listening can only occur in an atmosphere of responsibility and trust. Judgment and evaluation are typical and habitual human reactions. We have been accustomed to making quick judgments about whether or not something is desirable. We have learned to listen defensively with the intent of protecting our own positions: "I'll listen, but my mind is made up!" The problem comes when we don't listen to one another, when we make an evaluation of another person's point of view or frame of reference before we understand it.

Research suggests the adverse affects of a judgmental audience. Jack Gibb made a detailed study of group behavior by analyzing tapes of group discussions and reported three effects of judgment by the listener:

1. The listener is prevented from concentrating on the message as sent.
2. The listener distorts the message.
3. The listener misses the cues that indicate the motives, values, and emotions of the sender.[4]

Gibb's conclusion is that judgment arouses devastating doubts about ourselves that distort our ability to hear accurately. A judgmental atmosphere creates problems for the speaker as well as the listener. No doubt you have been in situations where it was difficult to share your thoughts because the listeners did not appear to understand or agree with what you were saying. The listeners in a judgmental condition may shake their heads in disagreement or interrupt the speaker. The speaker's attention may be diverted and delivery may suffer. It is frustrating to be put on the defensive when we are trying to communicate something important.

Listening with empathy requires that we temporarily suspend our own frame of reference and try to get into the speaker's inner world as he or she experiences it. This does not mean, however, that we necessarily agree with what the speaker has said, only that we genuinely understand the point of view and the feelings about it.

Empathic listening helps speakers understand themselves better. Carl Rogers has hypothesized that the more empathic our listening, the more willing and able the speaker will be to express feelings, give meanings to these feelings and try out new ideas.[5]

Empathic listening is a difficult skill, but we believe that it is such a powerful aid to communication that even when a person tries and only partially succeeds, the mere attempt may help the communication. Such an attempt is in itself an expression of respect for the speaker's views, a statement of caring in this situation, and most important, a desire for understanding.

While members of a group are sending and receiving verbal messages, they are simultaneously sending nonverbal messages. We shall next examine in greater detail nonverbal communication.

NONVERBAL COMMUNICATION

Social scientists have studied postures and gestures and attempted to "read a person like a book." We can tell a great deal about another person by his or her bodily communication, but problems result when we attempt to use generalized rules in order to create a certain impression. Researchers have suggested that when there is an incongruity between the verbal and the nonverbal messages, we tend to believe the nonverbal one. This reaction is based on the belief that nonverbal communication is less conscious and more revealing of a person's true internal state than words. Efforts to make our nonverbal communication appear conscious and strategic thus defeat the value of its unconsciousness.

Our bodies often betray deception. One study has suggested that when people are trying to be persuasive and strategic, they engage in higher rates of head nodding and gesturing, more facial expression and higher degrees of speech rate, speech volume, intonation, and smoothness of speech than when they are trying to be more objective.[6] In experiments, participants were asked to give persuasive arguments for stands on issues they did not hold as well as for stands they held. When deceitfully trying to convince other participants about something that they themselves did not believe in, the speakers had less-frequent body movements, leaned or turned away more from the other members, smiled more, and talked less (more slowly, with more speech errors). It appears that people are more animated in their movements when they believe in what they are arguing for and more controlled and contained when they are being deceitful.[7]

Gestures, particularly hand and arm movement (but including other elements of bodily movement, such as head nodding, slumping, foot shifting, etc.), perform several functions: illustrating an idea, expressing an emotional state, and signaling by using a conventional or agreed-upon sign. Illustration of an idea or object is usually connected to verbal speech. Nonverbal illustrations are iconic; that is, they show movements or relationships (shape, distance) with hands, arms, and so on that show similarity to an object or condition. They are especially useful in describing an idea that is difficult or inconvenient to explain in words, by use of pointing, showing spatial relationships and direction.[8] Another study has shown that people who have greater verbal facility also use more gestures.[9]

Although facial expressions generally are more dependable for inference of an emotional state, gestures and hand movements also display emotions. These movements are often diffuse, meaningless, and idiosyncratic (peculiar to individuals).[10] Hand movements especially convey the level of excitement of a speaker: hands waving, clutching each other, straining. Anxious speakers often exhibit such message-irrelevant but emotionally telling nonverbal signs despite the speaker's attempts to conceal them.

Gestures, especially hand movements, may reveal feelings and emotional states that persons don't intend to reveal.[11] Many of these feelings or attitudes are directed toward oneself.[12] Self-directed gestures may include covering the eyes, touching or covering parts of the face, and other hand movements designed to groom or hide parts of one's body. Such movements are frequently indicative of shame or embarrassment.[13] One research team asked subjects to view a film and then describe their feelings honestly in one interview and dishonestly in another. Observers were able to identify twice as many self-directed motions when the subjects gave dishonest reports; further, they rated the dishonest reports significantly lower in credibility.[14]

On the other hand, many people are quite aware that small, unobtrusive movements may reveal more of their emotions or feelings than they wish to reveal. To compensate, they may be fairly clever at deliberately using other movements to convey a contradictory impression. For example, artifice may be used to show confidence in order to conceal real anxiety. In such a case, gestures that can usually be taken as indexical (the result of an inner emotional state) are being faked; such gestures should be interpreted only with considerable care. As a participant in a group, you should be concentrating on your message rather than on yourself. You should be concerned with "How clear is my message?" rather than with "How do they see me?" If the topic you are discussing is truly important to you and important for the other members of your group, then your bodily actions will reflect this urgency.

As an observer, you can tell a great deal about the group by its nonverbal messages. For example, if a speaker sits facing away from other members of the group, a degree of aloofness or separateness is conveyed. Similarly, if all the members of the group are leaning forward, looking at each other, and speaking intently, then the group is obviously keenly involved and working together. A great deal of the coding discussed in the appendix is tied to nonverbal messages.

Communication Patterns

A major issue in the future development of small-group research is directly related to the study of communication patterns: whenever a group is studied, rather than considering only two or three variables at a time, many researchers are employing the systems research approach, measuring all known variables at once.

The study of communication patterns in groups is a major step in the direction of systems research in group behavior. Few scholars in small-group research have noted this point; consequently, exploratory efforts at systems research have not taken full advantage of the existing knowledge of all identifiable variables. But the approach employed is a significant start.

One approach that employs a systems research orientation is that taken by Bavelas in his study of "nets" in group communication.[15] "Nets" refers to the communication linkage between members of a group: Who speaks to whom? Bavelas diagrammed the net with arrows showing the initiator and receiver of each message. He clearly was interested in the relationships between communication patterns and other variables of group behavior. However, for the experiment, communication patterns were highly constricted, limited to either-or and some-or-none communication opportunities between selected individuals in a group. For example, one type of net would allow person A to communicate with person B, and B with C, but not allow A to communicate with C. Extensions were made of such "chain" patterns, together with the development of "circular" patterns and "wheel" patterns (one person at the "hub"). (See Figure 2.1.)

A further experimental condition, apparently imposed for a careful control of message content, was the limitation of communication to written messages. Such experimental conditions severely limit the value of inferences that may be drawn from the data so collected.

The primary concept developed from the group communica-

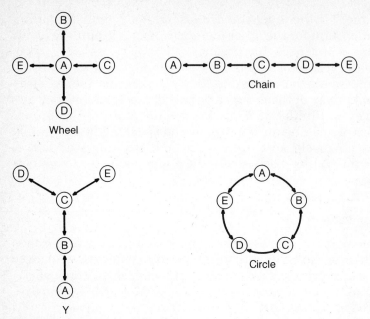

Figure 2.1 Patterns of communication.

tion net studies is that of *centrality.* This concept was operationally defined as the *sum* of linkages required for all members to communicate directly or indirectly or both with all other members of the group, *divided by* the *sum* of the linkages needed by one member of the group to communicate with each of the other members. Thus in an A–B–C–D–E chain, C has the highest centrality. Studies have typically determined the relationship between centrality and one or more of the major variables of group behavior. It has been determined that a position of high centrality in a group produces recognizable leadership role functions and higher status.[16] Shaw found that the degree of centrality was directly correlated with the number of messages initiated and received.[17] Leavitt found centrality directly associated with job satisfaction and role-function satisfaction. Although these findings may be true for the single individual enjoying high centrality, Shaw also found that the group in general shows more satisfaction with nets having less total centrality.[18] In another study Shaw found greater speed and accuracy of communication in nets having a greater degree of centrality, if the problem confronting the group was simple; however, if the problem was complex, nets with low centrality were faster and more accurate, probably because a complex problem more quickly taxes the abilities of the person in the central position, creating a saturation point or bottleneck.[19]

Consider the implication of the typical pattern of communication of two hypothetical football teams.[20] Head coaches have several assistants with specific assignments: offensive backfield, defensive linemen, offensive ends, and so on. The Wildcats head coach is quite independent, so he gathers information from each of his assistants and makes the strategy decisions himself (wheel pattern). The Raiders head coach relies heavily upon staff meetings in which the entire coaching staff participates in the decision making (circle). Thus, the Wildcats rely on a one-way process with little communication among the assistants, while the Raiders share in the pool of information and the decisions. The wheel pattern used by the Wildcats is highly centralized, while the circle pattern of the Raiders is decentralized. Which pattern is likely to be more successful?

For simple tasks the centralized pattern permits groups to perform better than the other patterns. The head coach of the Wildcats can piece the information together and make quick decisions. During a game this situation would be superior when decisions must be made quickly and the time for discussion is limited. However, as tasks become more complex, the centralized pattern is less satisfactory. Thus, in pregame strategy sessions the circle pattern of the Raiders is likely to be superior. Also, the Wildcat assistant coaches are more likely to become dissatisfied with their jobs and move on to other jobs.

Ultimately the greatest advantage would result from flexible communication patterns. Flexibility would permit a decentralized pattern before a game and a centralized pattern during the game itself.[21]

The studies on communication patterns and nets that we have cited are illustrative; many more have been completed with results essentially in agreement. The results obtained, however, must be viewed as mainly suggestive because of the limitations imposed by experimental conditions. Even so, the approaches made are important because of their proximity to a systems research orientation. This orientation holds the key to future definitive research on small-group behavior.

Brant Burleson and his colleagues hypothesized that an open exchange of information, opinions, and criticism is necessary for optimal decision making in complex tasks. They devised a study to determine whether groups employing such interaction procedures produce better decisions than groups employing either averaging or nominal decision procedures. Their work confirmed their hypothesis, even though two groups produced consensual decisions lower in quality than the conclusions that would be reached simply by averaging individual preferences. The researchers conclude: "Thus, while social interaction may not result in better decisions for all tasks, it is likely that social interaction will result in high quality decisions on 'everyday' group decision-making tasks."[22] Effective interaction will likely result in better decisions, whereas ineffective interaction or a lack of interaction will likely result in relatively poor decisions.

SUMMARY

Effective communication is the essence of group decision making. The ability of group members to speak and listen in such a manner as to share meanings permits the group to function as a unit. We have suggested skills that we feel are important to the speaker and the listener.

The effects of communication within a group have been studied in two ways: by careful observation by an outside researcher and by imposing some communication pattern on a group. Observation studies have shown that over time group members vary in the quantity and quality of their contributions. In this chapter we have examined the importance of both verbal and nonverbal messages within the group. Either as participants in a group or as observers of group process we should be aware of the range of messages and the outcomes of the options taken. The experimental study of patterns indicates that the more centralized the group structure (that is, the greater the extent to which one member can exchange messages with others), the greater the speed and accuracy in solving simple problems, and the lower the morale and satisfaction of the members.

Now that we have considered communication as the focal process in the group, let us consider how people's orientations impact upon the quality of decisions.

APPLICATIONS

2.1. In a small group, discuss the four communication intentions described in this chapter. How are these intentions reflected in different groups?

2.2. Select a television speech and as a group evaluate the speaker in terms of the logic or logical problems being demonstrated.

2.3. Divide your group into teams to play the game Charades. After each team has made a presentation, reflect and identify the behaviors that were iconic, indexical, and symbolic.

NOTES

1. I. A. Richards, "The future of poetry," *The Screens and Other Poems.* New York: Harcourt, Brace and World, 1960, p. 122.

2. R. Norton, *Communication Style.* Beverly Hills, Calif.: Sage, 1983.

3. G. Cronkhite, *Public Speaking and Critical Listening.* Menlo Park, Calif.: Benjamin/Cummings, 1978, pp. 38–39.

4. J. Gibb, "Defensive communication," *ETC,* 22 (June 1965), pp. 221–229.
5. C. R. Rogers, *On Becoming a Person.* Boston: Houghton Mifflin, 1961, pp. 330–331.
6. P. Ekman and W. Friesen, "Nonverbal leakage and clues to deception," *Psychiatry* (1969), 32, 80–106.
7. A. Mehrabian and M. Williams, "Nonverbal concomitants of perceived and intended persuasiveness," *Journal of Personality and Social Psychology* (1969), 13, 37–58.
8. J. Graham and M. Argyle, "A cross-cultural study of the communication of extra-verbal meaning of gestures," *International Journal of Psychology,* 24 (1975), 21–31.
9. J. C. Baxter, "Gestural behavior during a brief interview as a function of cognitive variables," *Journal of Personality and Social Psychology,* 8 (1968), 303–307.
10. P. Ekman and W. Friesen, "Nonverbal behavior in psychotherapy research," *Research in Psychotherapy,* 3 (1968), 179–216.
11. M. Rudden, "A critical and empirical analysis of Albert Mehrabian's 3-dimensional theoretical framework for nonverbal communication." Ph.D. dissertation, Pennsylvania State University, 1974, 12–22.
12. N. Freedman and S. T. Hoffman, "Kinetic behavior in altered clinical states: Approach to objective analysis of motor behavior during clinical interviews," *Perceptual and Motor Skills,* 24 (1967), 527–539.
13. P. Ekman and W. Friesen, "The repertoire of nonverbal behavior: categories, origins, usage, and coding," *Semiotics,* 1 (1969), pp. 49–98.
14. P. Ekman and W. Friesen, "Hand movements," *Journal of Communication,* 22 (1972), 353–374.
15. A. Bavelas, "Communication patterns in task-oriented groups," *Journal of the Acoustical Society of America,* 22 (1950), 725–730.
16. J. C. Gilchrist, M. E. Shaw, and L. C. Walker, "Some effects of unequal distribution of information in a wheel group structure," *Journal of Abnormal Social Psychology,* 49 (1954), 554–556.
17. M. E. Shaw, "Group structure and the behavior of individuals in small groups," *Journal of Psychology,* 38 (1954), 139–149.
18. H. J. Leavitt, "Some effects of certain communication patterns on group performance, *Journal of Abnormal Social Psychology,* 46 (1951), 38–50.
19. M. E. Shaw, "Some effects of problem complexity upon problem solution efficiency in different communication nets," *Journal of Experimental Psychology,* 48 (1954), 211–217.
20. This analysis is suggested by K. J. Gergen and M. M. Gergen, *Social Psychology.* New York: Harcourt Brace Jovanovich, 1981, pp. 448–450.
21. T. B. Roby, *Small Group Performance.* Chicago: Rand McNally. 1968.
22. B. B. Burleson, B. J. Levine, and W. Samter, "Effects of decision-making procedure on the quality of individual and group decisions." Paper presented at the Speech Communication Association, November 1983.

chapter 3

The Orientations
of People in Groups

People are truly social creatures. One's definitions and evaluations of "self" are largely reflections of judgments expressed by other people. Young children quickly learn to adapt to the people around them by putting on different masks, as it were, to incur favor and receive positive reinforcements. Reliance upon and adaptation to other people is the subject of this chapter.

Initially, we shall be concerned with the orientation of people within groups. What is going on within each participant that makes him or her want to participate in a particular group and determines the extent and degree of such participation? People bring with them to any group various attitudes and opinions, and these views typically influence group decisions. Throughout our lives we have developed dispositions that influence our interaction with other people. The extent to which someone enjoys being with other people reflects his or her individualized basic orientation. Anxieties, prejudices, biases, and defensiveness are also present in all of us to some extent. The bases of these orientations and attitudes begin in our infancy, when we depend upon other people for our survival. To cite all the dispositions potentially significant in group interaction would be impossible, but we can note certain general categories likely to be important in group decision making.

MOTIVATIONS TOWARD GROUP PARTICIPATION

Why do people choose to align with a particular group, give to the group, and even make sacrifices for that group? The answer to this question requires an examination of human motivation. The question becomes "To what goal is one motivated?"

Motivation may be viewed as a force that impels individuals toward, or repels them from, conditions, events, objects, or people. This, the traditional view of motivation, is concerned with behavior in terms of the goal that provides the stimulus. Obviously, people may perform one act for different reasons or different acts for only one reason. The need for social acceptance, for example, may impel one person to succeed in school and another to drop out of school.

Why do people seek election to school boards, city councils, and university committees? We are only able to infer in individual cases from the observed behavior of the person. All of a person's behavior—thoughts and actions—is directed toward the satisfaction of some drive, whether conscious or unconscious. Theory is not sophisticated enough to account for all behavior, but all overt actions of people seem to be goal directed.

The drive to align oneself with a group can be physiologically or psychologically based. We join a protest group, for example, because of fears concerning our livelihood, our neighborhood, or our society. Our fears may be legitimate or imagined, but the point is that they are effective in impelling us to take action.

In his well-known theory of human motivation Abraham Maslow presented a hierarchy of basic human needs.[1] A distinction is made between *primary motives,* which are physiologically based, such as the need for oxygen, food, and water and *acquired motives,* which are social in nature and may have cultural derivations. Maslow devised an elaborate hierarchy of motives. The hierarchy, starting with the most basic, and thereby strongest drives, suggests that acquired needs are perceived as significant only after the more basic needs are met. This hierarchy of "prepotency" is as follows:

Physiological needs. Participating in a group may provide the means to economic gain that can be translated into food and shelter. Even when minimal needs are met, we are all interested in obtaining more and better rewards.

Safety needs. A secure social environment is one of the possible goals of a decision-making group. For example, labor unions and professional associations are often concerned with job tenure.

Belongingness, or love, needs. Animals are rarely found in solitude, and human beings are no exception. We enjoy being with people and feeling that we "belong" to a group. A member of a street gang reported this feeling in the following words:

> The fellows in the gang are fast guys and good pals. We were like brothers and would stick by each other through thick and thin. We cheered each other in our troubles and loaned each other dough. Nothing could break our confidence in each other.[2]

The particular group we choose for affiliation and social reward is somewhat dependent upon personality factors. One person chooses a church for social rewards, while another chooses a motorcycle gang. All functional individuals have a need for some "sense of belonging."

Esteem needs. Within a given group is the opportunity to gain personal reputation and reinforcement. Intercollegiate debaters may be recognized as outstanding researchers or persuasive speakers by their peers. Recognition might also come for being the fastest runner or the most conscientious. The group provides an opportunity for a person to be identified truly as an individual. A person's self-esteem can be enhanced if others communicate that they value him or her as a human being and an important member of the group.

Self-actualization needs. Socialization is essential for self-actualization. In addition to monetary, vocational, and social rewards, the group provides the basis for self-fulfillment. Our personal definition of happiness and life satisfaction is formed by the groups with which we affiliate. Conversely, frustration and despair develop from our own failures or from the unrealistic expectations of a group.

Any one of these needs, or a particular element of one of them, may well become the mutual concern of members within a group seeking change in the environment. Certain threatening conditions may be the object of mutual concern, such as war, disease, natural disasters, crime waves, or societal disorganization. Basic rights may become the object of mutual concern, such as the freedom of speech, a procedure for achieving social justice, or the opportunity to obtain information or knowledge. The establishment or preservation of such conditions may not itself be a basic human need, but it may well appear to be basic when it is viewed as a *requisite* for the achievement of one or more of the primary human needs.

A complication in applying Maslow's theoretical constructs is that identical needs may inspire different actions, while different needs may inspire identical actions. While active participation on a church board may spring from different needs among the members, in a social club or professional activity it may spring from similar needs.

A different, but not contradictory, view has been presented by Robert Ardrey in *The Social Contract.*[3] Ardrey feels that humans share three innate needs with all other animals. The first and highest according to Ardrey is *identity,* the opposite of anonymity. The second is *stimulation,* the opposite of boredom. The third is *security,* the opposite of anxiety. These form a dynamic triad. The achievement of security and release from anxiety present us with boredom. This is the psychological process least appreciated by most of our social planners: As we achieve increased affluence and decreased economic anxiety, we are likely to produce a bored society. A bored society cannot be a reality, however, if we persist in our search for individual identity.

All of us need to feel secure in our environment. This security is based largely upon trust in others and freedom from threat. To the extent that a group provides an opportunity for people to feel secure, members will be attracted to its environment.

All of us need the intellectual and emotional stimulation that arise from social interaction. When we make an effort to attend a meeting, we are hoping to be challenged by new ideas and the potential for action; no one likes a dull meeting.

All of us need identity, too. Identification involves the transfer of attention from "I" to "we." Personal concerns for self are fused with concern for the group. The climate and atmosphere of the group must make individuals feel that they truly belong and that their best interests are being met by the group.

We believe that this conception—the triad of identity, stimulation, and security—forms a framework for examining the differences in personal actions. People may be pressed into seeking stimulation from a group by boredom that has been brought about by the achievement of security and the denial of identity. Experiences in groups may satisfy this need for stimulation, just as the group at other levels may have provided security and an opportunity for identification. Within a group in which communication flourishes and anonymity vanishes, identity becomes possible and stimulation is provided.

In all groups there is always the necessity to construct enough order for the group to act cooperatively on behalf of its individuals and yet to allow sufficient disorder for each member to fulfill his or her individual potential. Such disorder may be called freedom. The problem is to provide the delicate balance necessary for the amounts of order required by societal groups and disorder required by individuals.

PERSONALITY FACTORS OF GROUP MEMBERS

A number of scholars have devoted thought and research efforts to identifying those specific personality variables that directly and primarily influence interpersonal behavior. William Schutz set out to identify the "Fundamental Interpersonal Relations Orientations," FIRO,[4] those basic ways in which people characteristically orient themselves toward other people. Through analysis of a large number of research studies—parental, clinical, and small group—Schutz found agreement on the importance of three areas: *inclusion, control,* and *affection.* His work demonstrates how measures of these three variables can be used to test a wide variety of hypotheses about interpersonal relations, leading to a better understanding of interpersonal behavior. Each of these three dimensions can be divided into two parts: (1) behavior characteristic of three interpersonal needs actively expressed by an individual toward others (that is, need to control others, need to be controlled by them, and need of affection) and (2) the subjective degree to which an individual wants such behavior directed toward him or her.

> *Inclusion* concerns the entrance into associations with others. The need of inclusion involves being able to be interested in other people to a sufficient degree and feeling that others are satisfactorily interested in oneself. Behavior aimed at gaining inclusion is seen as an attempt to attract attention and interest.[5]
>
> *Control* is related to interactions involving influence and power. It includes the need to be controlled by respect for the competence of others and to control others by being respected by them. It is the need to feel adequate and reliable and also to understand the basis of legitimate control by others. Control behavior is related to decision making and is implied in terms like *authority, influence, dominance, submission,* and *leader.*[6]
>
> *Affection* includes the need to love and be loved and to feel lovable. It is implied in the terms *positive feelings, caring, cool, hate,* and *emotionally involved.*[7]

To have satisfactory interpersonal relationships, according to Schutz, the individual must establish in each of these three areas a balance between the amount of behavior he or she actively expresses and the amount he or she desires to receive from others.[8]

In Appendix A we shall present a rating scale modeled after Schutz's FIRO questionnaire that can serve as an instrument to call attention to group members' interpersonal needs.

Unquestionably the leading and most influential researcher on group process in the past 40 years has been Robert Freed Bales of Harvard University. In 1979 he and his colleague Stephen P. Cohen published a new system for analyzing groups[9] (this system is summarized in Appendix A). Their analysis is based upon a well-developed personality system. They suggest that people's personality styles vary on three central dimensions:

1. *Upward versus downward.* People vary in their activity level within a group. Some people will be active, outgoing, and opinionated, while others will be shy or retiring. A group member who frequently gives information to others, dramatizes the situation, or gives suggestions would fall on the upward end of the dimension. Someone who asks for opinions and information would be at the downward end.

2. *Positive versus negative.* People also differ in their friendliness and sociability. Some are friendly, while others seem to be cold and isolated. A person who frequently shows unfriendliness or disagreement or offers disparaging opinions would be placed toward the negative end of the dimension. Someone who agrees and seems friendly would be at the positive end.

3. *Forward versus backward.* Some people seem to take their group participation seriously and are interested in working toward group goals. Others seem to reject group goals and are more interested in themselves. People whose concerns are with group productivity are placed on the forward end of the dimension. Such people would give opinions, frequently ask for suggestions, or show tension.

Bales argues that full appreciation of personal style requires ratings on all three dimensions. Thus the person who is upward, positive, and forward is one who takes a great deal of initiative, is friendly, and is interested in group goals. He or she might be an ideal member of many decision-making groups. In contrast, a person who is downward, negative, and backward is inactive, unfriendly, and antagonistic to group goals. Usually such a person would create problems in a group.

The Schutz and Bales conceptualizations are somewhat different, but they do have some degree of commonality: Upward-downward is related to *control;* positive-negative is tied closely to *affection;* and forward-backward has overlap characteristics of *inclusion.* Such three-dimensional views of personality are consistent with the work of other researchers. In Appendix A we will present ways of observing and categorizing the personalities of members of a group.

PERCEPTIONS OF OTHERS

In perceiving, or having thoughts about another person, people note certain features, movements, and sounds and form a mental image. The process of perception is generally believed to accomplish two things:

1. People record the diversity of data they encounter in a form simple enough to be retained by their limited memory.
2. They mentally go beyond the data given to predict future events, and thereby minimize surprise.

These two accomplishments of perception, selective recording and prediction, become the basis for forming our impressions of other people. In forming our impressions of others, we observe their actions and expressive movements, we notice their voices, and we note what they say and do as they respond to us and other stimuli. From these data we make inferences about their cognitions, needs, emotions and feelings, goals, and attitudes. Our actions toward them and prediction of future interactions are guided by these judgments. Simultaneously, others are making judgments about us that will direct subsequent communications to us. If our judgments of each other are correct, effective interaction becomes possible. If, however, our observations or predictions of each other are incorrect, communication is hampered and difficulties may develop.

As we interact with people we see or hear them do certain things; from these observed behaviors we infer or guess that they have certain personality characteristics, motives, or intentions. For example, we may see them smile and conclude that they are "friendly." This process of inferring traits or intentions is known as *attribution* and has recently become the focus of much interest and study in social psychology.[10]

In the development and testing of attribution theory, research has tended to support the following principles: (1) Much of the behavior of others that can be observed is trivial or incidental and is not valuable for drawing conclusions regarding personality or intentions—we must be carefully tentative in the attribution process; (2) the observable behavior of others is often neatly designed to mislead or deceive us; and (3) their actions are often determined by external factors beyond their control and *not* by their internal states, personalities, or intentions. As a result of these limiting factors, we must use attribution with care; however, our experience tells us that in large measure it often works for us very well. This is essentially true for attribution of general dispositions or intentions on the bases of numerous observations over extended periods of time. Further research has indicated that we can sharpen the use of the attribution process if we pay special attention to two types of behavior: (1) that for which the observed person could have had only one or at most a very few possible reasons (for example, a young man marries a crabby, stupid, ugly old woman who is *wealthy*) and (2) behavior that deviates markedly from widely accepted social norms (for example, a middle-aged bachelor cooks all his food over an open fire in the middle of his living room).

A group member felt ill and abruptly left the group in the middle of a discussion. At the next meeting the other members were asked why they thought he had left. Responses included various reactions: The member was angered over the low quality of the discussion and left in disgust; he had an appointment; he thought he had arrived at a good stopping point; he was reacting emotionally to one of the comments made by a member of the group. None of the group guessed the true reason, but all were willing to make inferences concerning the behavior witnessed.

It seems that the experience, and the learning that accompanies it, are vital in making accurate judgments of others. Small children become quite adept at "reading" their parents for indications of "how far to go" before actual punishment becomes imminent. Cues of threatened punishment are often interpreted with great accuracy. The child, however, is not yet a discriminating observer and may try unsuccessfully to generalize from his or her parents to all adults. In kindergarten, attempts to cajole the teacher through baby talk and acting "cute" may prove to be inappropriate responses to threatened discipline.

Intelligence as well as maturity should obviously be related to our skill in judging people.[11] Two kinds of capacity (relevant to our judgment of others) are correlated with intelligence: the ability to draw inferences about people from observations of their behavior and the ability to account for observations in terms of general principles or concepts. Investigators have been particularly concerned with *self-serving* bias, the tendency to see oneself as the cause of one's successes but to attribute failure to outside sources.[12] In one experiment teams were formed and given responsibility for governing a fictitious country in the midst of a revolution. At intervals new information was provided about the nation's economy, people's attitudes, and the state of the revolution. Many decisions were called for, and since the outcomes were uncertain, the researcher varied either periods of consistent disaster or consistent success. After each period, the members of the teams were asked the causes of their success or failure. Overwhelmingly when the groups experienced failure, outside circumstances were at fault, but when their actions were successful, they rated themselves as being responsible for the outcome. This study has obvious implications for the results of all group decisions.

Some of the most serious distortions in perception of new acquaintances come from their chance resemblance to people who were once important to us. This is the process that Freud called transference. A gray-haired woman in a group may be seen as a mother-symbol; those who enjoyed childhood dependence on their own mothers expect a similar acceptance from her, and those who found their own mothers hateful will anticipate that kind of personal relationship and perhaps guard against it. A dominant male may be a father-figure against whom men who have never worked out their parental conflicts will rebel. An older man may be perceived as a godlike person who has the power to solve all our problems. These are familiar transference patterns, but there are many others. The young man with horned-rimmed glasses resembles a fellow we used to know; until we learned otherwise, we expected him to behave as our earlier acquaintance did. We may feel let down because he does not exhibit the lively sense of humor we imagined he would have, or we may feel relieved because he is not so critical as we had feared. Often we attribute to "intuition" those immediate flashes of feeling about new acquaintances that lead us to feel that they will prove trustworthy, malicious, superficial, or kind. Actually, those strong impressions can be shown on analysis to arise from some resemblance, in physique, speech, manner, or relative position, to someone whom we earlier knew as trustworthy, malicious, superficial, or kind.[13]

First impressions, in addition to what they tell us about others, tell us about ourselves. A genuine dislike for an exhibitionistic person may suggest how strictly we forbid expression of our own exhibitionist drives, whereas a feeling of attraction to such a person may suggest that we would like to live out our own drives in this direction. Rather than dismiss the value of first impressions, we should attempt to determine the bases of our reactions and remain tentative in our evaluations.

In an ideal decision-making group individual predispositions would be discussed and evaluated openly. Individual members would try to understand each other's opinions and be aware of their own biases. Unfortunately, however, this process of opinion exchange and readjustment does not always occur. Individuals cling to their initial biases, distorting the final group decision.[14]

To illustrate, James Davis has carried out extensive research on decision making in juries.[15] In one study, more than 800 students were asked about their general beliefs in rape trials. From their responses, three different types of predispositions were identified: proprosecution, moderate, and prodefense. Groups with each category of bias were shown a videotape on which an accused rapist admitted the rape took place but argued that the woman not only consented, but initiated the action. The woman testified that the

man had misrepresented himself as a police officer and subsequently raped her. After witnesses on both sides gave testimony and
lawyers gave summary statements, the students were asked to give
their opinions as to the defendant's guilt.

The students' preliminary biases had a strong effect on their
evaluation of the case. After 30-minute discussions, the six-person
groups who indicated a proprosecution bias were likely to vote
guilty while prodefense groups voted innocent. Skilled lawyers are
appropriately concerned during the period of jury selection.

GENERAL PREDISPOSITIONS

In addition to the specific biases that we hold on particular issues,
we may also have general predispositions that influence our interactions with other members of a group. Milton Rokeach has suggested that people function in a continuum of degrees of open- or
closed-mindedness.[16] This approach identifies the characteristic
way an individual receives and processes messages from others.
Extremely closed-minded people are characterized as highly dogmatic and described as follows:

1. Likely to evaluate messages on the basis of irrelevant inner
   drives or arbitrary reinforcements from external authority,
   rather than on the basis of considerations of logic
2. Primarily seeks information from sources within their own
   belief system—for example, "the more closed-minded a Baptist, the more likely it is that he will know what he knows
   about Catholicism or Judaism through Baptist sources"
3. Less likely to differentiate among various messages that
   come from belief systems other than their own—for example, an "extremely politically conservative person may perceive all nonrightists as extreme liberals"
4. Less likely to distinguish between information and the
   source of the information and will be likely to evaluate the
   message in terms of their perceptions of the belief system of
   the other person

Essentially, "closed" people are ones who rigidly maintain a
system of beliefs, who see a wide discrepancy between their belief
system and those belief systems different from theirs, and who evaluate messages in terms of the "goodness of fit" with their own belief
system.[17]

Conversely, the open person is likely to be more receptive to
messages that are disagreeable and to be tolerant of differences.
This person will be likely to contribute to a supportive climate in the
group.

A slightly more elaborate classification of interpersonal predispositions has been developed by Karen Horney.[18] Horney was among the leading psychiatrists in asserting that neurotic difficulties must be seen as disturbances in interpersonal relationships. In her theoretical work, she classified people into three types according to their predominant interpersonal response traits: (1) moving *toward* others; (2) moving *against* others; and (3) moving *away from* others.

According to Horney's system, *going toward* others ranges from mild attraction to affiliation, trust, and love. Such a person shows a marked need for affection and approval and a special need for a partner, that is, a friend, lover, husband, or wife who is to fulfill all expectations of life and to take responsibility for good and evil. This person "needs to be liked, wanted, desired, loved; to feel accepted, welcome, approved of, appreciated; to be needed, to be of importance to others, especially to one particular person; to be helped, protected, taken care of, guided."[19]

Behavior identified as *going against* others ranges from mild antagonism to hostility, anger, and hate. Such a person perceives that the world is an arena where, in the Darwinian sense, only the fittest survive and the strong overcome the weak. Such behavior is typified by a callous pursuit of self-interest. The person with this interpersonal orientation needs to excel, to achieve success, prestige, or recognition in any form. According to Horney, such a person has "a strong need to exploit others, to outsmart them, to make them of use to himself." Any situation or relationship is viewed from the standpoint of "what can I get out of it?"[20]

Behavior that is characterized as *going away* from others ranges from mild alienation to suspicion, withdrawal, and fear. With this orientation the underlying principle is that one never becomes so attached to anybody or anything that he, she, or it becomes indispensable. There is a pronounced need for privacy. When such people go to a hotel, they rarely remove the "Do Not Disturb" sign from outside their door. Both self-sufficiency and privacy serve their outstanding need, the need for utter independence. Their independence and detachment have a negative orientation, aimed at *not* being influenced, coerced, or obligated. To such a person, according to Horney, "to conform with accepted rules of behavior or to additional sets of values is repellant. . . . He will conform outwardly in order to avoid friction, but in his own mind he stubbornly rejects all conventional rules and standards."[21]

Horney summarizes the three types as follows:

Where the compliant type looks at his fellow men with a silent question, "will he like me?"—and the aggressive type wants to know, "how strong an adversary is he?" or "can he be useful to me?"—the detached person's concern is "will he interfere with me? Will he want to influence me or (will he) leave me alone?"[22]

An additional psychological dichotomy remains to be noted: cooperative-uncooperative orientations. A predisposition to behave according to one or the other orientation exists in every individual. We will discuss this topic, the social exchange theory of interaction, in the next chapter. Our approach is based largely on the thesis that people interact with others in order to obtain something from them: An individual's interpersonal needs can be satisfied only through others.

EXCHANGE THEORIES OF INTERACTION

Various researchers, notably Homans and Thibaut and Kelley, have surveyed related evidence and developed theoretical models of interaction as "social exchange."[23] These models are based upon the premise that the cost of interaction to the individual, that is, cost in terms of giving something to another person, is balanced against the potential reward in terms of satisfaction of a personal need.

According to exchange theorists, just as our business lives depend on the delivery of goods and services for payment, our social lives can be conceptualized as a process of giving and taking, bargaining for the best possible deal. You may find this view of human nature to be cynical and negative, but before you reject it, consider some of the insights of researchers from this perspective.

According to social psychologists Gergen and Gergen, exchange theories rest on four assumptions:[24]

1. Human action is motivated primarily by the desire to gain pleasure and avoid pain. Each individual has different perceived sources of pleasure or pain. Even a self-sacrificing individual who is giving up apparent physical pleasure is doing so to receive greater gains, such as esteem from friends or blessings from God.
2. The actions of other people are sources of pleasure and pain. Most people place value on other people's love, regard, attention, assistance, and respect. Since other people's feelings toward us are so important, we can be hurt by negative remarks and criticism.
3. By our own actions, we can obtain pleasure-giving actions from others. We thus trade our own actions for the actions of others, just as we trade currency. If you want to receive affection from your friends, a good strategy is to act warmly toward them.
4. People try to achieve maximum pleasure at minimum cost.

Thus, people will expend as little effort as possible to secure maximum rewards. This attempt to minimize the pain while maximizing the pleasure has been labeled the *MINI-MAX strategy.* People may try to cut costs in relationships by resorting to tricks and fakery that, if detected, make others resentful or hostile.

These assumptions have been tested in a number of laboratory experiments.[25] The exchange theory of MINIMAX works because people receive satisfaction from mutually pleasurable exchanges and develop rules that ensure the maintenance of these exchanges. When people disagree on what constitutes an equitable exchange, on how much cost or benefit is attached to an action, conflict develops.

This theory of cost and rewards is highly influential on small-group research in such areas as trust, cooperation, norms, conformity, and roles. These behavioral implications will be the focus of the next chapter. Interaction patterns in groups depend in large part on the perceived rewards and costs. As communication scholar Stephen Littlejohn has concluded: "Groups are more or less functional for people to the degree that they result in outcomes more favorable than those people would expect from other alternative relationships."[26]

SUMMARY

All that we are influences our behavior in a group situation. The total study of psychology would contribute only a portion of the data needed for any global generalizations. Nevertheless, we have attempted to focus attention on certain intrapersonal functions influencing the behavior of all individuals in a group. A study of a group cannot be made if factors such as the following are disregarded:

1. The motivations of the people to engage in interaction: What are the needs, drives, and modes of fulfillment of each individual member?
2. The individuals' attitudes and value orientations that exist prior to the meeting and that characteristically influence their behavior: Is there dissonance influencing potential action?
3. The individual and collective prejudices and biases brought to the group: Do they limit the decision-making potential?
4. The self-conceptions of individuals within the group: Is self-determination present? What levels of consciousness are present in the group?

5. The degree of individual openness and willingness to communicate honestly within the group: Are the individuals able to disclose honest feelings rather than merely fulfill role expectations?

From these frameworks of interpersonal orientations we shall proceed in the next chapter to examine the overt behaviors that we can identify as influencing group productivity.

APPLICATIONS

3.1. Analyze some of the groups to which you have identified yourself as belonging in terms of the priority of needs described in this chapter.

3.2. Within your group, share initial perceptions that have been changed as a result of your interaction. How has your communication changed as you have grown to know each other?

3.3. Analyze your participation in groups according to the MINIMAX strategy. Relate this theory to groups to which you no longer belong.

NOTES

1. A. H. Maslow, *Motivation and Personality.* New York: Harper & Row, 1954, pp. 80–106.
2. C. Shaw, *Brothers in Crime.* Chicago: University of Chicago Press, 1938, p. 96.
3. R. Ardrey, *The Social Contract.* New York: Atheneum, 1970.
4. W. Schutz, *FIRO, A Three-Dimensional Theory of Interpersonal Behavior.* New York: Holt, Rinehart & Winston, 1958. Reprinted as *The Interpersonal Underworld.* Palo Alto, Calif.: Science and Behavior Books, 1966.
5. Ibid., pp. 18, 21–22.
6. Ibid., pp. 18–20, 22–23.
7. Ibid., pp. 20, 23–24.
8. Ibid., pp. 25–33.
9. R. F. Bales and S. P. Cohen, *SYMLOG: A System for the Multiple Level Observation of Groups.* New York: The Free Press, 1979.
10. B. Weiner, " 'Spontaneous' causal thinking," *Psychological Bulletin,* 97 (1985), 74–84.
11. D. K. Simonton, "Intelligence and personal influence in groups: Four nonlinear models," *Psychological Review,* 92 (1985), 532–547.
12. G. W. Bradley, "Self-serving bias in the attribution process," *Journal of Personality and Social Psychology,* 36 (1978), 56–71.
13. S. Streufert and S. C. Streufert, "Effects of conceptual structure, failure and success on attribution of causality and interpersonal attitudes," *Journal of Personality and Social Psychology,* 11 (1969), 138–147.
14. See P. B. Smith, "Social influence processes in groups," *Psychological Survey,* 4 (1985), 88–108.
15. J. H. Davis, "Group decision and procedural justice," in *Progress in So-*

cial Psychology, vol. 1, ed. by M. Fishbein. Hillsdale, N.J.: Lawrence Erlbaum, 1980.

16. M. Rokeach, *The Open and Closed Mind.* New York: Basic Books, 1960, pp. 61–64.
17. Ibid.
18. K. Horney, *Our Inner Conflicts.* New York: Norton, 1945.
19. Ibid., pp. 50–51.
20. Ibid., p. 65.
21. Ibid., p. 78.
22. Ibid., pp. 80–81.
23. J. W. Thibaut and H. H. Kelley, *The Social Psychology of Groups.* New York: Wiley, 1959. G. Homans, *Social Behavior: Its Elementary Forms.* New York: Harcourt, Brace & World, 1961.
24. K. J. Gergen and M. M. Gergen, *Social Psychology.* New York: Harcourt Brace Jovanovich, 1981, pp. 384–385.
25. See for example, E. B. Foa and U. G. Foa, "Resource theory: Interpersonal behavior as exchange," in *Social Exchange: Advances in the Theory and Research,* ed. by K. G. Gergen, M. S. Greenberg, and R. H. Willis. New York: Plenum, 1980.
26. S. W. Littlejohn, *Theories of Human Communication.* Columbus, Ohio: Merrill, 1978, p. 272.

chapter *4*

Interpersonal Behavior in Groups

We spend a great amount of our lives in groups of various sorts—the family, friends, teams, work groups, and so on—but rarely do we take the time to stop and observe what is going on within the group; what do the members' behaviors mean? One of our main goals here is to note and categorize some of the behaviors to become better observers and better participants.

In the previous chapter we discussed the orientations or predispositions that people have that influence their subsequent activities in a group. In this chapter we will discuss specific categories of behavior that make a difference in the group interaction.

TASK, MAINTENANCE, AND SELF-ORIENTED BEHAVIOR

One way of studying the behavior of individuals in a group is to determine what the group's function, or purpose, seems to be. When a member says something, is that member trying to promote the accomplishment of the group task, to maintain relationships among members, or to meet a personal need or goal?[1]

The primary goal of the group is to deal with a common task-oriented problem; certain behaviors can be categorized in terms of roles that facilitate and contribute to the decision-making activities. A member may enact a wide range of such roles in a meeting, behaving relevantly to the group's fulfillment of its *task* in the following ways:

1. *Initiating.* Starts the group along new paths, for example, by proposing the task or goal or by suggesting a plan of attack for handling a problem
2. *Clarifying and elaborating.* Interprets issues and helps clear up ambiguous ideas or suggestions, focuses attention on the alternatives and issues before the group
3. *Seeking information or opinions.* Requests the facts and relevant information of the problem, seeks out expressions of feeling and values, asks for suggestions, estimates, ideas
4. *Giving information or opinions.* Offers facts and information needed by the group, is willing to state beliefs and offer suggestions and ideas
5. *Evaluating.* Helps establish standards for judgment, offers practical concerns such as cost, operations, and implementation of a proposal
6. *Coordinating.* Shows relationships between ideas and may restate suggestions to pull them together, summarizes and offers potential decisions for the group to accept or reject
7. *Consensus testing.* Asks to see whether the group is nearing a decision, sends up a "trial balloon" to test a possible conclusion

Types of behavior relevant to the group's remaining in good working order, having a good climate for task work, and having good relationships that permit maximal use of member resources— *group maintenance*—include:

1. *Harmonizing.* Attempts to reconcile disagreements, reduces tension, gets people to explore differences
2. *Gate keeping.* Helps to keep communication channels open by suggesting procedures that permit sharing remarks, facilitates the participation of everyone in the decisions
3. *Encouraging.* Is warm, friendly, and responsive to others; indicates by a remark or by nonverbal communication (nodding, smiling) the acceptance of others' contributions
4. *Compromising.* Offers compromises that may yield status when one's own idea is involved in a conflict, admits errors and is willing to modify beliefs in the interest of group cohesion or growth
5. *Standard setting and testing.* Tests whether a group is satisfied with its procedures, points out the norms that have been set for evaluating the quality of the group process
6. *Relieving tension.* Introduces humor or other relief in a tense situation, helps relax the group

Every group needs both task and maintenance to accomplish its problem-solving mission; both types of behavior make positive contributions to the group's productivity. Other forces that are active in groups disturb the work. These underlying emotional issues produce a variety of emotional behaviors that may interfere with or prove destructive to effective group functioning. We have discussed some of the underlying causes of such problems. A member may respond to group problems in the following *self-oriented* ways:

1. *Fighting and controlling.* Asserts personal dominance and attempts to get own way regardless of others. Fighting may be the aggressive reaction of hostility toward the aspects of the problem that appear to be blocking our progress. Deep in our biological nature lies a suppressed tendency to be angry, to retaliate, to hurt, to punish. This is one emotional mode of responding to a problem. Aggression may actively strike out or it may be passive and appear as a resentful refusal to apply effort to the solution of the problem. Unfortunately, the fighting response tends to elicit the same response from other members of the group.[2]
2. *Withdrawing.* Tries to remove the sources of uncomfortable feelings by psychologically leaving the group. This flight is the tendency of a person who wants to run away from problems. The student who is failing to solve his college-work problems can escape to beer parties and bull sessions. The urge to flee, like the urge to fight, is a social reality in the group situation. A whole group may flee by tacitly agreeing not to talk about certain subjects.[3]
3. *Dependency and counterdependency.* Reacts to people as authority figures. When certain people are confronted with a problem, their natural reaction is to wait for someone, a leader, to lead them to the solution. In all of us there seems to be a wish for a savior who is all-knowing and all-powerful. Perhaps this wish for a perfect leader is reflected in a companion behavior: the unwillingness to use the imperfect leadership resources available, particularly within ourselves, when confronted with a problem. Dependency may manifest itself in the guise of its opposite, counterdependency, a rejection of the efforts of anyone who is seen as an overt leader or authority figure.[4]
4. *Fixation.* Responds to a problem by unwarranted rigidity and persistence in a stereotyped response. Fixation is particularly likely to be present when a group is confronted with a problem of great magnitude that appears impossible to

solve. In such case there will be repeated attempts to use solutions that are ineffective in achieving the desired goals.[5]

This list of self-oriented behaviors could easily be expanded to include such defense mechanisms as *projection* and *alienation.* The main point, however, is to bring to our awareness the reality of emotionality as it affects the progress of groups.

Task and maintenance behaviors are the most significant categories of group behaviors identified in the research. In 1950 Bales published his original system for observing group behavior.[6] He identified three categories of positive maintenance activities: seems friendly, dramatizes (tension release by joking and showing satisfaction), and agrees; three categories of maintenance behavior were cited as negative: disagrees, shows tension, and shows antagonism. Six task categories that were cited could be either neutral or positive: asks for suggestions, gives suggestions; asks for opinions, gives opinions; and asks for orientations, gives orientations. The division of concern for people and concern for task will be one of the major issues in any group. Individuals' behaviors correlate to the personality types cited in the previous chapter.

TRUST AND COOPERATION

As people work together in a group, they must rely upon one another in order to achieve their mutual goal. Such confidence, even in risky situations, depends upon feelings of trust.[7] Closely akin to trust and often included in research is the concept of cooperation. For example, in early research on these topics, Morton Deutsch determined:

1. As there is an increase in an individual's confidence that his trust will be reciprocated, the probability of his engaging in cooperative behavior will increase.
2. As the ratio of anticipated positive consequences over negative consequences increases, the probability of his engaging in cooperative behavior will increase.[8]

A great deal of research in this area is based upon a theoretical model called the "Prisoner's Dilemma."[9] This model is based upon a situation in which police are holding two men suspected of armed robbery. Since there is insufficient evidence for conviction, the men are offered a deal. If they both confess, they are promised the minimum sentence for armed robbery, two years' imprisonment; if however, only one of the two confesses, he will be considered a state witness and go free, while the other will get a 20-year sentence. If neither confesses, they can be charged only with possession of firearms, which carries a penalty of six months in jail. Without an opportunity for discussion, the two are locked up in separate cells, unable to communicate.

What should the prisoners do? Since six months in prison is obviously their preference, it makes sense that neither of them confess. "But can I trust my cohort to reach that same conclusion?" — "Can I trust him?" — "If he confesses, he goes free and I go to prison for twenty years." — "Maybe I'd better confess and either go free myself or get no more than two years."

Note the depth of the dilemma. Even if they are able to communicate and reach a joint decision ("neither of us will confess"), their fate will depend on whether each feels he can trust the other to support the decision.

Decisions are typically based upon the degree of trust as group members attempt to determine what action others will likely take. Consider all the "real-life" applications of this dilemma—in arms control, labor negotiations, and divorce proceedings. In a summary of 50 years of research on trust and cooperation, Deutsch concluded that in the cooperative situation there were greater coordination of efforts, less homogeneity with respect to amount of participation, more specialization, more rapid decision making, more achievement pressure, more effective communication, greater productivity, and better interpersonal relations. He stated:

> To the extent that the results have any generality, greater group or organizational productivity may be expected when the members of subunits are cooperative rather than competitive in their interrelationships. The communication of ideas, coordination of efforts, friendliness, and pride in one's group which are basic to group harmony and effectiveness appear to be disrupted when members see themselves to be competing for mutually exclusive goals. Further, there is some indication that competitiveness produces greater personal insecurity through expectations of hostility from others than does cooperation. The implications for committees, conferences, and small groups in general appear fairly obvious.[10]

We shall address this topic again when we discuss conflict in Chapter 10. *Cooperation* and trusting behaviors are the keys to the successful functioning of groups and impact upon numerous other behaviors.

SUPPORTIVE AND DEFENSIVE BEHAVIOR

Closely akin to trust and cooperative behavior are behaviors labeled supportive. As with cooperation, trust appears to be essential to supportive behavior. Research in industry has demonstrated that high trust tends to stimulate high group productivity.[11] William Haney suggests reasons why communication practices are generally effective in a trusting, supportive organizational climate:

> First of all the members of such an organization, relatively speaking, have no ax to grind, nothing to be gained by miscommunicating deliberately. The aura of openness makes possible candid expressions of feelings and ideas. Even faulty communication does not lead immediately to retaliation, for others are not prone to presume malice on the offender's part, but instead "carry him," compensate for his errors. "That's not what he means to say." Moreover, a lapse in communication is viewed not as an occasion for punishment, but as an opportunity to learn from mistakes. Obviously, effective communication will do much to reinforce and enhance an existing trusting climate and the reverse is also true.[12]

Jack Gibb has identified characteristics of a supportive environment as one in which people express provisionalism, empathy, equality, spontaneity, and problem orientations and description rather than evaluation.[13] These "climates" may be defined as follows[14]:

Provisionalism. Members encourage flexibility, experimentation and creativity.

Empathy. Members attempt to listen and understand each other's feelings and values.

Equality. Members respect the positions of others, and no one is made to feel inferior.

Spontaneity. Ideas are expressed freely and honestly without hidden motives.

Problem orientation. There is open discussion about mutual problems without rushing to give solutions or insist on agreement.

Descriptive. Communications are clear and describe situations fairly, and perceptions are identified without implying a need for change.

Conversely, if people anticipate or perceive threat in a group, they are likely to behave defensively. Gibb states:

> The person who behaves defensively, even though he also gives some attention to the common task, devotes an appreciable portion of his energy to defending himself. Besides talking about the topic, he thinks about how he appears to others, how he may be seen more favorably, how he may win, dominate, impress or escape punishment, and/or how he may avoid or mitigate a perceived or an anticipated attack.[15]

He cites certain behaviors as contributory to defensiveness[16]:

1. *Evaluation* by expression, manner of speech, tone of voice, or verbal content, perceived by the listener as criticism or judgment, will produce defensive behavior.
2. Communication perceived as an attempt to *control* the recipient will produce defensiveness. It is interesting that if speech is said to be a social "tool," the implication is that the recipient has been "tooled."
3. *Stratagems* that are perceived as clever devices produce defensiveness; partially hidden motives breed suspicion. Persons seen as "playing a game," feigning emotion, withholding information, or having private access to sources of data will stimulate defensive responses.
4. An appearance of *neutrality* or lack of concern will heighten the need of defensiveness. A detached or impersonal manner (not caring) is usually feared and resented.
5. Conveying an attitude of *superiority* arouses defensive behavior. Any behavior that reinforces the recipient's feelings of inadequacy is a source of disturbance.
6. *Dogmatism* is a well-known stimulus of defensive behavior. If you know something "for certain," it is wise to determine whether or not anyone else wants to hear it from you and whether they want your answer to be offered tentatively or with final certainty.

Defensive behavior in one member of a group is likely to provoke defensiveness in others. A vicious circle is begun and becomes increasingly destructive as people stop listening to what is being said. Gibb notes: "As a person becomes more and more defensive, he becomes less and less able to perceive accurately the motives, the values, and the emotions of the sender."[17] Gibb's analysis of tape-recorded discussions shows a positive correlation between defensive behavior and losses of efficiency in communication. Thus distortions became greater when defensive behaviors were demonstrated in the groups.[18]

CONFORMITY AND INDEPENDENCE

Conformity as behavior can be defined as an individual's response to the pressure of a group. If people fall in line with the group, they demonstrate conformity; if they resist the group pressure, they display independence. Early research on this topic was performed by Solomon Asch.[19] In his classic experiment a group of seven to nine college students were instructed to announce publicly the length of one of three unequal lines. All but one of the students were confederates of the experimenter and were each instructed to give the same incorrect response. The experimental student sat near the end of the row, so that his announced decision would come after most other members'. Thus, the subject found himself a minority of one in the midst of a unanimous majority.

Of the students in the experimental group who were subjected to group pressure, only one fourth of them consistently rated the lengths of the lines correctly, whereas completely perfect reports were given by individuals in a control group free of any group pressure. The remaining three quarters of the experimental group made errors in the direction of the views of the majority. There was, however, great variation in the number of errors in this group, ranging from total adherence to the group views to very few errors.

Further analysis of the behavior of students who conformed revealed three categories of reactions:

Perceptual distortion. Some of the students were unaware that their estimates had been influenced and distorted by the group.

Judgmental distortion. Some of the students perceived the lengths correctly but decided that their perceptions were less accurate than those of other members of the group and decided to "go along." Thus they doubted their own perceptual capabilities.

Distortion of action. Some of the students perceived correctly and actually believed that they were correct, but they wanted to avoid being different from the others. Thus they conformed to the group's erroneous decisions rather than voice a difference.

Students who resisted group pressures were also able to be categorized into three groups:

Those who were confident of their perceptions

Those who believed strongly in the importance of independent judgments

Those who believed in taking effective action in the situation

Although there are numerous individual motives to account for the attention we pay to the expectations of others, the basic one seems to be that we care about what other members of the group think of us. As the group generates normative pressures, people respond as they do for the following reasons:[20]

1. The others will accept and like them, or will not reject them.
2. The group goal will be successfully attained.
3. The continuation of the group will be assured. People may also fulfill others' expectations as a by-product of informational, or cognitive, needs. Thus, if the group has an informational function, the others' expectations can serve as a guide for

   a. Gaining "correct" information about reality.
   b. Validating one's own opinions and making sure they are consistent with the opinions of others.
   c. Evaluating oneself and others.

The roles forced upon individuals are products of the interaction between their interpersonal orientations, the situational elements, and the demands of the group. The behavior is influenced by the individual's knowledge of the role, motivation to perform the role, self-concepts, and the other people in the group. Because each individual has a unique set of drives, attitudes, cognitions, and orientations, the ways they perform their various roles may be unique.

CHOICE SHIFTS—SAFE OR RISKY?

Consider the following situation. A man has been told that because of a tumor on his brain, surgery is needed. The man inquires into the dangers of the operation and is told that his chances of dying during surgery are one in twenty. He considers the alternatives, including his prospects if he does not have the surgery and has to make a decision. But what if the chances of death during surgery were one in five or five in ten or nine in ten? As you can see, the higher the possibility of death, the riskier the venture. A decision is likely to be made on the level of acceptable risk.

In early research, subjects were asked to respond privately to 12 dilemmas similar to this one, then to meet in groups to discuss and make a decision.[21] The group's decisions turned out to be much riskier than those made by individuals, and after discussion, each individual's decisions tended to have become riskier than they had been before the group interaction. This phenomenon, termed "risky shift," may have contributed to such decisions as the Soviet invasion of Afghanistan, the U.S. military actions toward Libya, and the NASA decision to launch the space shuttle *Challenger*.

Several possible explanations have been offered for this "risky shift" phenomenon of groups:

1. Groups diffuse responsibility. People in groups tend to feel less personally involved for the group decision. If people feel

they cannot be personally blamed for failure, they may feel freer to recommend riskier decisions.[22]

2. Our cultural values favor risk. Just as young people want to appear "cool," many people are inclined to go along with group pressure in the direction of more risk.

3. Group members are likely to be less inhibited. People may feel that constraints are released in the group, and people secretly long for the adventure of risk.[23]

4. Persuasive new arguments may be heard. During the interaction, novel arguments may be advanced that are likely to be persuasive.

Research by Michael E. Mayer found strong support for the fourth explanation.[24] His study included recorded messages and supported strongly the importance of persuasive arguments, but it did not rule out the possibility of social comparisons that are involved in the other explanations.

According to Mayer, people are more likely to accept "riskier" alternatives if someone has spoken out strongly and persuasively in favor of them. What we know from studies of salesmanship also affirms this phenomenon. We may be persuaded to buy something we never even considered, such as a time-share condominium, if a salesperson presents compelling economic reasons for ownership. Clever salespeople have learned to master the skills of promoting such "risky shifts" of attitude and behaviors.

Other research has shown that in some activities, people in groups may be influenced to become more cautious. Here the predispositions discussed in Chapter 3 come into play. If a majority in the group favors a riskier decision, the group will be more likely to move farther in that direction, and if a majority favors the conservative risk, the group will become more conservative. The group's position becomes more extreme as group members think up various arguments to demonstrate the validity of their position.

The best research on this point posits that group interaction will be likely to cause a group to take a more extreme stand—either riskier or more conservative—than ones favored privately by any member before the discussion.

SUMMARY

Several categories of behavior of individuals in decision-making groups have been noted as playing major roles in the interaction. Behaviors may be classified and recorded according to primary function: accomplishing a task, maintaining personal relationships, or being self-oriented, indifferent to the best interests of the group. Trust and cooperation in the group are closely interrelated and serve to promote the best interests of the group, while distrust and competition will result in severe problems. Defensiveness similarly interferes with a group's communication and makes it difficult if not impossible to interact effectively.

All groups exert pressure on members to conform. Judgment and perception can be distorted by blind conformity, while independent action must be able to be accommodated by the group. Finally we noted the tendency of a group to move to more definite decisions than would the members acting alone, sometimes resulting in a "risky shift" of judgment.

APPLICATIONS

4.1. Analyze your class group behavior in terms of task and maintenance behaviors. How have these dimensions changed through the course of your meetings?
4.2. Analyze the level of trust in your group. What incidents or topics have promoted greater openness and feelings of trust?
4.3. Analyze another group in terms of conformity pressures and tendencies to make either safe or risky decisions. What evidences of this behavior are you able to observe?

NOTES

1. These three broad groupings were originally cited by the National Training Laboratory in Group Development. See K. D. Benne and P. Sheats, "Functional roles of group members," *Journal of Social Issues,* 4 (1948), 41–49.
2. A. Zaleznik and D. Moment, *The Dynamics of Interpersonal Behavior.* New York: Wiley, 1964, pp. 161–172.
3. G. Egan, *Encounter: Group Processes for Interpersonal Growth.* Belmont, Calif.: Brooks/Cole, 1970, pp. 336–358.
4. Zaleznik and Moment, *Dynamics of Interpersonal Behavior,* pp. 155–158.
5. D. Krech, R. S. Crutchfield, and N. Livson, *Elements of Psychology.* New York: Knopf, 1969, pp. 426–428.
6. R. F. Bales, *Interaction Process Analysis: A Method for the Study of Small Groups.* Reading, Mass.: Addison-Wesley, 1950.
7. K. Griffin, "Interpersonal trust in small group communication," *Quarterly Journal of Speech,* 53 (1967), 224–234. Also see R. D. Heimouvics, "Trust and influence in an ambiguous group setting," *Small Group Behavior,* 15 (1984), 545–552.
8. M. A. Deutsch, "Trust and suspicion," *Journal of Conflict Resolution,* 2 (1958), 265–279.
9. A. Rapoport and A. M. Chammah, *Prisoner's Dilemma: A Study in Conflict and Cooperation.* Ann Arbor: University of Michigan Press, 1965.
10. M. Deutsch, "Fifty years of conflict," in *Retrospectives on Social Psy-*

chology, ed. by L. Festinger. New York: Oxford University Press, 1980, p. 481.

11. R. Likert, *New Patterns in Management.* New York: McGraw-Hill, 1961, pp. 101–105.

12. W. V. Haney, *Communication and Organizational Behavior Text and Cases.* Homewood, Ill.: Irwin, 1982, p. 13.

13. J. Gibb, "Defensive communication," *Journal of Communication,* 11 (September 1961), 141–148.

14. Adapted from J. I. Costigan and M. A. Schmeidler, "Exploring supportive and defensive communication climates," in *Developing Human Resources,* ed. by J. W. Pfeiffer and L. D. Goodstein. San Diego: University Associates, 1984, pp. 112–116.

15. Gibb, "Defensive communication," p. 141.

16. Ibid., pp. 142–148.

17. Ibid., p. 142.

18. Ibid., pp. 146–148.

19. S. E. Asch, "Effects of group pressure upon the modifications and distortion of judgments," in *Readings About the Social Animal,* ed. by E. Aronson. New York: Freeman, 1984, pp. 13–22.

20. C. A. Kiesler and S. B. Kiesler, *Conformity.* Reading, Mass.: Addison-Wesley, 1970, p. 33.

21. J. A. F. Stoner, "Risky and cautious shifts in group decisions: The influence of widely held values," *Journal of Experimental Social Psychology,* 4 (1968), 442–459.

22. M. A. Wallach, N. Kogan, and D. J. Bem, "Diffusion of responsibility and level of risk taking in groups," *Journal of Abnormal and Social Psychology,* 68 (1964), 263–274.

23. J. M. Jellison and J. Riskind, "A social comparison of abilities interpretation of risk-taking behavior," *Journal of Personality and Social Psychology,* 15 (1970), 375–390.

24. M. E. Mayer, "Explaining choice shift: An effects-coded-model," *Communication Monographs,* 52 (March 1983), 92–101. Background is also taken from Mayer's unpublished dissertation of the same title, from the University of Kansas, 1980, directed by Kim Giffin.

chapter 5

Logical Processes
and Phases
in Decision Making

Picture a group of people seated around a table discussing a common problem. Someone can be identified as a leader, and the participants take turns speaking and listening. Some of the conversation will be directly germane to the topic at hand, while other comments will seem irrelevant and possibly distracting to the progress of the group. Many of our students have been somewhat dismayed at the lack of sensible, logical progression on the part of the real-life decision-making groups they have observed, such as a city-planning commission or a local school board.

Disturbing as it may seem, irrelevancy and illogicality in decision making are fairly common in our society. This is probably true because no person or group can easily identify and evaluate all the possible interpretations and solutions to a given problem until what appear to be certain essential points have been covered more than once. One reason for this may be our inability to grasp all the related parts of a complex problem without focusing on some of them more than once. A second explanation may be that some people see aspects relevant to making a decision, but for some reason they do not verbalize these until after the logical, appropriate time. A third reason may be that some interpretations of the nature of a problem are not perceived by any member of a group until a proposed solution is explored in depth. For example, only recently have we fully recognized some national ecological problems when the U.S. government proposed solutions for acid rain; certain philosophical tenets of our governmental agencies were not seen as a part of the problem until we began asking these agencies to help implement what appeared to be solutions to other parts of the problem. Thus it is that frequently, as group members explore the potential value of a proposed solution to a problem, they unexpectedly uncover other facets or interpretations of the nature of the problem itself.

In the real world the variety of circumstances in which decisions are made is endless. The only way to cope with such variety is to examine approaches that help us understand how logical solutions to difficult problems can be found.

How can a number of individuals with differing backgrounds, values, and capabilities come to agree that a decision that effects all of them should be adopted? This question of social choice had been studied from a number of perspectives—mathematics, social science, politics, and philosophy. In this chapter we shall compare some of the existing theories of decision making and explore the logical processes that are vital to the successful functioning of a group.

GROUP DEVELOPMENT THEORIES

Scholars disagree over the likelihood of recurrent phases in typical groups' development. Many philosophical treatises and theoretical approaches have been elaborately detailed, usually based on what *logically* is needed or ought to work well. Many of the current ones are derived, at least in part, from John Dewey's masterful 1910 analysis of how we think when we think productively about a problem or a "felt difficulty."[1] An early study by Bales and Strodtbeck presented some evidence that task groups show the following phase-sequential behaviors in dealing with problems: a search for information or orientation on the selected problem; attempts to evaluate the situation and identify proposals for improving it; and exploration of ways of controlling group members' behavior regarding the situation, that is, attempts to reach a group decision on a plan of action. Bales and Strodtbeck viewed their results as more exploratory than definitive, as a presentation of a hypothesis in need of further study.[2]

Later, Schiedel and Crowell analyzed the content of the interaction of five small groups evaluating a metropolitan newsletter.[3] Their primary interest was the process used in the *development of ideas* in groups rather than testing the hypothesis that groups progress in a linear fashion through a sequential set of steps in reflective thinking. Their most interesting finding, as they saw it, was "the relatively small amount of time devoted to the initiation, extension, modification and synthesis of ideas, actions which would seem to comprise the very essence of the development of a thought." More than half of the comments recorded were statements *confirming, clarifying,* or *substantiating* ideas already presented to the group; less than one fourth of the comments were devoted to initiating, extending, modifying, or synthesizing ideas. They concluded:

> This oral play on an idea and the verbalizing of concurrence are probably the ways by which a group gets its anchoring. Group thought seems to move forward with a "reach and test" type of motion, that which seems to be elaborated at length with movements of clarification, substantiation, and verbalized acceptance. Little wonder that group thinking often proceeds slowly when the anchoring of group thought takes up practically half the total time.[4]

In a follow-up study, these two researchers focused directly on the feedback process thus defined: "Initial comment by X—Feedback comment by Y—Reaction comment X." Using this rather restricted definition of feedback, they found that for the five groups studied "thirty-five percent of the total discussion interaction was devoted to feedback activity." This feedback behavior was characterized by statements of agreement and clarification and was interpreted by the researchers as "a circular process which probably serves an anchoring function in the group communication process."[5] In a study of this feedback process, Dale Leathers demonstrated that the group member contributions involving high-level abstractions significantly disrupt group thought processes, producing responses that are confused, withdrawn, and tense.[6] In this way logical progression toward problem solving is deterred.

David Berg analyzed the content of 124 problem-solving discussions in 39 different task-oriented groups representing religious, political, educational, and other professional interests.[7] Using content analysis to identify themes discussed by these groups, he found that "although the discussion group did concentrate largely on task-related matters (91.7 percent of the time), over one-third of that time was taken up with questions of procedure." These were questions such as whether one subtopic, such as iron mining, should be discussed before another, such as agriculture. Berg also found that, even when the groups were focusing their attention on substantive (task-relevant) considerations, "they were able to sustain uninterrupted group attention for a mean time of only 76 seconds. Although the same themes frequently reappeared several times, groups were often unable to complete discussion of these topics."

Another theory of group development is that of B. W. Tuckman in "Development Sequence in Small Groups."[8] He identified four stages of group development: forming, storming, norming, and performing. This theory demonstrates that a group changes as it solves certain interpersonal issues and achieves certain tasks.

In the first phase, "forming," a group is primarily concerned with "Who's in charge?" and "What are we supposed to do?" and "Whom are we responsible to?" Individuals tend to depend on the designated leader to provide all the structure, to set the ground rules, to establish the agenda, and to do all the "leading." As far as one's task is concerned, one must identify one's "charge": What exactly has one been asked to do; what data does one already have to work with; what is the time frame within which one is to work; to whom is one accountable; what are the resources each member brings to the task? Too often, rather than providing for new members' dependency and orientation needs, groups just barrel along, taking up where the last meeting left off, with the frequent result that new members do not become effective on boards and committees for a long time.

The second phase, "storming," refers to the conflict experienced in groups as the members organize to get the work of the group done and to make decisions regarding who is going to be responsible for what; what are going to be the work rules and procedures (e.g., who will approach the candidates one would like to nominate to the board?); what are going to be the limits (e.g., how long will the group spend on this; how many buildings will it look at as possible facilities?); what is going to be the reward system (e.g., how many of the members ever thought of that in the committee work?); what are going to be the criteria by which they will know they have accomplished their task? People's effectiveness as a group depends on how well they solve these interpersonal conflicts over leadership and leadership structure, power, and authority.

The third phase, "norming," refers to the stage of development during which members of the group begin to experience a sense of groupness or cohesion, a feeling of catharsis at having resolved interpersonal conflict and of having "gotten their act together." They begin sharing ideas and feelings, giving feedback to each other, soliciting feedback, exploring actions related to the task (getting on with it!), and sharing information related to the task (through phone calls and formal and informal reports). They begin to feel good about their work and about being part of the group, and there is an emerging openness with regard to the task at hand. We have seen this happen on various committees on which we have served, and we have witnessed it in groups we have observed. There is a sense of flow, of something clicking, and this leads to brief indulgences in playfulness where people abandon the task and just enjoy being with one another. Everyone has probably been at meetings when this has occurred—everyone was joking, and every joke evoked hilarity, one never had such a good time as at that moment.

The fourth phase, "performing," is the culmination of the work as a group: People are both highly task oriented and highly person oriented. The group's tasks are well defined; members have a high degree of commitment to common activity, and they are able to support experimentation in solving problems. A trusting climate makes it safe to take risks.

A CONTINGENCY THEORY OF GROUP DEVELOPMENT

Communication researcher Marshall Scott Poole has objected to the traditional "phases" approach to studying groups; he believes that such models are too general and too vague to encompass the diversity of group activities.[9] Drawing from the same research we have cited, Poole identifies three "activity tracks" that decision-making groups require:[10]

1. *Task-process activities.* Those activities the group enacts to manage its task
2. *Relational activities.* Those activities that reflect or manage relationships among group members as they relate to the group's work
3. *Topical focus.* The substantive issues and arguments of concern to the group at a given point in the discussion

Poole also cites the importance of "break points" in the developmental process. He identifies normal break points, such as *topic shifts* and recesses or adjournments. *Delays* are a second type of break point, which signals a shift in the mood or tenor of the discussion, possibly even creating difficult or highly creative activities. *Disruptions* are the third type of break point, identified as either conflict or failure to reach a satisfactory solution.[11]

In addition to the activity types and the break points, another critical element in the description of development is the issue, "What is the object of this activity?" According to Poole:

> Components of task accomplishment will vary from task to task. For decision making these include recognition of the need for a decision, definition of the decision problem, diagnosis of the problem, search for and generation of solutions, adaption of solutions to the group's circumstances, consensus on criteria for an acceptable solution, selection of a solution, and implementation planning. These components make up a structure for decision that sets forth the logical priorities for accomplishing choice.[12]

Poole's description of developmental processes is based upon a view of group process as a set of interlocking tracks of activities oriented toward task accomplishment.

This contingency theory is helpful in predicting and explaining the general configurations or development for diverse sets of groups and conditions. Poole cites the greater flexibility of this multiple sequence model and provides an easier method for the empirical assessment of effects of varying techniques and approaches on group process.

THE CRITICAL ASSESSMENT OF PHASES

Researchers continue to debate the merits of research conclusions regarding both the validity and usefulness of studying groups in terms of phases.[13] Kenneth N. Cissna has reviewed the research that *does not* find sequential development in group processes. In his critical assessment he concludes:

> Not all groups will necessarily follow the full developmental sequence of the self-analytic or training group. . . . Other groups, perhaps well acquainted with one another or with the task, seem to skip the orientation or forming stage. Some groups accomplish very little productive work, missing the performing stage.[14]

The evidence that groups use a logical pattern of progression in problem solving is inconclusive, and research evidence that such a pattern facilitates effective problem solving is notably lacking. However, essays and textbooks for the past 50 years have advocated such a pattern.[15] In addition, casual observation of behavioral attempts to resolve personal difficulties frequently shows this pattern: (1) People express their feelings of difficulty. (2) They ask another person for confirmation of this feeling: "What do you think about the school drug problem?" (3) One or the other may suggest a possible solution: "Well, I think we should provide stiffer penalties." Or one may ask the other for a suggestion: "What do you think we should do about it?" (4) They may start to develop a plan of action: "Has anyone ever talked to the high school principal about stronger rules?"

In line with this point of view, group dynamics scholar Alvin Zander in 1982 described the four phases that he has observed groups characteristically move through:[16]

1. Describing the problem that requires a response and why a response is necessary
2. Identifying a number of possible solutions
3. Deciding on the best solution from among the alternatives
4. Taking action to implement the decision

When people are in trouble, such a pattern of interaction makes logical sense; however, many real-life group discussions do not follow such a pattern. Frequently, they slight or omit one phase or another. Our purpose here is to suggest a procedure that makes logical sense, to be followed in practice as well as you can work it out with your group. The point to be remembered is that at any given moment in a decision-making group discussion you need to know what you are doing. If at times you begin to feel you are in a light-weight skiff on a tumbled sea of more or less unrelated ideas or comments, the situation can be helped by reviewing the logical elements of problem solving and comparing your efforts to this ideal pattern. Ideas and contributions should never be arbitrarily cut off or derogated; they should be assessed as to whether they help the group move toward its goal, the solution of a mutual problem.

We suggest that the decision-making process ideally, or logically, consists of (1) identification of a group problem, including determination of the nature of concern shared by the group members; (2) analysis of the nature of the problem, including contributing factors, restraining factors, and the degree of intensity of the difficulty; (3) critical evaluation of the possible ways of trying to resolve the difficulty; and (4) development of a plan for group action designed to implement the problem solution agreed upon by the group. In the next chapter we shall examine these steps in detail.

In a recent meeting of a local school board, members argued strenuously on the relative value of three different suggested "solutions" to "the problem," only to discover (after generating negative interpersonal feelings) that different members of the group held different views on the nature of the problem. Members actually were considering the value of different solutions for different problems. In fact, a human-relations problem was generated by the poor performance of the group in its decision-making behavior.

PREDICTION FROM PAST EXPERIENCES

As we move from the familiar to the unknown, we are taking an intellectual step into the dark. We engage in such activities constantly in our daily lives. When we "decide" to eat at our favorite restaurant, for example, or even to show up at home for dinner, we are "predicting" on the basis of past experience that our needs *probably* will be satisfied better than if we went elsewhere.

The prediction of events involves reasoning, that is, identifying the reasons for believing that such events may occur. The act of identifying and evaluating such reasons requires, first, a knowledge of the relevant, or *similar,* past events; and second, a calculation of the likelihood, or *probability,* of similar events occurring under similar circumstances. If your group members can predict that selected conditions will very probably produce a set of desirable results, often the arranging of those conditions will help to achieve the results.[17]

The essential core of the reasoning process is the identification of *relevant similarities* between events. This involves a classification of past events according to some pertinent set of characteristics. It also requires observation of these events, by yourself or by someone else, with special attention to these selected similar characteristics.

As you attempt to use the reasoning process it is likely you will raise questions concerning any specific proposed solution. Your questions probably will be similar to the following:

1. Has a *similar* proposal been tried elsewhere?
2. Was that trial successful; that is, did it solve a *similar* problem?
3. Was it put into operation by persons *similar* to us?
4. Were there *no* costs or dangers that were *not similar* to those we can bear?
5. Has it been tried in other *similar* situations with *similar* results?
6. Were each of these other situations *similar* in essentially relevant ways?

In this list of questions the importance of identifying relevant similarities between observed past events and the result desired from adopting a particular plan of action should be obvious. However, the principle is important, and an illustrative example may be useful. Suppose you are helping a friend with preenrollment for next semester. You need to know in advance which courses are interesting and valuable. You have had three courses with Professor Smith. Other students have commented on finding courses with Professor Smith highly interesting and valuable. From your experience and the reports of other students you begin to form a *generalization:* Professor Smith's courses are interesting and valuable to students.

Forming generalizations covering selected characteristics of events and conditions is called *induction;* this process is basic to critical thinking and the scientific method. It is the process by which we establish reliable knowledge about our world, physical and social. As we use it we must be careful that we observe as many relevant similar events and conditions as possible. The particular characteristics in question (in the example given above, "interesting" and "valuable") must be noted with great care; it is most helpful if some method of quantification can be devised to measure such characteristics. (How much of interest was offered in Professor Smith's courses, or how valuable were they?)

The primary question in reasoning can be seen as one of relevant similarity: Is the unknown future event one of a set covered by the generalization we have formulated? In our example, will Professor Smith's course next semester be similar (in ways that matter to us: interesting and valuable) to those he has previously offered? We look carefully for information about these characteristics: Is next semester's course numbered and described the same as one previously offered? Does Professor Smith tell us it is similar, that he plans to teach it the same way and cover the same material? In all relevant ways we try to make certain that the future event in question will be one of a set about which we have formed our generalization. Traditional scholars of logic have called this process *deduction.* They usually illustrate this part of the reasoning process as follows: All of Professor Smith's courses are interesting; course 530 is one of Professor Smith's courses; therefore, course 530 is interesting. This paradigm is called a *syllogism;* we suspect that you have previously seen deductive reasoning illustrated this way. Actually, in this simplified approach the key issue of relevant similarity is neglected. What such reasoning can actually provide is this: Courses previously offered by Professor Smith have been interesting.

Next semester Professor Smith will offer a course that appears to be essentially similar to a selected number of courses he has previously offered. Next semester's course with Professor Smith *probably* will be interesting.

In this paradigm the issue of relevant similarity is clearly exposed. If the future events cannot be judged to be similar in relevant ways to those events about which the generalization has been made, then one's predictions regarding that future event will not be reliable. The practical application is this: As you try to evaluate various proposals to solve a problem, you must test the predicted results of each proposal (including the one you favor) in terms of its relevant similarity to previous experiences with such approaches.

The ability to predict the outcome of one or another proposed plan of action is vital to your group; however, that which is only probable is not certain. Consequently, you and your group should be interested in ways of determining the degree of likelihood, or probability, that a prediction will come true.

A degree of probability may be more specifically determined (calculated) to the extent that you are familiar with the laws of probability and you are able to obtain precise information about similar past events as we discussed in the previous section. We shall not go deeply into the laws of probability; our purposes will be served if we give the basic rule and an illustration to show the importance of understanding its application.

The basic rule for calculative probability is not very complicated, and very likely you have already used it many times. It is this: Divide the number of favored events (such as *interesting* courses) by the total number of events; for example if six out of eight courses offered by Professor Smith have been interesting, then we can say the *probability* that a future course will be interesting is six divided by eight, which equals a 75 percent probability.

As we have noted, the calculation of probabilities of future events has become a professional skill in industrial management; in many companies and government agencies it is given much time and attention as an aid to making decisions, especially to choosing among plans of action.

SUMMARY

In order for a group to be successful, logical processes must function. We have examined areas and ways in which logical analysis is important. As we attempt to predict future actions, we are dealing with degrees of uncertainty. Mathematical models may assist us in calculating the costs and potential gains from the available alternatives, and justifications can be made. In areas of values and inability to quantify, we still predict based upon our past experiences.

We have explained very briefly the reasoning process, focusing upon the core principle: a comparison of relevant similarities between observed past events and the event under discussion or the probable effect of adopting or implementing a proposed plan of action by your group, based on past effects. We have suggested the potential value of probability theory in making predictions.

APPLICATIONS

5.1. Analyze another group by the use of the phases discussed in this chapter. To what extent did the group follow sequentially these phases?

5.2. With appropriate permission, transcribe a short group interaction and record, as you listen, topic shifts, delays, and interruptions. How do these "break points" influence the discussion?

5.3. From the transcribed discussion, analyze the reasoning processes employed. Were probabilities accurately assessed and demonstrated?

NOTES

1. J. Dewey, *How We Think.* Boston: Heath, 1910.
2. R. F. Bales and F. L. Strodtbeck, "Phases in group problem solving," *Journal of Abnormal Social Psychology,* 46 (1951), 485–495.
3. T. M. Schiedel and L. Crowell, "Idea development in small discussion groups," *Quarterly Journal of Speech,* 50 (1964), 140–145.
4. Ibid., p. 143.
5. T. M. Scheidel and L. Crowell, "Feedback in small group communication," *Quarterly Journal of Speech,* 52 (1966), 273–278.
6. D. G. Leathers, "Progress disruption and measurement in small group discussion," *Quarterly Journal of Speech,* 55 (1969), 287–300. See also

D. G. Leathers, "Testing for determinant interactions in the small group communication process," *Speech Monographs,* 39 (1971), 182–189.

7. D. M. Berg, "A descriptive analysis of the distribution and duration of themes discussed by task-oriented small groups," *Speech Monographs,* 34 (1967), 172–175.

8. B. W. Tuckman, "Development sequence in small groups," *Psychological Bulletin,* 63 (1965), 384–399.

9. M. S. Poole, "Decision development in small groups III: A multiple sequence model of group decision development," *Communication Monographs,* 50 (December 1983), 321–341.

10. Ibid., p. 326.

11. Ibid., pp. 330–331.

12. Ibid., p. 331.

13. See, for example, D. R. Siebold, "Criticism of communication theory and research: A critical celebration," *Central States Speech Journal,* 30, (1979), 25–39; Randy Hirokawa, "Group communication and problem-solving effectiveness: An investigation of group phases," *Human Communication Research,* 9 (1983), 291–305.

14. K. N. Cissna, "Phases in group development: The negative evidence," *Small Group Behavior,* 15 (1984), 28.

15. M. A. Bell, "Phases in group problem-solving," *Small Group Behavior,* 13 (November 1982), 475–495.

16. A. Zander, *Making Groups Effective.* London: Jossey-Bass, 1982, p. 14.

17. B. Fischhoff and M. Bar-Hillet, "Focusing techniques: A shortcut to improving probability judgments," *Organizational Behavior and Human Performance,* 34 (1984), 175–194.

chapter 6

The Problem-Solving Format

No group is like another group; no meeting is exactly like another. Every group is so different that it is difficult to generalize about decision making.

As we noted in the previous chapter, researchers have been trying to determine how real-life groups reach conclusions. The concern of this chapter is how decisions *ought* to be made, not necessarily how they *are* made. In group situations calling for a problem to be solved, members identify ways of dealing with the problem and then select the most satisfactory alternative. For the process to proceed logically, four steps need to be followed:

1. The group identifies the common problem.
2. The problem is analyzed.
3. Solutions are proposed and evaluated.
4. A decision is made and steps are taken to implement it.

Each component in this format deserves consideration, and we shall provide our suggestions for how a group *should* function to arrive at the best solution.

IDENTIFYING A COMMON PROBLEM

To solve a problem the first step clearly is to gain an understanding of the problem. Without this step, confusion can easily frustrate a group. Confusion on the nature of the problem can pull the group apart and may keep it from ever achieving a solution. Remember: "If we aim at nothing, we are pretty likely to hit it." The unchecked assumption that everybody in a group understands the problem (that is, sees it the way we do or has the same basic concern we do) is entirely unwarranted in the experience of most decision-making groups.

To clarify a mutual concern with others you start with tentative, trusting behavior, clearly stating your personal view of the situation *and how you feel about it.* Your comment may be something like this: "I see a need to reconsider course requirements for the English major, and I feel this need is very important." The keynote elements are "I see . . . and "I feel. . . ." These elements indicate a personal viewpoint (not the only possible viewpoint) and signify that another group member may see or feel differently.

At this stage your interpersonal manner, way of stating your viewpoint, and attitude toward other members can indicate a good, or poor, understanding of this phase of the decision-making process. You must state clearly and honestly your viewpoint and your feelings; by all means be genuine and sincere, and *show your expectation that others in the group will do the same, comfortably disagreeing as necessary.* Your manner of stating your viewpoint and feelings should be genuine and honest, not prescriptive; it should deliberately and overtly tell other members you can tolerate expressed differences of viewpoints or feelings when *they* state *their* position.

As each group member in effect says "This is the way I see it . . ." and "This is the how I feel about it . . . ," the *nature* and *degree* of common concern can be diagnosed. If honesty prevails, it will become apparent whether a group can work well together on the problem previously thought to be of mutual concern. All members must be prepared to discover that others do *not* share their view and concern. In fact, it may be discovered that there is no common concern at all. In such a case it is better to discover this earlier than later; it can save time, energy and, possibly, hurt feelings.

Identifying Possible Concerns

Some understanding of the nature of ordinary common concerns frequently identified by groups may be helpful. People join each other for many reasons, as we suggested in Chapter 2. From a perspective of the group three general areas of interpersonal needs may be reiterated:

  1. *The need of people to interact with other people.* This need has been called "the interpersonal imperative."[1] It is just

this simple: People need to be with people part of the time, at certain times—some more and some less. Many times groups are formed on this basis: The members like each other and enjoy being with each other. Very simply, they find each other attractive as people, and their mutual concern may appropriately be how to enhance their enjoyment of being together. If they like each other and enjoy just being together, their mutual concern is easily met without formal plans or group action, and there is no problem other than that of getting together. Problems (initial concerns) of time and place may surface; but if decisions are easily reached, the main concern of the group may be pursued by enjoying each other's company.

2. *The need to achieve personal status.* Being an accepted member of a high-status group is often the primary mutual concern of members of sororities, fraternities, and country clubs. The mutual concern focuses on the status of the organization and its recognized membership. If these goals are indeed personal concerns of the group members, and if they are clearly identified and accepted as the group members' goals, and if by becoming a member in good standing satisfactory personal status can be enhanced, then the group members' mutual concern very likely will be met in a satisfactory way. Verification that their goals *are* the primary mutual concern of members is continuously necessary; if members happen to suggest that such a group should "support a worthy community cause," such as integration of schools or county zoning, these suggestions may create confusion and misunderstanding. In such cases verification of the real nature of the group members' concerns can be helpful, even if eventually some members together create a new community action group. It cannot be overemphasized that the individual's primary concern is the only solid basis for interaction in groups. In a social-status group a very appropriate mutual concern might be how to enhance the social status of the group.

3. *The need to produce a change in social environment.* For the most part this is the basic mutual concern of most group interaction. The decision-making may take many forms. It may be to develop a new arrangement (contract) between group members, for example, reaching an agreement upon the route and times for departure of members of a surburban car pool. It may be to negotiate a contract between members of one group and members of another group, for example, arranging an agreement on time and place for a game with another community softball team. It may involve working

out an agreement between members of your group and the various members of different echelons within a large organization; for example, attempting to develop a new Women's Studies major in a state university.

The precise nature of the social change desired by a group may take the form of a *physical task*—for example, purchasing property and building a new center for youth activities. On the other hand, the desired change may be a new *procedure*—for example, allowing students to preenroll and avoid being denied admission to academic courses of their choosing.

In a very general way the possible mutual concerns for desired social change are encompassed by a list of individual needs that motivate people to action. Maslow's hierarchy of human needs, discussed in Chapter 2, provides a framework for understanding the basis of such change.

These mutual concerns are often expressed as questions that require different kinds of answers, such as the following:

1. *Questions of fact.* Seek to determine whether a statement is essentially true or false. Such questions often require empirical data and scientific research: "Have homicides increased in the country this year?"
2. *Questions of value.* Seek to discover the value orientations and judgments of group members. Such questions require interpretation of data: "Was Reagan a good president?"
3. *Questions of policy.* Seek to find a way of changing a situation so that it is more nearly that which is desired. The answer lies in some form of action: "What policy of advising should be employed at the university?"

The primary point to be learned from this step is that you should not *assume* that you and other members of your group share a mutual concern about an alleged problem area or situation; rather, you should carefully determine the actual degree of shared concern.

ANALYZING A PROBLEM

By definition a problem consists of a situation or condition in which what currently exists is not what you prefer. For example, an undependable car may be what you have, and a dependable one is what you want. In some cases, that which *exists,* such as a practice of racial discrimination in selling houses, may not be the condition which you believe "ought" to exist. Often people become impatient with one another in discussing what "ought" to be. Often they could more quickly and easily accept one another's descriptions of a condition they would like to have than pronouncements of what "ought" to exist. Stating what you *want* and how it differs from what *is* allows others to deal with you as a human being rather than as a questionable spokesperson for imperative and immutable laws on what ought to be.

In its simplest terms the process of problem analysis consists of determining the *difference* between what you have and what you would like to have. However, the determination of this difference can be a difficult and complex procedure when it is performed by a group; varying personal views of the difference may be voiced, many of which have at least some real merit.

Determining the Scope of the Problem

To analyze a problem in detail properly we must determine the size or extent of the difficulty involved. The group may find a problem to be multifaceted and far reaching. For example, a minority group in a large city may be faced with numerous social and economic conditions that require change, such as poor housing, few job opportunities, limited financial credit, poor facilities for education, few opportunities to gain needed experience, poor motivation to put forth great effort, and little expectation of achieving desirable ends; indeed, the scope of such problems may be tremendous. On the other hand, in the case of a family in which the mother is killed in an auto accident, the scope of the problem may not be very extensive. In both examples, however, the *intensity* of the perceived need may be very great; the amount of emotional investment on the part of members of both groups may, indeed, be great.

Thus, to analyze a problem, we need first to determine its scope. How large is it? How many people are involved? How many forces are at work? Are social, economic, and political forces involved? Or is it a matter of obtaining a little more money?

Identifying Impelling and Constraining Forces

We have earlier suggested that a problem situation is one in which there is a difference between the way things are and the way you want them to be. Lewin borrowed a concept from the physical sciences and offered it as a way of understanding social problems;[2] it is sometimes called *force-field analysis.* This diagnostic technique is based on the principle that any sociopsychological situation is the way it is at any given moment because sets of counterbalancing forces are keeping it that way. The technique of force-field analysis seeks to identify these forces.

To acknowledge and identify the forces at work in a problem is important to a group's success. Let's look at an example. A student-faculty committee agrees that a required course is not satisfactory; the course requirement needs to be changed. What forces are involved? Some committee members may feel that the basis of the problem is blind adherence to tradition; other members see it as lack of acceptance of graduates by hiring officials in industry; others see it as arising from the difficulty of securing instructors with special training or experience; others see it as mainly stemming from the high cost of obtaining special instructional materials or equipment; and other members believe that the basic difficulty lies in a low morale or poor motivation among instructors to change their classroom methods. You can immediately think of other factors possibly involved in such a problem.

The point we wish to make is that a consideration of various forces in a problem can be well worth your while. Unless you deliberately look for these forces, you and others in your group may surprise each other by the degree of confusion generated by some members who think that a problem is simple when others are making it so complex! The lamentable feature of such confusion frequently is that the group members *started the analysis of the problem with a cohesive agreement* that it is of mutual concern (that is, that it *exists*), and what seemed like a battle half won has turned into a shambles.

What specifically can you do to avoid this confusion? You can ask your colleagues carefully and deliberately to make a list of those forces that are *impelling* change in the present undesirable condition and to make a similar list of those forces that are currently holding back or *constraining* change.

In the illustrative example of the problem of course requirements, your lists (in part) might look like these:

Impelling Forces

1. Inability of students to apply or use material learned
2. Inability of students to grasp concepts presented
3. Repetition of material previously learned by students
4. Unimportance to hiring officials of material learned
5. Etc.

Constraining Forces

1. Cost of new equipment for instruction
2. Difficulty of finding specially trained instructors
3. Resistance to change by school administrators
4. Vested interests (for example, the difficulty of finding new assignments for the present staff)
5. Etc.

Almost all problems have these basic components of *impelling* forces and *constraining* forces. Our point is this, and it is one frequently neglected by problem-solving groups: Adequate analysis of a problem requires careful consideration of these two sets of forces, those impelling and those constraining. No solution that neglects either set can be optimal.

In actual fact we have been presenting a procedure for identifying what are commonly called the *causes* of a problem. Thus far we have avoided using the word because we have found it to be misleading. When people think of causes of a problem, their thinking frequently is overly simplistic. They tend to think of *A* as caused by *B,* a single cause (or at most two or three). Usually they identify only impelling forces as causes and neglect consideration of constraining forces. Often a *problem solution* requires a modification of the constraining forces much more than of those that are impelling. *And* as we have indicated, most problems faced by groups are not simple but complex, involving numerous constraining and impelling components.

Analyzing Problem Intensity

The degree of intensity of a problem may be determined by noting the degree of dissatisfaction with the present condition. This dissatisfaction can be the result of physical hardship, economic deprivation, personal injustice, or violation of a moral or ethical principle.

It should be easy to understand that any present condition may be viewed quite differently by various members of a group. Members may feel differing degrees of dissatisfaction; this can be the result of differing values or value systems. Even the members of a group having a solid core of mutual interest in a situation will often disagree on the intensity of dissatisfaction with the current condition. This statement may be difficult for you to believe or accept. On the surface it may seem paradoxical that members can agree on their *interest* in a problem area and differ in their feelings of the *need to do something* about it. However, such a situation does occur, and it can impede a group's effectiveness. Group members' degree of commitment to solving a problem will be the direct result of their view of the intensity of the problem, that is, their emotional investment in the situation. And their degree of commitment will directly affect the group's efficiency in implementing a workable *problem solution.*

In some cases as a member of a decision-making group, you are deeply concerned about the severity of a problem that has been identified as being of mutual interest to those in your group, only to find that few others in the group actually think it is important. This may be frustrating to you, and you may wonder how the others can possibly "be so blind"; alternatively, you may wonder what's "wrong" with *you* that only you see the problem as being important. What can be done when there is such lack of agreement?

It is important that group members ask each other for their views regarding the *intensity* of a problem. If members agree quicky and easily, they can move along to determine its precise nature. If they don't agree on its intensity, it is then necessary for those disagreeing to explore the differing *sets of values* that underlie their disagreement.

Full exploration and discussion of differing sets of values underlying each group member's view of a problem's intensity can help the group reach a better understanding of each member's attitude toward the problem. It can provide common ground for considering possible solutions. Such discussion *may* show that this group, at this time, cannot hope to agree on *how quickly* or *at what cost* a course of action should be adopted. If this is reality, the group needs to face it. At worst, members can agree that they cannot hope to reach agreement, and they will have a basis for understanding why this is so. However, in most cases a discussion of the relevant value systems can produce mild changes by individuals in the direction of group agreement. In many cases common ground can be found, understanding of each other increased, and agreement reached on the general degree of intensity of the problem.

The major point to be made is this: It has been our observation that *disagreement among group members more frequently occurs regarding the degree of intensity of a problem than on the facts of the situation being considered.* If the disagreement is on intensity (based on differing values), no amount of "checking out the facts" can resolve this disagreement. In the face of such disagreement in a group, members who say, "Well, let's just look at the facts" are headed for trouble. If they mean "Let's look at *our interpretation* of the facts based upon *our sense of values,*" they should say so, and there is then some possibility of others understanding them, particularly if they will give other members the same opportunity.

In reality a disagreement over the intensity of a problem is *not* a disagreement about the facts of the problem situation but about how much commitment one should have to one or another basic value or value system.

Much frustration and heightened emotional behavior occur when *a review of "the facts" of the case is agreed on as correct, but a solid sense of disagreement remains* because of differing value systems. Group members at a loss for words, then look away from each other in disbelief, suspicion, distrust. This sometimes happens in families with teenage children over something like the use of a car. Such a disagreement based on different value systems can bring a family to a highly frustrating impasse. Members feel that they have been reasonable, they have done "all they know how to do," they have tried to do what should have been done, and still they have not found common ground with such "unreasonable" people ("hardheads," "bigots," "fools"). Such a feeling of frustration with a so-called unreasonable person can produce name calling that is also unreasonable and may have a heavy effect on interpersonal relations in the group.

The analysis of problem intensity is serious business. In this section we have deliberately belabored the point. In decision-making groups you ignore it at your peril; the result may be interpersonal difficulties that are hard to resolve and could have been avoided. Such problem-analysis elements cannot entirely be divorced from human relations; conversely, excellent human relationships in a group cannot substitute for careful problem analysis.

Setting a Group Goal

Much difference exists between sharing a mutual concern and defining a group goal. The primary difference is the degree of specificity. When a group sets a goal, it should be *specific enough for members to tell when it has been achieved.*

As the group works on the identification of a specific goal, it will become apparent that what is exactly the concern for some members is not exactly the concern of other members. As members attempt to clarify the area of primary group concern, they must be prepared to make minor adjustments and compromises with each other in order, eventually, to adopt a goal that meets the concerns of most and to which all members can make a functional commitment.

This group goal must be specific for three reasons. First, the members must be able to know what type of proposal will take them to their target. Second, they must be able to tell when, if ever, a specific problem has been solved. Third, an effectively high commitment and concerted group effort cannot be maintained forever; within some reasonable period of time the group will need to feel that something specific has been accomplished.

The group goal should be specified in terms of an event, procedure, or environmental condition that can be observed and agreed on by all members. If the goal is to produce a music festival (an event), some example of a music festival needs to be cited or described so that all members understand the nature of the event desired. If an improved campus-voting procedure is the specified goal, then a well-known example of the desired procedure should be cited; if such a plan is unavailable, the basic *principles* of the desired procedure should be identified in detail. For example, the group should state those issues that would be brought to a vote, when and where such voting would occur, and how the votes would be counted and reported. If an environmental change is the group goal, the group should specify exactly what part of the local situation should be changed and what it will look like when the desired change has been achieved.

The importance of goal specificity cannot be overemphasized. Our work in observing and counseling decision-making groups has led us to the conviction that groups fail, bog down, lose member commitment, and develop interpersonal dislike and irritation more because of lack of specific goal identification than for any other reason. This is the point: If a group aims at nothing in particular, it is likely to achieve just that—nothing in particular, with appropriate dissatisfaction or disgust.

Obtaining Relevant Information

We run a high risk of being misunderstood as we present the following suggestion: *Almost the last thing you should do in analyzing a problem is get the facts.* In making this suggestion we do not wish at all to deny the value of getting precise information. Rather we wish to emphasize the importance of the question "Whose facts?"

Whose facts? Pertaining to what? For what purpose? *Relevant* facts in any given situation will be determined in part by a thorough analysis (as we have suggested above) of impelling and constraining forces. Getting "the facts" too soon, that is, without complete consideration of these forces, can produce a lopsided (although very factual) view of a problem.

In addition, group members' value systems (as described above) will determine some facts to be relevant and some not directly related to the problem *as they see it.* Checking out the value systems of different members can help to identify different types of factual information seen to be relevant by the group members.

An illustrative example may help to clarify this principle. It recently came to our attention that in at least one major city in this country contraction of a venereal disease is, by city statute, a criminal act. In this city a ten-year-old boy contracted gonorrhea from his baby-sitter! His parents were aghast when, upon treatment, the incident had to be reported by the medical health officer to the city police. They started forming a group with other parents "to do something about this problem." It should be obvious to you, the reader, that the nature of factual information required was seriously influenced by impelling forces, such as increased incidence of venereal disease among teenagers, and by constraining forces, such as the influence of police action in deterring the spread of such disease. In addition, the relevancy of some types of factual data was influenced by the parents' desire to protect their children from being given a "police record" through ignorance or the illegal acts of others. Further, the value systems of public health officials, law enforcement officers, public school officials, and juvenile court officials eventually influence the degree of relevancy of certain other kinds of factual information.

In analyzing complex problems it is important to look carefully at impelling and constraining forces, noting how the value systems of interested persons influence the degree of relevancy of certain types of information. It should now be clear that obtaining *relevant* factual information is absolutely essential in problem analysis. The degree of difference between what exists and what is desired cannot be assessed without careful consideration of the pertinent facts.

What is the *nature* of factual information? In raising this question we do not mean to imply that an adult reader is totally ignorant of the nature of scientific data. We assume that you, the reader, are an educated person. Our aim is to point out frequently misunderstood principles and to contribute clarity to your thinking in this important area.

Let's start by agreeing that to an educated person a fact is the existence of a condition, object, or event possible of verification. An example might be the daily flow of traffic between Anaheim and downtown Los Angeles. Or it might be the incidence of venereal disease in Wichita. It may be the number of Hispanic Americans enrolled for the coming fall in Camelback High School.

In order that reports on such conditions may be used in a decision-making group the condition must be *observed* (seen, heard, or otherwise determined), certain elements must be *counted* (if a number of certain variables are involved), and then the observation must be *reported* by people. Thus, to a decision-making group, factual information is usable if it is in the form of a *factual statement.* So our question now is this: What are the requirements of a factual statement?

People in groups can seldom go to the site of the condition or situation itself and do all their own observing and counting. (When they can, they should do so, of course, but even when they do, they must check on each others' observations, because human error in observing and counting is notorious.) In most problem-solving groups the *practical* concern is this: Should reported data available to the group be accepted as factual? After much deliberation we have adopted the following definition of a factual statement. It is a statement that obtains a high degree of acceptance on the part of those persons in whom you have confidence regarding their ability to observe and to report such data.

When a problem has been analyzed effectively, the next step is to evaluate the proposed solutions.

EVALUATING PROPOSED SOLUTIONS

The procedure for evaluating suggestions (even when operationally described) deserves special attention. In evaluating various suggested approaches, or plans of action, your group will be interested in achieving two objectives: (a) choosing that proposal that will be most satisfactory for your group and (b) obtaining members' agreement and commitment. This group commitment eventually will be necessary if you are to implement the chosen solution and make it work as envisioned.

Informal observation of task groups and practical experience in solving problems have made many people aware of three basic criteria that can be used to evaluate any proposed plan of action:

1. Will this proposal produce the desired changes in the current situation? Will it meet the need for change as we have identified it?
2. Can this proposal be implemented by us? Is it a workable suggestion?
3. Does this proposal inherently contain serious disadvantages?

These criteria have been found useful for evaluating proposals that involve plans of action or changes in current policies—that is, proposals which may be resolved by agreeing upon a plan of action or a change in existing policy. Such issues are called policy issues or questions of policy. For groups dealing with them the three criteria suggested above may be used to evaluate proposed changes in policy or plans of action. Let's look at each of these criteria in some detail.

Criterion 1: Meeting the Need for Change.   This requires you to go back to the results of your force-field analysis and compare your impelling and constraining forces with the actual changes suggested by the proposal. Does the suggested plan of action actually propose a change in one or more of the impelling or constraining forces? We used the example of a student-faculty committee working on the problem of course requirements; one of the impelling forces was the inability of the students to apply or use the course material currently taught. The first criterion for evaluating a proposed change in policy could be met if the proposal changed the course material in such a way that the concepts involved could be used in practical applications by the students. Of course, any proposal that changes a number of significant impelling or constraining forces will be evaluated as more desirable than a suggestion relating to only one of these forces. Thus *each proposal must be* *evaluated in terms of its probable effect on each of the impelling and constraining forces earlier identified.* It is easy to see that the quality of work done by your group as it produces an analysis of the problem will directly affect the way in which it is now able to evaluate various suggested proposals.

Criterion 2: Implementing the Proposal. This is crucial and frequently neglected by decision-making groups. It is crucial because, if a proposal cannot be implemented, it is not practical. Care should be taken that suggestions are not branded impractical without being given careful thought and consideration; sometimes plans that are *new* to a group are too quickly called impractical. Eventually it must be possible to implement any proposal of real value. In addition, implementation must be possible *by your group.* If such is not the case, you have identified a new problem for your group: *How can your group influence people who can implement this proposal?* Your group will have to deal with this problem, going the full route of force-field analysis, evaluating various proposals, adopting and implementing a plan designed to influence others who can take decisive action. Such an approach should be avoided if your group can think of any possible plan of action that it can implement without having to rely on influencing outsiders.

Criterion 3: Inherent and Serious Disadvantages in the Proposal. This requires you to look for inherent *dangers* or *severe costs* to your group. Inherent dangers usually consist of risks that your group cannot afford to take. For example, a student-faculty committee dealing with curriculum problems may evaluate proposed extension courses as inherently risky because of the difficulty of establishing the validity of such courses to the satisfaction of the hiring officials, who may refuse to give proper consideration to such training. Costs are judged to be unreasonable if they are greater than the benefits that would be derived from the adoption of a given proposal or if they are greater than the costs of alternative proposals that can achieve the same results. Government agencies in recent years have made the phrase "cost analysis" famous. We will explore this topic in Chapter 8.

IMPLEMENTING A DECISION

After decision-making group members have reached agreement on the appropriate or best solution to a problem of mutual concern, they will need to give special attention to putting that solution into operation. A chosen solution does not ordinarily become operative just because it is approved by a group; individual group members must make sure that it is actually put into practice. It is at this point that so many "action groups" fail; many committees are remiss in making an effort to see that a prepared plan is "followed through" to completion.

We shall deal with two issues: (a) developing a plan of action for your group members to follow and (b) mobilizing the resources external to your own group. In dealing with the first issue we shall assume that your plan is one that can be put into operation by your own group members without the help of people outside your group. For the second issue we shall suggest ways of implementing a plan that requires the help or cooperation of people who are not in your problem-solving group. These two approaches are significantly different, but at various times each one may be necessary.

Developing a Detailed Plan of Action

In essence, a detailed plan of action is one that organizes the efforts of the members of your group. The objective is to arrange for the most capable member to do a needed job at the most appropriate time with the necessary equipment or material. Haphazard efforts or poor planning can result in poor group effort as well as a severe loss of interpersonal regard and trust. Lack of an effective plan of action for implementing a proposed solution to a problem can, in fact, result in the ultimate breakup of your group.

At the heart of any effort for developing a detailed plan of group action must be a strong *commitment* on the part of your members to the group effort. They must be willing not only to do their part individually but also to acknowledge the superior capabilities of other members in doing certain tasks or assuming certain roles. The key concept here is *interdependence* between group members; they must work together as a team, assuming individual responsibility as well as relying upon each other.

If your group members are highly committed to achieving a chosen solution to the problem, and if they are willing to work together as a team, you are ready to develop a detailed plan of action involving five steps:

1. Identifying Specific Steps to Be Accomplished. Detailed planning starts here. Various members suggest things to be done, one item at a time. A list should be kept by a member, preferably on a blackboard or drawing table so that all can see. At some point you will need to be sure that all essential steps are identified. In addition, a chronological arrangement of these steps will be helpful. It is not uncommon for highly committed members to volunteer to perform some of these steps as they are being identified; such offers should be tentatively encouraged and reevaluated later in terms of the entire plan and its relation to an optimal use of the group's complete resources of time and energy.

In making your final list of detailed steps to be accomplished, start with today: What needs to be done *now?* The immediate enthusiasm of the group should be put to work; nothing should be put off or delayed if it can be started at once. Your final list should conclude with a step that operationally completes, or finalizes, the changed state of affairs your proposal is supposed to achieve.

2. Determining Required Resources. As you complete your list of steps to be taken, you will need to identify equipment, machines, material, and other resources needed in each step. The use of computers, office machines, offices, meeting places, and so on should be considered. Arrangements should be made so that at the appropriate time and place the required resources will be available. In some instances you will need to become informed as to where and how certain items can be obtained. These arrangements should be made a part of your detailed plan for implementing your chosen solution to the group problem and not be left to chance.

3. Agreeing upon Individual Responsibilities. If there is high commitment to the proposed plan of action, the group members should find it fairly easy to assess individual interests and capabilities. Both personal desire and capability should be considered as individuals take on certain obligations. General group agreement should be obtained as individual responsibilities are determined; in essence, the individual's responsibility should be to the group, not to one or two of its members or to himself or herself alone. As individual responsibilities are determined, all involved should be acquainted with the overall plan as well as with the details of their area of responsibility. In addition, they should know how, when, and where they will obtain the equipment or material needed. They should also determine the amount of help, if any, they will need from other group members and should plan with them how their help will be used.

4. Providing for Emergencies. Our experiences show us that few plans, even when well developed, work perfectly without mishap. Accidents occur, unforeseen barriers are encountered, and some persons become ill or find that their capabilities were overestimated. Your overall plan should provide for such unforeseen emergencies; some group members should have the responsibility of handling such problems if they arise. In the military it is common to have some units in reserve, "just in case." Some people in your group should have the responsibility to anticipate and provide contingency plans for crises.

5. Planning for Evaluation of the Proposed Plan. One of the present writers once worked for an oil pipeline company whose policy was to identify a problem, analyze it, select a plan of action, put the plan into operation, and go on to another problem. Only if a plan failed or worked poorly was it brought up again for further attention. However, a management consultant pointed out the value of systematically evaluating each "solution" after it was put into action. He suggested that the most appropriate time to plan or arrange for such evaluation was during the detailed planning of the program implementation. At this time procedures for evaluation could be built into the overall procedure; equipment for collecting performance data could be installed while other installations or modifications were being made. In this way total disruption and confusion would be reduced. The company adopted his suggestions and found them very useful.

We similarly recommend that your group include an evaluation of the proposed plan of action as one of the basic elements in implementing the plan. Seek information on the following items: (1) Did the predicted change actually occur; that is, did the proposal, when implemented, meet the need earlier identified by the group? (2) Did the plan, when implemented, cost no more (demand no more time, energy, or money) than predicted? (3) Were there any unforeseen risks or dangers after the plan was put into operation? Only if such questions are answered can a new policy or procedure be properly evaluated.

Mobilizing External Resources

In some cases your group will face problems that cannot be solved through the efforts of your group members; they will then need the help of persons outside your group. If the degree of help thought to be needed is significant, your group should redefine the problem as a *community* responsibility; that is, a social problem needing to be brought to the attention of the larger unit of society of which your group is only a part. This operation is not easy and is somewhat complicated. It will require procedures and skills of advocacy in addition to skills of group interaction. In part, however, the procedures of problem identification and analysis, as well as ways of evaluating proposed solutions, as described in previous sections, will be of value to you.

One effective approach is to reorganize yourselves into a new, larger group involving the entire community, or unit of society, having a concern or interest regarding this problem. If this can be done, well and good, and all that you have learned about working together as a group may be called upon in this new social environment. In many situations, however, the larger social unit may not share the concern felt by the members of your own smaller group. They have the resources and, in fact, they have the problem (although they do not recognize it), but you have the concern. In such a case you must think both for yourselves and for them and, when possible, explain your thinking to them, hoping they will adopt your proposed plan of action.

The first step is to follow standard procedures of group problem solving. Meet with other concerned persons, identify clearly this mutual concern, analyze impelling and constraining forces, identify the possible approaches, evaluate the suggested alternatives, and develop a detailed plan of action. In doing these things, however, you must also inform yourselves regarding the thinking of the "others" in the community or larger social unit. You must familiarize yourself with their thinking, their feelings, their other primary concerns, and their biases or "blind spots."

Starting with your concern, you must analyze and solve their problems *as if you were they.* This, of course, is never easy, but as best you can, you must do it. While this procedure is in progress, you will discover areas of their thinking you cannot accept. What should you do?

First, make sure you have obtained an accurate understanding of their thinking: Invite them to your meetings, ask for their opinions, read their published statements, and interview their spokespersons. If you are satisfied that you clearly understand their views but you still disagree, you must bolster your personal courage, because you will probably need it. Do not adopt their thinking if you honestly disagree with it; do not "find where the people want to go and get out in front" just to be liked by them. If you are not sincerely in agreement, quite likely you will be found out, and you will then be neither liked nor effective.

If you cannot satisfy both yourself and others, seek *to understand* their view. *Eventually, however, you must satisfy the demands of your own logic and conscience, and then you must, as honestly and clearly as you can, offer to them the essence of your thinking.* You must, in fact, become an advocate of your beliefs. As an advocate you will attempt to get them to adopt your analysis of the problem and your proposed plan of action.

SUMMARY

We have suggested an idealized format to aid decision-making groups in solving problems. First, groups are encouraged to compare the existing condition with the specific condition desired. This can be done by determining the scope of the problem, identifying the impelling and constraining forces, and noting members' perceptions of the intensity of the problems. Second, a realistic group goal must be set. Third, the group must obtain relevant information by evaluating the statements purported to be factual and determining the degree of acceptance of the statements by others.

In this chapter we have attempted to suggest appropriate ways of evaluating various proposed solutions to a problem when your group members have (1) previously agreed on an area of mutual concern and (2) made a careful analysis of the problem. We have admitted that many groups do not follow this sequence of consideration; however, we have held that groups can profit from looking at their problem-solving efforts in light of the logic of these sequential steps. The final section of the chapter has been devoted to suggestions for gaining the support of those outside your group when the resources of the larger community are required.

APPLICATIONS

6.1. Again refer to the transcription of the group made in the previous chapter. To what extent were the four steps suggested in this chapter followed?

6.2. In groups in which you have participated, have appropriate efforts been made to obtain relevant information? What sort of research was characteristic of your experience?

6.3. Formulate a model showing the impelling and constraining forces of the group discussion that you have transcribed.

NOTES

1. K. Giffin and B. R. Patton, *Fundamentals of Interpersonal Communication.* New York: Harper & Row, 1976, pp. 44–65.
2. K. Lewin, *Field Theory in Social Research.* New York: Harper & Row, 1951; see especially pp. 188–237.

chapter 7

Leadership

A group of adults was asked to list the behaviors of effective leaders they had witnessed. The group offered the following list:

shows knowledge	is flexible
is confident	provides feedback
is analytical	keeps focus on the task
delegates	is group centered
provides structure	is energetic
is hardworking	is honest
leads by example	listens carefully
is creative	is willing to make decisions

How do you respond to this list? Are there other behaviors you would add to the list or ones you feel are suspect?

Scholars and researchers have been extremely interested in the phenomenon of leadership. Bernard M. Bass revised and expanded in 1981 the *Handbook of Leadership,* originally compiled by Ralph M. Stogdill.[1] This sourcebook summarizes and interprets more than 5,000 books and articles on the dynamics of leadership written since 1940. It is highly recommended as a resource for exploring in greater detail the rich resources available on this topic; in this chapter we shall merely be able to give an overview of the theories and suggest general findings of the research.

Leaders, like groups, vary in their characteristics. Different situations and circumstances require different functions to be performed if a group is to move closer to its goal. We view leadership as a role that provides for vital group needs by exerting influence toward the attainment of group goals. Leadership, according to this definition, is a process. It is present no matter who the individuals are who are taking leadership roles or what their influence is.

CHARACTERISTICS OF LEADERS

What kind of person is most likely to become a leader? A number of researchers have attempted to identify the traits of people who are generally regarded as effective leaders. For example, as long ago as 1915 investigators who were looking at the relationship between leadership and *height* found that executives in insurance companies were on the average taller than subordinates, university presidents were generally taller than presidents of small colleges, and railway presidents were taller than station agents.[2] Such single-variable studies are now easily dismissed because of their lack of sophistication. Researchers then turned to internal traits.

Studies of personality traits of leaders indicate that people in leadership roles are more self-confident than other people, are better adjusted and show greater empathy and interpersonal sensitivity than other people.[3]

Bass summarizes his analysis of more than 200 studies on traits of leadership as follows:

> The leader is characterized by a strong drive for responsibility and task completion, vigor and persistence in pursuit of goals, venturesomeness and originality in problem solving, drive to exercise initiation in social situations, self-confidence and sense of personal identity, willingness to accept consequences of decision and action, readiness to absorb interpersonal stress, willingness to tolerate frustration and delay, ability to influence other persons' behavior, and capacity to structure social interaction systems to the purpose at hand.[4]

This evidence that leaders have different traits from nonleaders must be interpreted with caution. Exceptions to all these general trends can be found, and having these traits does not guarantee that a person will assume positions of effective leadership. Causality is also subject to scrutiny. Possibly, if you are elected to a position of leadership, your self-confidence will increase, you will be better adjusted, and you will become more sensitive to others.

In a study of the selection and performance of leaders, researchers at the New Jersey Institute of Technology discovered a high correlation between the number of verbal comments made by a group participant and the participant's anticipation that few or numerous comments indicated leadership potential. In a controlled experiment that allowed the researchers to know in advance the correct answers to a group problem, there was no correlation between the quality of the leader's prediscussion solution and the likelihood of his or her being selected as a leader. They state: "Thus, we see that it is the relatively verbose person who becomes leader, not the person with the most knowledge about the problem the group would try to solve."[5]

STYLES OF LEADERSHIP

The classic dichotomy of contrasting styles of leadership has been the authoritarian-democratic. In an extensive study of groups of children in summer day camps, White and Lippitt were concerned with the effects on productivity and on membership satisfaction of three different styles of leadership, which they called authoritarian, democratic, and laissez-faire.[6] Adult leaders were trained to proficiency in the leadership styles. The distinctions in leaderships are shown in Table 7.1.

The major results were the following:

1. Democratic leadership led to more and better productivity than did laissez-faire leadership.
2. Autocratic leadership led to more productivity than did democratic leadership over a short period of time (in the long run democratic leadership tends to higher productivity). On the other hand, the quality of work was consistently better in democratic groups, compared with that in autocratic groups.
3. When autocratic leaders were absent, the group tended to "fall apart"; this did not happen in democratic groups.
4. Members of democratic groups were more satisfied than members of laissez-faire groups; most of the members were more satisfied with democratic leadership than with autocratic leadership, although a few were more satisfied under autocratic leaders.
5. There was least absenteeism and fewest dropouts under democratic leadership.
6. Autocratic leadership was characterized either by the greatest incidence of hostility and aggressiveness among members or by the greatest apathy, depending on the group. On the other hand, autocratic groups displayed the least "talking back" to leaders.

Similarly conceived studies have applied similar conceptual schemes to the study of effective supervisory and administrative behavior. The conclusion seems inescapable that, to the extent that

Table 7.1   LEADER BEHAVIOR IN THREE "SOCIAL CLIMATES"

Authoritarian	Democratic	Laissez-faire
1. All determination of policy made by leader	1. All policies a matter of group discussion and decision, encouraged and assisted by leader	1. Complete freedom for group or individual decision; minimum of leader participation
2. Techniques and activity steps dictated by the authority, one at a time, so that future steps are always largely uncertain	2. Activity perspective gained during discussion period; general steps to group goal sketched and, when technical advice needed, two or more alternative procedures suggested by leader	2. Leader supplying various materials, making it clear he or she would supply information when asked, but taking no other part in discussion
3. Particular work task and work companion of each member usually dictated by leader	3. Members free to work with anyone; division of tasks left up to group	3. Complete nonparticipation of leader
4. Dominator tending to be "personal" in praise and criticism of work of each member; remaining aloof from active group participation except when demonstrating	4. Leader "objective" or "fact minded" in praise or criticism, trying to be regular group member in spirit without doing too much of the work	4. Leader infrequently spontaneously commenting on member activities, unless questioned; no attempt to appraise or regulate course of events

Source: R. White and R. Lippitt, "Leader behavior and member reaction in three 'social climates,'" in *Group Dynamics,* 3rd ed., ed. by D. Cartwright and A. Zander. New York: Harper & Row, 1968, p. 319.

group members participate in the making of decisions that affect them, they will have greater productivity and greater satisfaction.[7]

Jack Gibb has equated the authoritarian style with defensive behavior. Defensive leaders believe that the average person cannot be trusted, so their role is to supervise and control. They rely on subterfuge and manipulation through extrinsic rewards. A cycle of fear and distrust is created. As Gibb states:

Defensive leaders use various forms of persuasion to motivate subordinates toward the organization of goals, but often the results are either apathy and passivity or frenetic conformity. Persuasion is a form of control and begets resistance, which may take many subtle forms. Open and aggressive cold war between teachers and administrators, for instance, is an obvious form. More common—and less easy to deal with—is passive, often unconscious resistance such as apathy, apparent obtuseness, dependent demands for further and more minute instructions, bumbling, wheelspinning, and a whole variety of inefficiencies that reduce creative work.[8]

As an alternative to such defensive leadership, Gibb suggests:

The key to emergent leadership centers in a high degree of trust and confidence in people. Leaders who trust their colleagues and subordinates and have confidence in them tend to be open and frank, to be permissive in goal setting, and to be noncontrolling in personal style and leadership policy. People with a great deal of self-acceptance and personal security do trust others, do make trust assumptions about their motives and behavior. The self-adequate person tends to assume that others are also adequate and, other things being equal, that they will be responsible, loyal, appropriately work-oriented when work is to be performed, and adequate to carry out jobs that are commensurate with their levels of experience and growth.[9]

Openness thus begets openness.

An experiment attempted to determine the effects of different leader verbal styles on group members. Leaders were trained to be either speculative (open) or confrontive. Confrontive-led members perceived their leaders to be charismatic, strong, and powerful and tended to intimidate members during the group's formative stage. In the speculative-led groups, members spoke more and saw their leaders as peers. While the leader style in this experiment had an effect on the group process, no correlation was found with the members' satisfaction scores or the types of leaders on member's self-concept scores.[10]

SITUATIONAL LEADERSHIP

A number of social critics suggest that had the World War II not occurred, history would have ignored Winston Churchill. He was considered dogmatic, authoritarian, impatient, and opinionated. In the crisis of war, however, England needed such a leader to inspire the people in a single-minded mission. Thus, these critics believe it was a case of history making the man, rather than of the man making history. The perspective illustrates the *situationist* concept, which posits the view that most people have the potential to serve as leaders if the conditions and circumstances favor their unique talents.

An example of research on this topic was conducted by Arthur Hastorf, who was interested in seeing whether shy, quiet people who are often unnoticed in groups have the potential for leadership.[11] After observing groups of four students discuss a case-study (from behind a one-way mirror), the individual whose participation was next to the lowest in each group was selected for the experiment. During the experimental phase the subjects were told that shielded panels in front of each of them would display either a red or a green light, as determined by human relations experts in the observation room. The green light was a signal to talk more, and the red light suggested silence. The shy person was thus able to be encouraged to talk more and the more talkative members encouraged to less participation. As expected, the quiet person's contributions increased substantially.

A subsequent phase to the study dispensed with the lights, and the participants were allowed to talk as much as they pleased. During this final discussion, the new leader did not relinquish his position. This study then suggests that most people have some leadership potential, and given the opportunity and encouragement, they can learn to take command. As new leaders without experience emerge, people are likely to be skeptical of their potential, but the situationist would predict that the leader will be viewed as more capable after taking leadership. The 1986 emergence of Corazon Aquino as president of the Philippines is a good example of this phenomenon.

The best-known proponent of situational leadership effectiveness is Fred E. Fiedler with his *Contingency Model of Leadership.*[12] This model specifies the kind of situation in which a leader with a high LPC (*L*east *P*referred *C*oworker) score will be more effective than a leader with a low LPC score, and vice versa. The score is obtained by a semantic differential as shown in Figure 7.1. A leader is thus asked to think of the coworker with whom he or she could work least well. The ratings for each item are coded from 1 to 8 and added together. A leader who is quite critical in rating his or her least preferred coworker will obtain a low LPC score, while a lenient leader will obtain a high LPC score.

From considerable research, Fiedler observed that a high LPC leader tends to have close interpersonal relationships with people and is more person-oriented than task-oriented. The low LPC leader is committed to task objectives, often at the expense of people. The precise behavior of the two types of leaders vary depending on the situation.

In Fiedler's model, the relationship between leader LPC scores and leader effectiveness depends on a complex situational variable with multiple components. The variable is called either "situational favorability" or "situational control," defined by the extent to which the situation gives a leader influence over subordinate performance. Situational control is usually measured in terms of three aspects:

1. *Leader-member relations.* A leader who has the loyalty and support of the group can rely on members to comply en-

Instructions:

People differ in the ways they think about those with whom they work. On the scale below are pairs of words that are opposite in meaning. You are asked to describe someone with whom you have worked by placing an *X* in one of the eight spaces on the line between the two words. Each space represents how well the adjective fits the person you are describing, as in the following example:

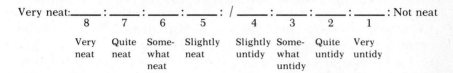

Now think of the person with whom you can work least well. It may be someone you work with now or someone you knew in the past. It does not have to be the person you like least well but should be the person with whom you had the most difficulty in getting a job done. Describe this person as he or she appears to you.

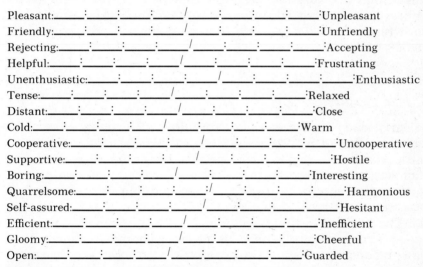

Figure 7.1 Example of an LPC Scale. Adapted from F. E. Fiedler, *A Theory of Leadership Effectiveness.* New York: McGraw-Hill, 1967.

thusiastically with directions, while a leader who is disliked may have group members ignore directions or subvert policies.

2. *Position power.* A leader with substantial position power is able to administer rewards and punishments as incentives for compliance, while leaders without such power must rely on other means of influence.

3. *Task structure.* A task is highly structured when a detailed description of the product, service, or goal of the group is

available to determine how well the work has been performed. If the task is unstructured, the leader cannot easily
determine how well group members are performing.[13]

Fiedler has found that leader-member relations are the most
important determinant of situational control, followed by task structure and finally by position power. When the situation is either very
high or very low in situational control, leaders with low LPC scores
will be more effective than leaders with high LPC scores. In the
intermediate area, leaders with high LPC scores will be more effective. Fiedler has proposed an explanation for this relationship suggesting that the particular motive hierarchy of some leaders makes
them more likely to use the kind of leadership behavior appropriate
for that situation.[14]

Fiedler's model and the methodology of the validation studies
have been severely criticized in the last few years. Critics suggest
that the LPC score is speculative and inadequately supported. The
causal links are questionable, without strong justifications for an
arbitrary system of weighing variables.[15] The debate continues, and
more research is being conducted attempting to determine the
model's validity and utility.

TASK AND MAINTENANCE FUNCTIONS

An early analysis of the leadership duties of business executives
made by Barnard in 1938 suggested that two dimensions must be
considered: achievement, or the performing of the group task, and
efficiency, or keeping the members satisfied.[16] These two dimensions parallel the functions of task and maintenance described in
Chapter 4.

The leadership functions related to task accomplishment include helping set and clarify goals, focusing on information needed,
drawing upon available group resources, stimulating research,
maintaining orderly operating procedures, introducing suggestions
when they are needed, establishing an atmosphere that permits
testing, rigorously evaluating ideas, devoting oneself to the task,
attending to the clock and the schedule, pulling the group together
for consensus or patterns of action, and enabling the group to determine and evaluate its progress.

The group maintenance functions of leadership include encouraging participation by everyone in the group, keeping everyone
in a friendly mood, responding to the emotional concerns of group
members when that is appropriate, promoting open communication, listening attentively to all contributions, encouraging with positive feedback, showing enthusiasm and good humor, promoting

pride in the group, judging accurately the changing moods of the group, and providing productive outlets for tensions.

The performance of both task and maintenance roles, then, is essential if a group is to move toward its goal. These roles are constantly being filled, adequately or inadequately, through the participation of group members. To some degree, therefore, all good members help in fulfilling these necessary leadership roles.

Robert Blake and his associates refined the theoretical view of leadership as it relates to managerial behavior in industry with his Managerial Grid.[17] Figure 7.2 shows the grid with its two dimensions, concern for people and concern for task accomplishment. On the basis of questionnaire surveys and responses to value statements, Blake categorized people as follows: the "bureaucrat," unconcerned with either dimension (1,1); the "country-club manager," interested in people but not in tasks (1,9); the "taskmaster," high on tasks but low on people (9,1); the firm but fair "compromiser" (5,5); and the "ideal," concerned greatly with both task and people (9,9). Blake believes that it is possible to attain a maximal concern for both production and people simultaneously.

Some task groups are so concerned with what they are doing that they ignore problems of maintenance, sweeping them under the rug. Conversely, other task groups are so concerned with creat-

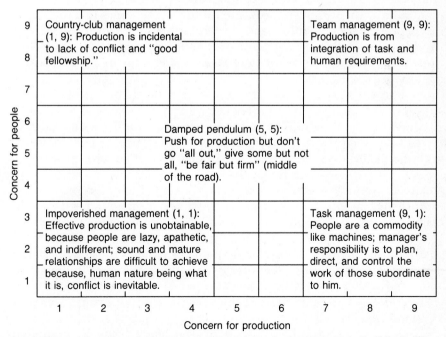

Figure 7.2 The Managerial Grid. From R. R. Blake, J. S. Mouton, and A. C. Bidwell, "The managerial grid: A comparison of eight theories of management," *Advanced Management-Office Executive,* 1 (September 1962), 13.

ing a warm, acceptant atmosphere and analyzing personal functioning that they allow the development of frustrations in the area of task accomplishment. Groups need a balance of both task and maintenance functions if they are to be effective. In most groups, especially those with a formal leader, these functions must be assumed by the leader if he or she is to lead effectively. Failure in either category will give rise to an unofficial or informal leader who takes over neglected roles.

In leaderless groups the two functions are assumed typically by two different people, a "task specialist" and a "maintenance specialist." The task specialist is seen as having the best ideas and plays an aggressive role in moving the group toward a solution of its problems; this person may, however, thereby incur hostility.[18] The maintenance specialist is highly liked and is concerned with solving the socioemotional problems of the group, resolving tensions and conflicts within the group and preserving its unity.[19]

Extending Blake's Managerial Grid model, Hersey and Blanchard developed a situational leadership theory based upon the variable of follower "maturity."[20] Maturity is defined as "the capacity to set high but attainable goals (achievement motivation), willingness to take responsibility, and education and/or experience."[21] Measurement is made regarding a particular task to be performed and may differ from subordinate to subordinate and task to task. According to their theory, as subordinate maturity increases to a moderate level, the leader should use more relationship-oriented behavior and less task-oriented behavior. As subordinate maturity increases further, the leader should decrease the amount of both types of behavior (see Figure 7.3).

The causal relationships implied by the theory are shown in Figure 7.4. The leader can alter the maturity level of subordinates by using developmental interventions consisting of reduced directives and delegating greater responsibility. If the subordinate responds positively, the leader reinforces by praise and encouragement. This theory and model has also been seriously criticized in terms of the absence of validation studies and the omission of other significant situational variables.[22] However, it makes a positive contribution with its emphasis on flexible, adaptable leader behaviors.

Research by Sandra Ketrow supports an attributional theory of leadership. She found that people judge as leaders those who match an implicit set of valued leadership behaviors. Subjects in her study chose procedural specialists most often as leaders, but viewed task-oriented specialists as most influential in a small-group decision-making discussion.[23]

Beatrice Schultz has confirmed that leaders can be predicted based upon members' ratings of communication function. Leadership is thus defined by those functions that move a group toward its

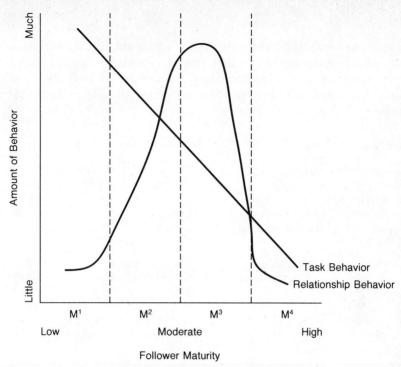

Figure 7.3 Situational leadership behavior prescriptions. From P. Hersey and K. H. Blanchard, *Management of Organizational Behavior.* Englewood Cliffs, N.J.: Prentice-Hall, 1977, p. 161.

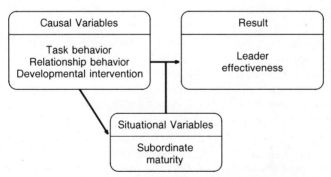

Figure 7.4 Causal relationships in situational leadership.

goals: setting goals, giving directions, and summarizing. Leader competence was determined by actions related to goal setting or direction giving.[24]

GROUP-CENTERED LEADERSHIP

In contrast to the theories just cited, in which the leader serves to motivate, direct, and evaluate the group's outcome, Bradford contends that better results can be attained by using a group-centered approach.[25] According to this view of leadership, the group as a whole must share the responsibility for its effectiveness, and maintenance functions are considered as important as task-oriented functions. Bradford summarizes the contrast between traditional and group-centered leadership as follows:[26]

Traditional Leadership

1. The leader directs, controls, polices the members, and leads them to the proper decision. Basically it is his or her group, and the leader's authority and responsibility are acknowledged by members.

2. The leader focuses his or her attention on the task to be accomplished, brings the group back from any diverse wandering, performs all the functions needed to arrive at the proper decision.

3. The leader sets limits and uses rules of order to keep the discussion within strict limits set by the agenda. He or she controls the time spent on each item lest the group wander fruitlessly.

4. The leader believes that emotions are disruptive to objective, logical thinking and should be discouraged or suppressed. He or she assumes it is his or her task to make clear to all members the disruptive effect of emotions.

5. The leader believes that he or she should handle a member's disruptive behavior by talking to the member away from the group; it is the leader's task to do so.

6. Because the need to arrive at a task decision is all-important in the eyes of the leader, the needs of individual members are considered less important.

Group-Centered Leadership

1. The group, or meeting, is owned by the members, including the leader. All members, with the leader's assistance, contribute to its effectiveness.

2. The group is responsible, with occasional and appropriate help from the designated leader, for reaching a decision that includes the participation of all and is the product of all. The leader is a servant and helper of the group.

3. Members of the group should be encouraged and helped to take responsibility for its task productivity, its methods of working, its assignment of tasks, and its plans for the use of the time available.

4. Feelings, emotions, and conflict are recognized by the members and the leader as legitimate facts and situations demanding as serious attention as the task agenda.

5. The leader believes that any problem in the group must be faced and solved within the group and by the group. As trust develops among members, it is much easier for an individual to discover ways in which his or her behavior is bothering the group.

6. With help and encouragement from the leader, the members come to realize that the needs, feelings, and purposes of all members should be met so that an awareness forms of being a group. Then the group can continue to grow.

Bradford recognizes that group-centered leadership requires considerable skill on the part of both leader and group member. Traditionally oriented leaders may be afraid to risk sharing control or dealing openly with emotions. Even in the absence of strong validation checks under experimental conditions, personal experience leads us to favor and encourage the group-centered approach. While all groups do not have the maturity to employ such an approach, we believe that this style of leadership will promote greater trust and commitment to the group. The interpersonal skills and sensitivity to the well-being of others can be developed if the risks are taken and appropriate time is available.

LEADERSHIP BEHAVIORS

In keeping with the task/maintenance functions of leadership, specific leadership behaviors can be identified that enhance the group-centered approach. The following list is a composite drawn from the work of Bales,[27] Bradford,[28] and Benne and Sheats.[29]

Task Orientation

1. *Initiating-structuring.* To present a problem to the group, to propose an objective and get the group's approval, to introduce a procedure for the group to use in solving a problem or making a decision, to develop an agenda listing topics to be discussed and issues to be decided, to suggest that the group is ready to proceed to a different activity, to direct the discussion back to the task after it has wandered off track, to recess or end the meeting

2. *Stimulating communication.* To seek specific information from group members, to ask members for their opinions, to encourage members to contribute their ideas, to provide specific information yourself

3. *Clarifying communication.* To reduce confusion or clear up a misunderstanding by asking a member to elaborate what he or she has said, by restating in a different way what someone has said, by asking a group member how he or she interpreted another member's comment, by interpreting ideas and defining terms, or by integrating separate ideas to show how they are related

4. *Summarizing.* To review what has been said or accomplished so far, to review ideas and facts offered during a lengthy period of discussion, to list or post ideas as they are suggested and ask the group to review them

5. *Consensus testing.* To check on the amount of agreement among group members regarding objectives, interpretation

of information, evaluation of different alternatives, and readiness to reach a decision

Maintenance Orientation

1. *Gatekeeping.* To regulate and facilitate the participation of group members, to suggest ways of increasing participation, to encourage contributions by quiet members and prevent dominant members from monopolizing the discussion
2. *Harmonizing.* To smooth over conflict between members or mediate it by suggesting compromises, to reduce tension with humor, to ask members to reconcile their differences in a constructive manner, to discourage personal attacks, insults, and threats
3. *Supporting.* To be friendly and supportive to group members, to be responsive to their needs and feelings, to come to the aid of a member or help the person save face, to show appreciation for the contributions of members
4. *Standard setting.* To suggest norms and standards of behavior (e.g., objectivity, fairness), to encourage the group to establish norms, to remind the group of norms that it established previously, to point out implicit group norms and check how members really feel about them
5. *Process analyzing.* To examine group processes in order to identify process problems and dysfunctional member behavior, to point out process problems to the group, to ask members for their perception of the group meetings (e.g., effectiveness of communication, degree of trust, amount of cooperation, effectiveness of procedures, etc.)

SUMMARY

Leadership is certainly an important consideration in the relative success or failure of any group. In this chapter we have surveyed approaches to the study of leadership by looking at characteristics of effective leaders, styles of leadership, situational and contingency factors, and suggested group-centered leadership as a goal to be pursued.

In essence we concur with Bernard Bass, who summarized his monumental survey of the research and theory on leadership as follows:

The real test of leadership lies not in the personality or behavior of the leaders, but in the performance of the groups they lead. Groups, when free to do so, appear to select as leaders members who create the expectation that they will be able to maintain goal direction, facilitate task achievement, and ensure group cohesiveness. Whether objectives are long-term to develop the group or short-term to maximize current performance will make a decided difference. The behaviors furthering task accomplishment are not necessarily the same as those fostering cohesiveness. Some leaders are extremely effective in furthering task achievement. Others are exceptionally skilled in the art of building member satisfaction and intermember loyalty, which strengthen group cohesiveness. The most valued leaders are able to do both.[30]

APPLICATIONS

7.1. With a group of classmates, compile a list of the behaviors you believe exemplify effective leaders. Compile another list of characteristics typical of poor leaders. How do they compare with the list at the beginning of this chapter?

7.2. Apply the concept of situational leadership to one of the groups you have observed. How would you predict the members of the group would have filled out the LPC scale?

7.3. Analyze one of the groups observed using the Managerial Grid. Relate the interpretation to the concept of group-centered leadership.

NOTES

1. B. M. Bass, *Stogdill's Handbook of Leadership.* New York: The Free Press, 1981.

2. C. A. Gibb, "Leadership," in *The Handbook of Social Psychology,* ed. by G. Lindzey and E. Aronson. Reading, Mass.: Addison-Wesley, 1969.

3. K. J. Gergen and M. M. Gergen, *Social Psychology.* New York: Harcourt Brace Jovanovich, 1981, p. 321.

4. Bass, *Stogdill's Handbook of Leadership,* p. 81.

5. S. R. Hiltz, M. Turoff, and K. Johnson, "The effects of human leadership and computer feedback on the quality of group problem solving via computer," paper presented at the International Communication Association, May 1984.

6. R. White and R. Lippitt, "Leader behavior and member reaction in three 'social climates,' " in *Group Dynamics,* 3rd ed., ed. by D. Cartwright and A. Zander. New York: Harper & Row, 1968, pp. 318–335.

7. See, for example, K. Griffin and L. Ehrlich, "The attitudinal effects of a group discussion on a proposed change in company policy," *Speech Monographs,* 30 (1963), 337–379.

8. J. R. Gibb, "Dynamics of leadership," *Current Issues in Higher Education,* a publication of the American Association for Higher Education, 1967, 27.

9. Ibid., p. 31.

10. S. Barlow, W. D. Hansen, A. J. Fuhriman, and R. Finley, "Leader communication style—Effects on members of small groups," *Small Group Behavior,* 13, No. 4 (November 1982), 518–531.

11. A. H. Hastorf, "The 'reinforcement' of individual actions in a group situation," in *Research in Behavior Modification,* ed. by L. Krasner and L. P. Ullmann. New York: Holt, Rinehart and Winston, 1965.

12. See, for example, F. E. Fiedler, *A Theory of Leadership Effectiveness.* New York: McGraw-Hill, 1967. See also F. E. Fiedler and L. Mahar, "A field experiment validating contingency model leadership training," *Journal of Applied Psychology,* 64 (1979), 247–254.
13. F. E. Fiedler, "The contingency model and the dynamics of the leadership process," in *Advances in Experimental Social Psychology,* ed. by L. Berkowitz. New York: Academic Press, 1978, pp. 62–65.
14. Ibid., pp. 59–112.
15. L. H. Peters, D. D. Hartke, and J. T. Pohlmann, "Fiedler's contingency theory of leadership: An application of the meta-analysis procedures of Schmidt and Hunter," *Psychological Bulletin,* 97 (1985), 275–285.
16. C. Barnard, *The Functions of the Executive.* Cambridge, Mass.: Harvard University Press, 1938.
17. R. R. Blake, J. S. Mouton, and A. C. Bidwell, "The managerial grid: A comparison of eight theories of management," *Advanced Management-Office Executive,* 1 (September 1962), 12–16, 36.
18. R. F. Bales, "The equilibrium problem in small groups," in *Working Papers in the Theory of Action,* ed. by T. Parsons, R. F. Bales, and E. A. Shils. Glencoe, Ill.: Free Press, 1953.
19. J. W. Thibaut and H. H. Kelley, *The Social Psychology of Groups.* New York: Wiley, 1959.
20. P. Hersey and K. H. Blanchard, *Management of Organizational Behavior.* Englewood Cliffs, N.J.: Prentice-Hall, 1977.
21. Ibid., p. 161.
22. G. A. Yukl, *Leadership in Organizations.* Englewood Cliffs, N.J.: Prentice-Hall, 1981, pp. 143–144.
23. S. M. Ketrow, "Valued leadership behaviors and perceptions of contribution," paper presented at the Speech Communication Association, San Francisco, November 1983.
24. B. Schultz, "Predicting emergent leaders: An exploratory study of the salience of communicative functions," *Small Group Behavior,* 9, No. 1 (1978), 109–114.
25. L. P. Bradford, *Making Meetings Work.* La Jolla, Calif.: University Associates, 1976.
26. Ibid., p. 13.
27. R. F. Bales, *Interaction Process Analysis.* Reading, Mass.: Addison-Wesley, 1950.
28. Bradford, *Making Meetings Work.*
29. K. D. Benne and P. Sheats, "Functional roles of groups members," *Journal of Social Issues,* 4 (1948), 41–49.
30. Bass, Stogdill's *Handbook of Leadership,* p. 598.

chapter *8*

Group Characteristics and Their Effects

When called upon to describe a person, we might start listing characteristics that distinguish him or her from others. Similarly, in describing a group we ask, "What are the distinguishing characteristics of this group?" We shall look at the group as an entity with definite properties. In this chapter we shall consider group characteristics that have been demonstrated to affect or be affected by interaction among group members.

We shall examine such characteristics as norms of the group, group cohesiveness, group task, group size, and gender makeup of the group.

NORMS

If a collection of people is characterized as a "group," certain norms and conformity behavior may be identified. The concept of group norms has been derived from long usage in sociopsychological studies. It identifies the ways that members of a group behave and ways that are thought by them to be proper. A group norm has been defined as a "shared acceptance of a rule."[1] Members come to expect how other people will behave and how they themselves are expected to behave.

Group norms are particularly important to an understanding of the interactions in a group. If people are to be able to interact, they must have some common areas of agreement around which to organize their attitudes, values, perceptions, and cognitions. In the absence of such norms no stability or orderliness is possible, and chaos will result. Cooperation presupposes bases of mutual agreement.

If we conceive of norms as shared expectations about beliefs and behaviors, then it follows that certain things in the life of the group will be deemed appropriate and that there will be a certain approved way of doing things. Thus groups have the capacity to influence the behavior of their members.

Groups establish norms in order to fulfil a variety of needs. Norms may serve to keep a group together, to provide information, and to regulate the social interactions of the group. For example, norms may establish that interpersonal hostility is not to occur among members of the group and may only be directed toward people outside the group.[2]

An example of the positive use of norms may be found in Alcoholics Anonymous. People who were apparently unable to cope individually with their drinking problems have been able to change their behavior through affiliation with that organization. In testimonial meetings the members see that others share their experiences and problems and in effect speak the same language. If they are able to accept the norms of the group and adhere to the rules established, then the program can be successful.

Other examples of norms' dictating behavior are the rigorous enforcement of output regulations in industrial unions and of "squealing" to the police among street gangs, which can bring dire results. One study of norms in a group of workers at Western Electric revealed the following standards of behavior:[3]

1. You should not turn out too much work. If you do, you are a "ratebuster."
2. You should not turn out too little work. If you do, you are a "chiseler."
3. You should not tell a supervisor anything that will act to the detriment of an associate. If you do you are a "squealer."
4. You should not attempt to maintain social distance or act officious. If you are an inspector, for example, you should not act like one.

The researchers actually identified these norms, which were more or less subconscious among the workers. Norms are found in other groups, too, such as fraternities, sports teams, and living units.

The rigorous observance of norms may result in conformity. Conformity extends from overt behaviors to perceptions and attitudes. In Chapter 4 we cited the Asch study as demonstrating the way in which our perceptions are affected by group pressures. Our cognitions and evaluative standards are likewise influenced by group norms. How we view foreign aid, the things we believe, and the judgments we make obviously will be influenced by the groups in which we interact. We are more likely to speak out only if we feel in accord with the attitudes of others.

How do these group norms emerge? Festinger has suggested two ways.[4] First, people seek to validate their beliefs; if their beliefs cannot be verified by checking facts personally, then what everyone else believes must be true. If the other members of a male group endorse sexual discrimination, then that belief becomes social reality; jokes are made at the expense of women, and only a heretic could endorse a woman for the presidency. Second, if a group is to survive and be effective, interactions among the members must be coordinated. Norms regulating the conduct of the members are, therefore, instrumental to the survival and success of the group.

Kiesler and Kiesler cite examples of norms that are likely to emerge in groups:

1. When individuals are committed to each other because of situational factors (e.g., they work together) or because their interaction has aroused emotional ties, they want future interaction to be as smooth as possible. Norms requiring "polite" behavior or "moderate" attitudes may become strong. In one experiment, either subjects were committed to working with their partners in the future, or would never see them again. Some subjects heard a bogus tape in which their partners insulted the experimenter. The insult involved expressing extremely negative attitudes about secretaries—the experimenter's former occupation. The subjects' reactions to this *faux pas* depended on whether or not they would have to work with their partners in the future. If they were not committed to future interaction, they tended to ignore their partner's behavior. But when they were committed, they openly expressed concern that their partners act "correctly."

2. Sometimes the success of the group goal will depend on the members' expressing extreme attitudes and personal feelings, or on the enactment of less "cultured" behaviors. Students at Yale University participated in a group "problem-solving" experiment. The atmosphere of the experiment was varied to create different group goals. In one condition, the experimenter formally and carefully presented the experiment as if it were very important to him. In another condition, he was dressed sloppily, and casually introduced the experiment as if it were an extra duty. Throughout the experiment, a confederate acted impolitely and disrespectfully. Another "control" confederate acted normally. Later in the session, subjects rated the two confederates. The data showed that, compared to the normal confederate, the impolite confederate was disliked. But negative reactions to him were much greater when the atmosphere of the experiment was serious rather than casual. Presumably, the serious dress and demeanor of the experimenter encouraged the group members to be formal and task oriented; the goal might have been to get the job done or to please the experimenter. Since

in that case norms requiring attention to the task, respect for the experimenter, and politeness would be important, it is not surprising that the subjects disliked the confederate who fooled around.

3. The group serving an informational function for its members is often less concerned with manners and the pleasantness of interaction. Instead the group imposes standards that will provide the maximum amount of the desired information, and the least disquieting means of evaluating others and oneself. In discussing some data from the World War II studies of the American soldier, Kelley . . . noted that combat veterans had "a strong group code against any tendencies to glamorize or express eagerness for combat." We can guess that in the face of danger, unambiguous information on how to behave was essential for survival. Moreover, unrealistic bravado would have contradicted the evidence of the senses. Of course, the green troops were also insecure and in need of information. But without the evidence of combat, optimistic evaluations of the situation would be the most comfortable and self-enhancing kinds of information to have. Hence, the emergence of "blood and thunder" norms would reduce anxiety while increasing "manliness" and patriotism—that is, until war became a reality.[5]

Norms vary in the ease with which they can be learned. Some are formally codified, as in bylaws; others may be easily recognized and verbalized by members; others are less explicit and become apparent only when they are violated. A new teacher on a Native American reservation was invited to a "spirit breakfast" honoring a deceased member of the tribe. She refused some of the food as it was passed to her. Although no one made any direct comments, she subsequently probed their repeated references to the occasion and learned that it is expected that each person take a portion of every dish. Her act was deviant because it violated a shared idea about what should have been done on that particular occasion.

Sanctions enable the group to maintain its norms and punish violators. They carry two messages, which may or may not be explicit. The first relates an act to a norm directly: "What you have done goes against the rules." The second is concerned with future actions: "You must cease and desist." Like all actions, sanctions themselves are subject to norms. Bad looks, silence, and the ignoring of a person may suffice to reinforce behavior perceived as deviant.

Having examined norms and conformity behavior, let us consider the forces that determine the strength of norms and their influence on the behavior of group members; these forces are called group cohesiveness.

COHESIVENESS

As we have just noted, conformity may be thought of as an individual's adherence to group expectancies. Similarly, conformity is greatest when a group is cohesive. The two dimensions are interdependent and closely related.

Although "cohesiveness" as a term is used widely, the definition and conceptualization cause problems. Cohesiveness refers to the overall attraction of group members to each other and the way in which they "stick together." Members have a sense of belonging and are dedicated to the well-being of the group. Indirectly, cohesiveness refers to morale, teamwork, or so-called group spirit of the group.[6] In a review of experimental group research Bednar and Kaul went so far as to suggest that there is little cognitive substance to the concept of cohesion and that the term "be dropped from the empirical vocabulary and that more representative alternatives be found."[7]

This conceptual problem has been attacked by researchers who have examined constructs thought to be related to cohesion. Stokes has suggested three such constructs:[8]

1. *Attraction to individual members of the group.* This factor was suggested earlier by Zaleznik and Moment who stated the strong connectedness between norms and cohesion:

   Norms of behavior tend to be strong when members are attracted to and identify with the group. Work groups create conditions for identification simply because membership is economically important to the individuals. We do not lightly undertake to leave jobs and abandon existing work groups. When group members, in addition, have few other group memberships the value of the group is enhanced for them. This phenomenon is seen most clearly in minority group formations. Where ethnic barriers prevent free movement among groups in a society, the restricted opportunities for membership result in strong systems of norms because the attraction to the group is high for its members.[9]

2. *The instrumental value of the group.* A group will thus be cohesive or attractive to its members to the degree that they see it as meeting their needs and as being helpful to them. This construct has also been supported by previous research. If members of a group feel included, liked, and respected, they come to depend on the group for these reinforcements. As people with similar needs find similar reinforcements, a cohesive group develops. Even one dissatisfied member, however, may damage the morale of the entire group. In one study groups of college students were assigned tasks relating to dart throwing. In certain groups a confederate was planted, who expressed the opinion that the task was trivial, dull, and impossible of accomplishment. These groups had significantly lower levels of aspiration and satisfaction than did the other groups.[10]

3. *Risk-taking behaviors that occur in the group.* Since cohesive groups are more likely to permit risk taking in the form of self-disclosure and expression of hostility and conflict than are less cohesive groups, it seems reasonable to suppose that these behaviors in turn may lead to greater cohesion.[11]

Stokes found a high multiple correlation of these three constructs with cohesion. He suggests:

Conceptualizing cohesion as a combination of the three constructs suggested in this article might have heuristic value. Perhaps understanding the relation of cohesion to outcome would be facilitated by a more precise operationalization of cohesion. *It could be that certain aspects of cohesion are more important for certain types of groups.* Therapy groups, for example, might require risk taking for positive outcomes, whereas a problem-focused counseling or self-help group's success on outcome measures would depend more on members' finding one another attractive as individuals.[12]

A continuing contribution to the conceptual problem with cohesiveness is that researchers have treated it as both a dependent and an independent variable. We feel attracted to groups whose members we like, and we tend to like the individual members of groups to which we are attached.[13]

How is cohesiveness achieved? Groups maintain their norms and solidarity through systems of rewards and punishments. Rewards come through the satisfaction of individual needs already discussed. Punishment or sanctions occur when members deviate from group expectations. The sanctions may be direct or indirect. Isolation, withholding of communication, and denial of other satisfactions provide corrective feedback. Persons who deviate from the group norms are not likely to be accepted as friends by other members of the group. Schachter tested this assumption by inviting students to join a club organized to discuss topics of lively interest. Three paid participants attended each meeting, of whom two conformed to the beliefs of the group and one took a clearly deviant position. The deviant member was rejected, while the other two participants were accepted. Rejection of the deviant was stronger in groups with high cohesiveness and where the deviancy concerned matters highly relevant to the purposes of the group. This finding is consistent with the expectations that cohesive groups develop stronger norms. The conforming members received a steady, but low, amount of communication from other members. A confederate, called by the group a "slider" (one who moves from deviance to conformity), received a large number of hints from fellow members to conform. As sliders moved toward conformity, the number diminished. They received the greatest number when the group attempted to change their views. When their deviancy became fixed, group members ceased communicating with the deviants in an unconscious attempt to isolate him or her.[14]

One of the major effects of cohesiveness is the group's influence over its members. As Cartwright states: "There can be little doubt that members of a more cohesive group more readily exert influence on one another and are more readily influenced by one another."[15] Cartwright points to the research of Thibaut and Kelley, in which the power of a group over a member appears to depend on what the member expects to receive from the group as against what the member believes he or she can receive from any other available group. The individual, then, is much more dependent upon a group that he or she considers the best available.[16] A positive personal consequence of increased cohesiveness seems to be greater acceptance, trust, and confidence among members, resulting in a sense of security and personal value. People feel free to disagree and even express hostility; suppressed feelings sometimes become a hidden agenda.[17]

A negative aspect of cohesiveness will be discussed in Chapter 11. For now, we point out that when a cohesive group's need for unanimity overwhelms a member's realistic appraisal of alternative courses of action, *groupthink* evolves.[18]

The interrelationships between norms, conformity, and cohesion are obvious but should be viewed with caution. With different definitions and methodologies, the studies cannot easily be compared.[19] More of a multidimensional approach such as has been tried by Stokes will help us in the future to better understand these processes.

TASK

Most groups have some task or external purpose that can provide a basis for evaluation of the effectiveness of the group. Groups may be superior at solving some kinds of tasks, while individuals may be better at other kinds. Steiner has developed a taxonomy of different group tasks and specifies for each a "prescribed process" that, if followed, will lead to maximal group performance.[20] He distinguishes among four types of work, each with different requirements:

1. *Additive tasks.* Shoveling snow and collecting charitable contributions are examples of additive tasks. Each member's product can be added to the others' to yield the total group product. The more people, the greater the productivity. Few decision-making groups encounter additive tasks.
2. *Conjunctive tasks.* Mountain climbers or members of a marching band perform conjuctive tasks. All the members perform similar activities and all depend on each other for group success. Adding another member may not increase productivity; in fact just as a group of mountain climbers can move no faster than its slowest member, a group engaged in a conjunctive task can only be as efficient as its least proficient member. In decision-making groups that delegate research responsibilities, the group can only be as accurate as its least reliable source of information.

3. *Disjunctive tasks.* Working on a complex mathematical problem in a group usually depends on the proficiency of the most competent member. There is no division of labor, and the product does not depend on the summed efforts of individuals.

4. *Discretionary tasks.* Most decision-making groups are dealing with tasks in which the offerings of one individual may be accepted or rejected, and the skills of various members may be combined in a variety of ways to yield a product. Members may combine their efforts in any way they wish, and the group product depends on the manner in which efforts are coordinated. Rather than relying on one expert, the group depends on how the members' efforts are balanced and coordinated.

Steiner argues that for each kind of task, productivity depends on *process gain* versus *process loss.* Process loss includes the time spent deciding how a group is to function. For a committee to be effective, the time spent together must produce a product superior to the work of the members if they had worked individually. Does the process of interaction promote gain or cause loss?

One study has attempted to answer the questions by comparing individual judgments to group judgments. Davis devised mathematical techniques for establishing how in practice a group combines its individual views to form a group product.[21] Working from a knowledge of preferred individual solutions to a problem and of a historical group's actual decision, various hypothetical decision rules were tested out. For example, the probability that jurors would change their verdict from guilty to not guilty, or vice versa, was closely matched to how large a majority initially preferred that verdict. While this decision reflected normative social behavior, the degree of certainty that the decision was correct correlated with the size of the minority.

Hackman and Morris have used a *Job Diagnostic Survey* to predict the potential of a particular task to induce high performance motivation.[22] They classify the factors influencing the task effectiveness under three headings:

1. The level and utilization of member knowledge and skill
2. The nature and utilization of task performances and strategies
3. The level and coordination of members' effort

While these broad classificatory headings certainly include many of the relevant variables, Hackman and Morris concede that until we have a much clearer view of which types of tasks require which types of organizational structure and influence processes, attempts to enhance group performance will have to rest on diagnoses of each specific situation. They see a usefulness for three types of such attempts, in line with their three headings above: Modification of the group's composition, redesign of tasks, and modification of group norms. However, they emphasize that inadequately thought-out interventions may make matters worse rather than better. Job redesign schemes, such as job enrichment, often fail through inattention to detail, while interventions focused on the interpersonal relationships within a group sometimes neglect task variables.

Groups must be conscious of whether or not assumed tasks can best be handled by the group as a whole or through individual efforts. Complex tasks and decisions allow members to compare views and develop a more accurate picture of reality than that of any individual member. Such interaction can also reduce biases and provide a check for accuracy. If the individual members have a strong desire for group success, if new goals are based on past levels of successful performance, if all members know that the group needs their best efforts, and if a mechanism for providing feedback on results is available, then a group's performance is likely to be better.[23]

The prospect of working together to solve a group problem may require a new pattern of interpersonal relationships. Enemies may have to work together, and friends may have to stay apart, until the task is completed. Sometimes even norms must be broken or changed. Group members must realize that to work effectively with another does not necessarily mean to like the other. Actors in a play may not be on close personal terms, but the joint needs of a successful theatrical production may require them to work together cooperatively. The group goal thus supersedes the varied individual goals. "I can receive positive reinforcements from the audience only if the total production is a good one." The satisfactions are not likely to be as high, however, as in situations when the success of others reinforces the individual.

In general, then, people are committed to the group task when they conceive and accept the group goals; commit their personal resources, skills, intelligence, and energy toward accomplishing it; and give its accomplishment higher priority than their own goals, the group's norms, and the existing pattern of interpersonal relationships among members, including their own popularity and personal comfort.

GROUP SIZE

The number of persons in a group affects both the communication participation among members and the quality of interaction. However, the relationship between the size of the group and the group's effectiveness is complex.

Bales in his studies at Harvard counted acts of initiation by each member in groups of varying size. In groups of three or four the initiation was spread evenly; as the group size was increased from five to eight members, the groups were dominated by the more aggressive members and the quiet ones participated less. With further increases in group size, dominance by aggressive initiators increased.[24]

Research by Slater has shown that the quality of the interaction varies with group size. Comparing the ratios of groups of two to seven members over four discussion sessions, he found that as group size increased, the index of inhibition decreased and that, as members became better acquainted through the course of the meetings, the inhibition levels dropped more for the larger groups than for the smaller. He felt that, as size increased, the consequences of alienating other people became less and less severe. As he states:

> In the larger group, physical freedom is restricted while psychological freedom is increased. The member has less time to talk, more points of view to integrate and adapt to, and a more elaborate structure into which he must fit. At the same time he is more free to ignore some of these viewpoints, to express his own feelings and ideas in a direct and forceful fashion, and even to withdraw from the fray without loss of face.[25]

Members of five-person groups expressed complete satisfaction; no members reported their group as being too large or small. Larger groups felt themselves disorderly and their members too aggressive, competitive, and given to wasting time. The smaller groups (with fewer than five members) complained that they were too small and that members were prevented from expressing their ideas freely for fear of alienating one another.[26]

How does size affect group productivity? Gibb discovered that the total number of ideas increases with an increase in group size, but not in direct proportion to the number of members.[27] In larger groups the members tend to stifle contributions as the more aggressive tend to dominate; the members contribute less and complain that group direction is lacking. In addition, a group with more than six members may cope with its size by forming functional subgroups within itself.[28] Zander makes this practical suggestion: "A person assembling a decision-making group will do well to restrict the group's size because give-and-take is more rapid and widespread in a small group than a large one."[29]

GENDER MAKEUP OF THE GROUP

In recent years attention has been directed to the consideration of the influence of gender on the activities within a group. Baird reviewed a body of research and concluded that men tend to be more task oriented while women are more maintenance oriented. He reported that men tend to talk more, initiate topic changes, interrupt more, and be more objective. Women were said to be more opinionated, more positive in responses, and more likely to withdraw from unpleasant interactions.[30]

In a later study Bradley reported that women who demonstrated task competency were shown friendliness, reason, and fewer displays of dominant behavior by male counterparts. She also reported, however, that such women were not particularly well liked.[31]

Such research must be evaluated in terms of the changing roles of women and men. Until recently large numbers of women had not been seen in roles of leadership and decision making in the organizational context. As women moved into such roles, the male norm was the standard to which the women were made to adhere. Issues of power and control were seen to be in the masculine domain, while maintenance concerns were feminine and secondary.

We have cited considerable research that shows that an androgynous model of decision making, a balanced concern for task and relationships, is likely to be the best suited for effective ongoing group interaction. Women, when given the opportunity, have learned quickly the skills of the instrumental problem solver. To this point, men have been less adaptive and have changed little in expounding their communication competencies to include empathic listening, sensitivity to nonverbal messages, and greater responsiveness to metacommunication.

Lafferty and Pond have studied groups of five people working on a group survival task that can be scored in terms of accuracy of accomplishment. The most successful group both in terms of final score and of average gain over individual scores was made up of five women. In declining rank of accomplishment were (2) groups of three females and two males, (3) groups of four females and one male, (4) groups of four males and one female, (5) groups entirely of men, and (6) groups of three males and two females.[32] Perhaps you can provide some inferential explanations of why the sexual makeup of the groups provides these results.

SUMMARY

In this chapter we have noted some distinctive characteristics of groups that greatly affect a group's effectiveness and likelihood of success. The variables we call norms, conformity, cohesiveness, task, and size are so dynamic and fluid that each affects and is affected by each of the other factors. Morale is highest when members feel that they are trusted to get the task done (cohesiveness).

The degree of effectiveness will be determined by the amount expected by fellow workers (conformity to norms) and by the motivation supplied for high productivity (commitment to task). Any change in the size or gender makeup of a group can change its effectiveness. These characteristics are so interrelated that it is difficult to consider them in isolation.

APPLICATIONS

8.1. List the norm that you can identify as operative within your group. Have these norms changed during the course of your meetings?

8.2. How would your group conceptualize cohesion? What factors do you feel are important in promoting cohesion in a given group?

8.3. Discuss the variables of group size and gender makeup in the groups you have observed. Can you identify differences that would have appeared had the groups been larger, smaller, or with a different combination of women and men?

NOTES

1. T. M. Newcomb, R. H. Turner, and P. E. Converse, *Social Psychology.* New York: Holt, Rinehart & Winston, 1965, p. 254.

2. J. M. Innes, "Group structure," in *Social Psychology,* ed. by G. Gardner. Sydney: Prentice-Hall, 1981, p. 136.

3. F. J. Roethlisberger and W. J. Dickson, *Management and the Worker.* Cambridge, Mass.: Harvard University Press, 1943, p. 512.

4. L. Festinger, "Informal social communication," in *Group Dynamics,* ed. by D. Cartwright and A. Zander. New York: Harper & Row, 1968, pp. 182–191.

5. C. A. Kiesler and S. B. Kiesler, *Conformity.* Reading, Mass.: Addison-Wesley, 1969, pp. 35–36.

6. S. Drescher, G. Burlingame, and A. Fuhriman, "Cohesion—or: An odyssey in empirical understanding," *Small Group Behavior,* 16, (February 1985), 3–30.

7. R. L. Bednar and T. J. Kaul, "Experimental group research: Current perspectives," in *Handbook for Psychotherapy and Behavior Change,* ed. by S. Garfield and A. Bergin. New York: Wiley, 1978.

8. J. P. Stokes, "Components of group cohesion," *Small Group Behavior,* 14 (May 1983), 163–173.

9. A. Zaleznik and D. Moment, *The Dynamics of Interpersonal Behavior.* New York: Wiley, 1964, p. 109.

10. D. Rosenthal and C. N. Cofer, "The effect on group performance of an indifferent and neglectful attitude shown by one group member," *Journal of Experimental Psychology,* 38 (1948), 568–577.

11. Stokes, "Components of group cohesion," 165–166.

12. Ibid., 170.

13. B. H. Raven and J. Z. Rubin, *Social Psychology: People in Groups.* New York: Wiley, 1976, p. 253.

14. S. Schachter, "Deviation, rejection, and communication," in *Group Dynamics,* ed. by D. Cartwright and A. Zander. New York: Harper & Row, 1968, pp. 165–181.
15. D. Cartwright, "Nature of group cohesiveness," in *Group Dynamics,* ed. by D. Cartwright and A. Zander. New York: Harper & Row, 1968, p. 104.
16. Ibid. Based on J. W. Thibaut and H. H. Kelley, *The Social Psychology of Groups.* New York: Wiley, 1959.
17. A. Pepitone and G. Reichling, "Group cohesiveness and the expression of hostility," *Human Relations,* 8 (1955), 327–337.
18. I. L. Janis, *Victims of Groupthink: A Psychological Study of Foreign Policy Decisions and Fiascos.* Boston: Houghton Mifflin, 1972.
19. Drescher et al., "Cohesion—or," 27.
20. I. D. Steiner, *Group Process and Productivity.* New York: Academic Press, 1972.
21. J. H. Davis, "Social interaction as a combinatorial process in group decision," in *Group Decision Making,* ed. by H. Brandstatter, J. H. Davis, and G. Stocker-Kreichgauer. London: Academic Press, 1982.
22. J. R. Hackman and C. G. Morris, "Group tasks, group interaction process and group performance effectiveness: A review and proposed integration," *Advances in Experimental Social Psychology,* 8, ed. by L. Berkowitz (1975), 47–99.
23. A. Zander, *Making Groups Effective.* San Francisco: Jossey-Bass, 1982, pp. 65–66.
24. R. F. Bales, F. L. Strodtbeck, T. M. Mills, and M. E. Roseborough, "Channels of communication in small groups," *American Sociological Review,* 16 (1951), 461–468.
25. P. E. Slater, "Contrasting correlates of group size," *Sociometry,* 21 (1958), 129–139.
26. Ibid., 137–139.
27. C. A. Gibb, "The effects of group size and of threat reduction upon creativity in a problem-solving situation," *American Psychology,* 6 (1951), 324 (abstract).
28. J. M. Innes, "Group performance," in *Social Psychology,* ed. by G. Gardner. Sydney: Prentice-Hall, 1981, p. 165.
29. Zander, *Making Groups Effective,* p. 21.
30. J. E. Baird, "Sex differences in group communication," *Quarterly Journal of Speech,* 62 (1976), 179–192.
31. P. H. Bradley, "Sex, competence and opinion deviation: An expectation states approach," *Communication Monographs,* 47 (1980), 105–110.
32. J. C. Lafferty and A. W. Pond, *The Desert Survival Situation.* Plymouth, Mich.: Human Synergistics, 1985.

chapter 9

Conflict and Cooperation

What does the word *conflict* mean to you? To many people it means quarreling, arguing, and fighting. We suggest, however, that there is a positive dimension to conflict. Just as we know that conflict is inevitable because of the differences in people, we know that without conflict there would be no innovation, creativity, or challenging of existing norms and practices. The key to whether conflict should be viewed positively is in the method of its resolution.

In this chapter we shall examine the concept of conflict as it occurs both within a group and between groups. Opportunities and avenues for cooperation will be explored as means of resolving problems.

We recognize that conflict often involves strong feelings. When people are required to make decisions on ego-involving issues, intellectual judgments may give way to emotion. Any theoretical model should take into account the potential of strong negative feelings and actions.

INTERDEPENDENCE AND CONFLICT

One characteristic of the small group that we cited in Chapter 1 is interdependence. Each member depends on the others, so members unavoidably influence each other. This interaction is circular, with cause producing effect and effect turning into cause and feeding back to the original cause. Raven has, in fact, defined conflict as "any situation in which people are *negatively interdependent*—with respect to goals, means, or both."[1]

Figure 9.1 illustrates this interdependence by means of a situation in which graduate students prepare for their next meeting. Each graduate student has agreed to read five articles and be prepared to discuss them at the next class session. To the extent that they all want a good discussion, they are positively interdependent with respect to goals. If they anticipate an exam graded on the "curve" (relative to other students), they will feel competition with other students and be negatively interdependent concerning goals. If they anticipate being graded individually rather than comparatively, their goals will be independent.

Note in Figure 9.1 how the means also prompts different responses: Since the articles are too long to copy, a system of sharing has to be arranged. Such a system prompts negative interdependence in competition over the papers. If each student has a set of

		Goals		
		Positive interdependence	Independence	Negative interdependence
Means	Positive interdependence	Subgroup division of labor; joint discussion at next meeting. (A)	Subgroup division of labor; noncurved exam at next meeting. (D)	Subgroup division of labor; curved exam at next meeting. (G)
	Independence	Everyone does own reading (multiple copies); joint discussion at next meeting. (B)	Everyone does own reading (multiple copies); noncurved exam at next meeting. (E)	Everyone does own reading (multiple copies); curved exam at next meeting. (H)
	Negative interdependence	Everyone does own reading (limited copies); joint discussion at next meeting. (C)	Everyone does own reading (limited copies); noncurved exam at next meeting. (F)	Everyone does own reading (limited copies); curved exam at next meeting. (I)

Figure 9.1 Raven's model of means-goals interdependence. From B. Raven, *Social Psychology: People in Groups.* New York: Wiley, 1976. p. 189.

articles, they can act independently. If the group divides the assignment into subgroups, each with different articles to read and report on, they will act positively interdependent.

This model helps to explain the alternatives available in any group situation. In Chapter 4 we discussed the "Prisoner's Dilemma" as an example of a mixed-motive problem. Such mixed motives are likely to be present in any group. Our society values and takes pride in recognizing differences in people—in backgrounds, values, ethics, needs, desires, and abilities. Because we are interdependent, and because each of us is different from everyone else, we can anticipate situations of conflict. If on the other hand, we were all alike with the same perceptions, values, and so on, the value of the group process would be negated. Our contributions would be redundant.

Kemp has, in fact, proposed a "creative handling of conflict" by consideration of the following points:[2]

1. Productive conflict arises because group members are so bound together that their actions affect one another; that is, they have accepted the fact that they have become interdependent.
2. Conflict occurs because people care. Often group members who have great creative differences share a very deep relationship. Because they care about one another and the group as a whole, they are willing to make, if necessary, a costly emotional response to help improve a situation.
3. Each member has different needs and values. These differences become evident and produce conflict unless the members repress their individual differences and assign the direction of the group to an authority figure. Sometimes, members allow themselves to be taken over by such a leader, rather than accept the fact of their differences.

Animals, when confronted by an aggressive opponent, have several options: They can submit to the aggressor; they can take flight; or they can stay and fight. In human terms, to submit would be to become submissive, allowing someone to dominate you; to take flight would be to become independent by leaving the group or relationship; to fight means to remain interdependent and work through the conflict either positively or negatively. Let us consider these options in the small group.

CONFLICT WITHIN THE GROUP

There are numerous sources of internal group conflict. Any perceived changes, ranging from leadership roles to group structure to activities to new membership, may provoke conflict. The conflicts are inevitable; the nature of the group will determine whether they are handled openly or reduced to the level of a hidden agenda. Even the changing nature of an individual member may introduce conflict. In a teenage gang the members' interests and maturity levels may change at different rates of time.

Conflict situations in groups may be classed as two types, *distributive* and *integrative*.[3] A distributive situation is one in which a person can win only at someone else's expense, such as in a poker game. An integrative situation is one in which the members of the group integrate their resources toward a common task, as in working together on a jigsaw puzzle. Research teams work in an integrative manner, whereas a buying and selling transaction involves distributive or mixed-motive bargaining.

The National Training Laboratories has identified two opposite modes of behavior, called Approach A and Approach B. Approach A is associated with behavior in distributive social situations; Approach B, with behavior in integrative.[4]

Approach A

1. Behavior is purposeful in that one's own goals are pursued.

2. Secrecy.

3. Accurate personal understanding of own needs, but these are publicly disguised or misrepresented: Don't let them know what you really want most, so that they won't know how much you are really willing to give up to get it.

4. Unpredictable, mixed strategies, utilizing the element of surprise.

5. Threats and bluffs.

6. Search behavior is devoted to finding ways of appearing to become committed to a position; logical, non-rational, and irrational arguments alike may serve this purpose.

7. Success is often enhanced (where teams, committees, or organizations are involved on each side) by forming a bad stereotype of the other, by ignoring the other's logic, by increasing the level of hostility. These tend to strengthen in-group loyalty and convince others that you mean business.

Approach B

1. Behavior is purposeful in that goals held in common are pursued.

2. Openness.

3. Accurate personal understanding of own needs and accurate representation of them.

4. Predictable; while flexible behavior is appropriate, it is not designed to take the other party by surprise.

5. Threats or bluffs are not used.

6. Search behavior is devoted to finding solutions to problems and utilizing logical and innovative processes.

7. Success demands that stereotypes be dropped, that ideas be given consideration on their merit regardless of sources, and that hostility not be induced deliberately. In fact, positive feelings about others are both a cause and an effect of other aspects of Approach B.

8. A pathological extreme occurs when one assumes that everything that prevents the other from reaching his or her goal also must facilitate one's own movement toward one's own goal; thus, one would state one's own goals as being the negation of others' achievement.

9. Etc.

8. A pathological extreme occurs when one will assume that whatever is good for others and the group is necessarily good for oneself. Cannot distinguish own identity from group or other person's identity. Will not take responsibility for own self.

9. Etc.

Engaging in the distributive approach causes problems for the task-oriented group. Among the problems are the following:

1. Development of we-they and superiority-inferiority complexes within the group. The group may splinter if the distributive behavior is sustained.
2. In groups with internal competitive pressure, individuals tend to overestimate their contributions and unrealistically downgrade the work of others.
3. Under competitive pressures group members think they understand one another when in fact they do not. These distortions in perception may cause areas of agreement to go unrecognized.[5]

Labor-management negotiations characteristically use this distributive approach in a between-groups pattern of interaction. Labor wins at management's expense. An integrative approach would attempt to discover ways that both parties might gain. We shall discuss this possibility in greater detail when we suggest alternative modes of handling conflict.

Conflict of the integrative type can have positive benefits for the group. Only when members feel comfortable in the group can conflict safely emerge. Basic problems cannot usually be resolved without some conflict because of the different values, feelings, and perceptions of the members. For the conflict to center on issues rather than on personalities and exaggerations, an acceptance of individual differences and some degree of mutual trust are required. While distributive situations are based on a "win-lose" premise, the integrative approach provides an opportunity for "win-win."

Group conflict may either bring out the best in a group or literally tear the group apart. The overall social structure of the group may determine which occurs. As sociologist Lewis Coser states: "Conflict within a group frequently helps to revitalize existent norms; or it contributes to the emergence of new norms. In this sense, social conflict is a mechanism for adjustment of norms adequate to new conditions."[6]

In a study of conflict in organizations, Kabanoff found the cause often to be structural incongruencies in the distribution of influence. While acknowledging other variables, he found major causal factors:

> For example, if interpersonal relations are poor between two persons in an interdependent work system, the felt hostility may push the parties involved toward assertive influence modes while their interdependence pushes them toward cooperative modes. The outcome may be a joint function of these two "forces" or may reflect the "dominant" relationship in the conflict. A high level of hostility may dominate the choice if interdependence is relatively slight, but the reverse may be true if interdependence is very high.[7]

An implication of this study is that conflict is intimately linked to potential influence relations and tactics.

Janis and Mann have approached group decision making and conflict from a psychological perspective. Their "conflict theory of decision making" analyzes the coping patterns used by people faced with major decisions. The theory assumes that *stress* engendered by decisional conflict is a major determinant of failure to achieve high-quality decisions. They identify five major patterns for coping with stress:

1. **Unconflicted adherence.** The decision maker complacently decides to continue whatever he or she has been doing, ignoring information about the risk of losses. There is little or no stress.
2. **Unconflicted change** to a new course of action. The decision maker uncritically adopts whichever new course of action is most salient or most strongly recommended. Again, there is little or no stress.
3. **Defensive avoidance.** The decision maker escapes the conflict by procrastinating, shifting responsibility to someone else, or constructing wishful rationalizations to bolster the least objectionable alternative. Defensive avoidance is associated with high stress.
4. **Hypervigilance.** The decision maker searches frantically for a way out of the dilemma. He or she impulsively seizes upon a hastily contrived solution that seems to promise immediate relief. The full range of consequences of the choice are overlooked because of emotional excitement, perseveration, and limited attention. In its more extreme form, hypervigilance is known as "panic." It is associated with great emotional stress.
5. **Vigilance.** The decision maker searches painstakingly for relevant information, assimilates information in an unbiased manner, and evaluates alternatives carefully before making a choice. Vigilance is associated with a moderate level of psychological stress.

Table 9.1   DECISION COPING PATTERNS

Conditions	Stress Level	Coping Pattern
No conflict	Low stress	Unconflicted adherence or unconflicted change
Conflict + pessimism about finding a good alternative	High stress	Defensive avoidance (procrastination, buck passing, rationalization)
Conflict + time pressure	High stress	Hypervigilance (panic)
Conflict, but optimism about finding a good alternative + believe sufficient time	Moderate stress	Vigilance

Source: Based on I.L. Janis and L. Mann, *Decision Making.* New York: Free Press, 1977.

Janis and Mann maintain that coping patterns occur both predecisionally and postdecisionally, because conflict may persist even after a choice is made. The model indicates that the coping patterns are determined by the presence or absence of three factors: (1) arousal of conflict (because of the awareness of serious risks for whichever alternative is chosen), (2) optimistic or pessimistic expectations about finding a better alternative, and (3) belief that there is sufficient (or insufficient) time to search and deliberate before a decision is required.[8]

Table 9.1 summarizes the determinants of the coping patterns and their associated level of psychological stress. Janis and Mann claim that the five coping patterns are linked dependably with the conditions specified in Table 9.1. This leads to testable implications about the antecedents of vigilant decision making, the nature of the relationship between magnitude of psychological stress and decision coping pattern, and the kinds of interventions necessary to counteract use of the nonvigilant patterns.[9]

CONFLICT BETWEEN GROUPS

Whether we are aware of it or not, our future goals and fortunes are greatly affected by the states of harmony or conflict between groups. Problems of intergroup relations include conflict between political groups, religious groups, economic groups, labor and management, and young and old, as well as across international boundaries.

The classic study of conflicts between groups was made by Sherif and Sherif. They studied groups of young boys, 11 and 12 years old, at camp sites under experimentally manipulated conditions. The boys were all selected from stable, white, Protestant families from the middle socioeconomic level; they were well adjusted and had no past records of behavioral problems. No cultural, physical, or economic differences were present in the sample. In a "robbers' cave" experiment, two groups were formed separately and kept unaware of the presence of the other until competitive tournament games in various sports between the two groups were arranged. A series of mutually frustrating events arose naturally in the course of the tournament activities. Stealing and burning of the opponent's flag, raiding of cabins, and name calling resulted. The experimenters tested and validated the following hypotheses:

1. **When members of two groups come into contact with one another in a series of activities that embody goals which each group urgently desires but which can be attained by one group only at the expense of the other, competitive activity toward the goal changes with time into hostility between the groups and among their members.** Prizes were offered in the sports contests, and cumulative scores were kept for the various events, which included baseball, football, a tug of war, a treasure hunt, and tent pitching. Good sportsmanship deteriorated as the events progressed, and the cheer "2-4-6-8, who do we appreciate?" changed to "2-4-6-8, who do we appreci-hate?" Accusations of "dirty players" and "cheaters" abounded and led to overt physical attacks.

2. **In the course of such competitive interaction toward a goal available only to one group, unfavorable attitudes and images (stereotypes) of the out-group come into use and are standardized, placing the out-group at a definite social distance from the in-group.** Members of each group were asked to rate their fellow members and the opponents in the other group during the height of friction. Adjectives applied to the in-groups were "brave," "tough," and "friendly," while the out-group members were "sneaky," "smart alecks," "stinkers." The ratings were assigned on the basis of "all of them are . . ." to "none of them are . . ."

3. **Conflict between two groups tends to produce an increase in solidarity within the groups.** Pride and group solidarity increased as the conflict and hostility grew. After the tournament, the sociometric choices became exclusively restricted to one's own group, and members of other groups were rejected. At a beach outing, each group stuck together despite many distractions.

4. **The heightened solidarity and pride in the group will be reflected in an overestimation of the achievements of fellow members and in a lower estimation of the achievements of members of the out-group.** A game of bean toss was introduced, in which the goal was to collect as many of the beans scattered on the ground as possible within a limited time. A judgment was called for by exposing, with an opaque projector, the supposed collection

of each individual. Actually, 35 beans were exposed each time. The members of each group overestimated the number of beans collected by their fellow group members and made significantly lower estimates of the performance of the out-group members.

5. **Relations between groups that are of consequence to the groups in question, including conflict, tend to produce changes in the organization and practices within the groups.** In one group the leadership changed hands when the leader who had emerged prior to the conflict was reluctant to take aggressive actions. In the other group a boy perceived as a low-status bully during group formation emerged as a hero during the intergroup encounters.[10]

In the study it became unmistakably clear that overt differences are unnecessary for the rise of intergroup hostility, social distances, stereotyped images, and negative attitudes in a group of "normal" youngsters. Although physical appearance, language, and culture may serve to intensify differences, conflict itself becomes a major contributing variable.

In order to understand the complex relationship between the competitive and hostile aspects of conflict and to understand how it develops, Deutsch has listed seven questions that should be carefully examined:

1. What are the two parties like? Are they equal or unequal in relative power? What weapons or methods do they have available to them?
2. What is the prior history of their relationship? Have the two parties generally been friendly or unfriendly to one another? Do they have a history of trust or distrust? Here one can ask whether the conflict is primarily due to hostility.
3. What issues or disagreements have led to the present conflict? Are they ideological or related to scarce resources? What goals or means are incompatible? Here one can examine the extent to which there is competitive conflict.
4. What is the situation or environment in which the conflict occurred? Are there legal or moral restraints that oppose or favor the use of certain weapons or strategies? Is there a tradition or ethic that favors cooperation or conflict?
5. What third parties are involved as audiences or possible participants? Does one of the parties want to save face before a third party, so that a strong nonconciliatory stance might seem appropriate? Or does a third party press for a peaceful resolution? If so, does the third party maintain peace with force or with censure, or does it serve as a conciliator?
6. What are the strategies and tactics that have been employed during the course of conflict? Can we characterize the bases of power (re-

ward, coercion, expertise, legitimacy, reference, and information) that each party utilizes in attempting to achieve its ends? Is there free communication, or is interaction restricted?

7. How does the conflict affect the participants? How do the techniques, strategies, and weapons used by each party affect both that party and the opposition? Here one should look for the ways in which competitive conflict might lead to hostile conflict. Alternatively, one could examine how a conciliatory strategy might or might not reduce hostility.[11]

PROMOTING COOPERATION

Under what circumstances will cooperation emerge in a group? This question has intrigued social scientists for a long time. We know that people are not angels, that they tend to be selfish and look after themselves first, yet we also know that cooperation does occur and that our civilization is based on it. Exchange theorists assume that people will attempt to gain as much as they can at minimum cost. As people receive satisfaction from mutually pleasurable exchanges, rules develop to insure continuation of such exchanges.

Problems arise when people disagree on what constitutes equitable exchange, what the costs and rewards actually are. And, as we observed in Chapter 4, discussing the "Prisoner's Dilemma," how much can you trust another person both to report honestly and to do what he or she promises to do?

Axelrod has developed a "cooperation theory" based upon his investigations of individuals who pursue their own self-interest without assistance from a central authority forcing them to cooperate.[12] The pursuit of self-interest when behavior is not guided is greater in a group using the "win-lose" alternatives implicit in a situation.

Axelrod's theory grows out of the Prisoner's Dilemma model. The Dilemma is actually an abstract formulation of very real situations in which what is best for *each* person individually leads to mutual defection, whereas *everyone* would have been better off with mutual cooperation. Players too often merely take turns at exploiting each other. Axelrod attempted to find the most reasonable and predictable way to promote cooperation.

Professional game theorists were invited to participate in a computer tournament based on the Prisoner's Dilemma. Scholars from different academic disciplines designed programs that exemplified a *rule* to select the cooperative or noncooperative choice for each move; knowledge of all previous moves was built into the program. The winning entry, TIT FOR TAT, was submitted by Professor Anatol Rapoport of the University of Toronto. This program was not only the simplest, but the best. TIT FOR TAT simply starts with a cooperative choice and thereafter does what the other player did on the previous move. For example, if one player chooses green and one chooses red, the red choice wins. If both choose red, they both lose, while if they both choose green, they both win. With TIT FOR TAT the player establishes that in each subsequent round, he or she will replicate the choice of the opponent in the previous round. Thus, if you vote green in the first round, this player votes green in the second round. Axelrod summarizes the basis for its success:

> What accounts for tit for tat's robust success is its combination of being nice, forgiving and clear. Its niceness prevents it from getting into unnecessary trouble. Its retaliation discourages the other side from persisting whenever defection is tried. Its forgiveness helps restore mutual cooperation and its clarity make it intelligible to the other player, thereby eliciting long-term cooperation.[13]

The remaining problem is that trial and error is slow and costly as people learn how to achieve rewards from cooperation. Within the small group, conditions should promote mutually rewarding strategies based on reciprocity. As Gergen and Gergen have commented, "The most promising means of increasing cooperation may be the improvement of communication."[14] Reciprocity in the interdependent group should suggest, "If I help you to win, I win too."

At the intergroup level Sherif and Sherif used what they called "superordinate goals" to bring the boys in the "robbers' cave" experiment out of the state of conflict. The operating principle was that "if conflict develops from mutually incompatible goals, common goals should promote cooperation.[15] Camp activities were planned in such a way that desirable goals could not be achieved by the efforts of only one in-group; both groups were forced to cooperate toward the common goal. One such goal involved repairing a sabotaged water-supply system. Others included cooperatively raising money to obtain a movie that both groups wanted to see and moving a stalled food truck. All the tasks were accomplished by the cooperative efforts of the two groups.

After the boys had participated in these cooperative activities, sociometric tests were again administered. The results revealed that attitudes toward members of the out-group had clearly changed. While the friendship choices remained primarily within each in-group, the choices of out-group member friends had increased, and there was less total rejection of out-group members. As Sherif says:

> Our findings demonstrate the effectiveness of a series of superordinate goals in the reduction of intergroup conflict, hostility, and their by-products. They also have implications for other measures proposed for reducing intergroup tensions.

It is true that lines of communication between groups must be opened before prevailing hostility can be reduced. But, if contact between hostile groups takes place without superordinate goals, the communication channels serve as media for further accusations and recriminations. When contact situations involve superordinate goals, communication is utilized in the direction of reducing conflict in order to attain the common goals.[16]

The identification and utilization of superordinate goals seem to have genuine effectiveness in reducing intergroup conflict.

SUMMARY

Although conflict is inevitable, it may be positive in some instances, negative in others, and irrelevant in still others.

Within a group a distributive approach to conflict problems leads to distrust and competition, whereas an integrative approach promotes openness and cooperation.

Between groups, sustained conflict over mutually desired goals attainable to only one group provokes hostile and aggressive acts, social distance, negative stereotypes, and also internal group solidarity and changed relationships. Establishing superordinate goals provides a framework of cooperation among the rival groups and effectively reduces the negative conflict.

Cooperativeness leads to coordination of effort, productivity, good human relations, and other positive benefits. Competitiveness leads to distrust and insecurity. The implications for all groups are readily apparent.

APPLICATIONS

9.1. Characterize one of the groups you have observed in terms of Raven's model of means-goals shown in this chapter.

9.2. If you have observed overt conflict in a group, analyze the behaviors demonstrated and what you would infer to be the causes.

9.3. Compile a list of the ways in which conflict may actually help in group decision making. Supply as many specific examples as you can.

NOTES

1. B. Raven, *Social Psychology: People in Groups.* New York: Wiley, 1976, p. 189.
2. C. G. Kemp, "The creative handling of conflict," in *Perspectives on the Group Process,* ed. by C. G. Kemp. Boston: Houghton Mifflin, 1970, p. 262.
3. This analysis was made in the *1968 Reading Book* of the National Training Laboratories Institute of Applied Behavioral Sciences.
4. Ibid.
5. These consequences and others are reported in R. R. Blake and J. S.

Mouton, "Reactions to intergroup competition under win-lose conditions," *Management Science* (July 1961).

6. L. Coser, *The Functions of Social Conflict.* New York: Free Press, 1964, p. 154.

7. B. Kabanoff, "Potential influence structures as sources of interpersonal conflict in groups and organizations," *Organizational Behavior and Human Decision Processes,* 36 (1985), 128–129.

8. I. L. Janis and L. Mann, *Decision Making.* New York: Free Press, 1977, pp. 45–80.

9. For validation studies, see L. Mann, "Decision-Making," in *Australian Psychology,* ed. by N. T. Feather. Sydney: Allen and Unwin, 1985, pp. 218–235.

10. M. Sherif and C. W. Sherif, *Social Psychology.* New York: Harper & Row, 1969, pp. 239, 221–266.

11. M. Deutsch, *The Resolution of Conflict: Constructive and Destructive Processes.* New Haven: Yale University Press, 1973.

12. R. Axelrod, *The Evolution of Cooperation.* New York: Basic Books, 1984.

13. Ibid., p. 54.

14. K. J. Gergen and M. M. Gergen, *Social Psychology.* New York: Harcourt Brace Jovanovich, 1981, p. 405.

15. Sherif and Sherif, *Social Psychology,* p. 266.

16. M. Sherif, "Superordinate goals in the reduction of intergroup conflicts," *American Journal of Sociology,* 63 (1958), 356.

chapter 10

Factors That Limit Group Effectiveness

Most of us have been members of groups that we thought functioned quite effectively; we got the job done well and felt a sense of satisfaction both in the product and in the process of working together. We may also have participated in groups that never measured up to expectations and hopes: Either the group process did not run smoothly, or things were never accomplished.

Throughout this book we have considered a number of variables that influence the effectiveness of the group. In this chapter we shall focus on three major problem areas that must be dealt with wisely if a group is to make sound decisions: procedural problems, process problems, and personality problems.

PROCEDURAL PROBLEMS

For the group to function effectively, procedures that promote sound decisions must be agreed to and followed. Three procedural problems confront many groups: role conflicts, problem analysis, and means of evaluating alternative proposals.

Role Conflicts and Procedures

Role ambiguity occurs when members of a group do not understand clearly the kind of participation that is expected of them. Role expectations differ a great deal in the range of behaviors demanded and the degree of their specification. Some groups develop rules and rituals and agree to follow formalized parliamentary rules. The extent of the formality of procedures imposes limits on spontaneous interaction. The absence of systematized procedures, on the other hand, will lead to wasted time and inability to determine with clarity when a task has been completed.[1]

When all members of the group are initially equal, a struggle for status and leadership may result.[2] Gaining the leadership role will depend on individual initiative, assertiveness, competence, and esteem. If the leader tries to dominate the discussion with her or his own ideas ("content control"), rather than insuring that the group proceeds in a systematic manner, then the group will be dissatisfied and unproductive. Like any dominant or high-status member, the leader can discourage the contribution of ideas and inhibit critical evaluations of proposals by the group.[3]

When members are of unequal status, for example, in a meeting chaired by the boss, role ambiguity of a different kind may emerge. Does the boss want an honest opinion or merely to be supported by the group? As Zander states:

> . . . members cannot confidently anticipate what style higher-status persons will use when exercising their power. The subordinates' uneasy reactions to this uncertainty are compounded because they realize that powerful persons can, by definition, use their influence in ways that satisfy themselves alone, ignoring the desires or displeasures of subordinates.[4]

Problem Analysis

In many decision-making groups one finds an impetuous urge to look at alleged solutions to an identified problem. Some members take a stand on a solution that appeals to them before the group has properly identified all of the impelling and constraining forces.

The point is this: It is logical that the most reasonable solution cannot be selected unless each one of the relevant impelling and constraining forces has been given careful consideration. In addition, it is psychologically important that all members feel satisfied that their particular insights into the forces inherent in the problem have been expressed and given adequate consideration by the group. This is necessary if the members are later to give their full commitment and support to the problem solution chosen by the group.

It should be clearly understood that when members indicate too early that they favor a particular solution (that is, before the other members of the group have analyzed the problem), they very possibly may have picked the solution that the group will eventually select as the best one, and yet, even so, this is no justification for shortcircuiting the analytical process. It is not enough that one or another member comes up with the best solution; the individual psychological needs of the other members must be met by letting them express their interpretation of the nature of the problem.

Studies of the ways in which groups go about this analytical process tend to show that they do not neatly move from problem identification to analysis to solution;[5] rather, they tend to make erratic progress. They move on and off their logical course, gaining some bits of insight and agreement at various intervals, sometimes circling back to reaffirm a point or position earlier expressed but not clearly grasped by all, until eventually all members seem generally satisfied that the pertinent points have been given adequate consideration. Thus, to avoid premature emphasis on possible solutions, bright and well-informed members must deliberately exercise patience; they must wait for the others to process their thoughts and to analyze adequately for themselves the impelling and constraining forces inherent in the problem. Statesmen and public leaders learn that they must wait for their constituents to realize the nature of changing and emerging conditions; the wiser ones exercise patience with their followers, even the ones who have proper concern but cannot so quickly grasp a complex situation. The price you must pay for being highly intelligent is that in group action you must wait for the others to cover the same ground you perceived in rapid fashion. Be helpful to the others if they are willing to accept your help. Otherwise, be patient; there is no other way.

Evaluating Proposals

Unfortunately, much time is wasted in groups while evaluating alternative proposals. Often the absence of a consensus on the criteria for rendering judgment forces a group to go "round-and-round" without centering in on the action to take.

Parkinson has published a scientific spoof of bureaucracy and group meetings that has a ring of truth. For example, his "Law of Triviality" states that when a group is discussing financial matters, "the time spent on any item of the agenda will be in inverse proportion to the sum involved."[6] The finance committee will make a speedy decision on the allocation of $14 million for a new building but discuss at length a proposal calling for $2,150 for refreshments at a national conference. The occasionally bizarre results of some group meetings has prompted the observation that a camel is a horse designed by a committee.

PROCESS PROBLEMS

Many factors that impede effective group decision making can be identified within the process itself. Such problems are usually ones of degree. For example, both too little and too much cohesion can lead to problems. The same is true of conformity pressures. We shall first examine the two topics of cohesion and conformity, and then the problems associated with the logical-thinking process.

Cohesion—Too Little or Too Much

As we noted in Chapter 8, cohesiveness is important to the well-being of any group. Members must want to be affiliated and feel a commitment to group outcomes if the group is to be successful. The problem is with the degree of cohesion. Too little presents problems in morale and results in member dropouts. Too much can also present problems.

Irving Janis analyzed a number of significant real-life groups that reached unfortunate decisions, such as the U.S. defense decisions regarding Pearl Harbor prior to World War II and the ill-fated attempt to invade Cuba at the Bay of Pigs in 1961. His analysis of the data revealed a tendency for cohesive members to conform too readily to group norms and to reinforce one another indiscriminately. He labeled this phenomenon "groupthink" and suggested eight symptoms:

1. An illusion of invulnerability, shared by most or all the members, which creates excessive optimism and encourages taking extreme risks
2. Collective efforts to rationalize in order to discount warnings that might lead the members to reconsider their assumptions before they recommit themselves to their past policy decisions
3. An unquestioned belief in the group's inherent morality, inclining the members to ignore the ethical or moral consequences of their decisions
4. Stereotyped views of enemy leaders as being too evil to warrant genuine attempts to negotiate or as too weak and stupid to counter whatever risky attempts are made to defeat their purposes
5. Direct pressure on any member who expresses strong arguments against any of the group's stereotypes, illusions, or commitments, making clear that this type of dissent is contrary to what is expected of all loyal members
6. Self-censorship of deviations from the apparent group consensus, reflecting each member's inclination to minimize him- or herself to the importance of personal doubts and counterarguments
7. A shared illusion of unanimity concerning judgments conforming to the majority view (partly resulting from self-censorship of deviations, augmented by the false assumption that silence means consent)
8. The emergence of self-appointed mindguards—members who protect the group from adverse information that might shatter its shared complacency about the effectiveness and morality of its decisions[7]

Janis's analysis is supported by laboratory evidence suggesting that groups do have the power to isolate themselves from outside influence.[8] Recall that we have discussed how people create their own social reality. By filtering their perceptions and withholding conflicting opinions, people in groups may in fact exacerbate the individual potential for self-deception.

Yet Janis does not suggest that cohesion must necessarily give rise to "groupthink." He proposes that individuals be assigned the role of critical evaluator and that a high priority be placed on airing doubts and uncertainties. Possibly the agenda can be altered to pay greater attention to the competing alternatives to initial preferences. If the group leader openly welcomes new ideas, the pressure toward "groupthink" will be lessened.[9]

Conformity Pressures

Just as too much cohesion can cause problems, so also can too rigid an attempt to establish and maintain norms. In Chapter 4 we cited the reactions of conforming group members in the Asch experiments resulting in distortions of perception, judgment, and action. Pressure is created within the group as the majority tries to force deviant members to comply with norms.

Social-impact theory offers other insights into how individual freedom is able to be retained in the group. Latané and Nida suggest that three factors determine a group's impact on deviant members:

1. *The number of group members.* The more people applying the pressure, the greater the likelihood of conformity.
2. *The strength of the group.* The stronger the characteristics that attract the deviant member to the group, the greater the likelihood of conformity.
3. *Immediacy.* The greater the closeness in time and space, the greater the impact.[10]

Thus, the group's ability to keep its members in line depends on the size of the group, the attractiveness of what the group has to offer, and the physical and temporal closeness of the members.

Some degree of conformity is necessary for the well-being of the group. The difficulty lies in balancing the conformist responses with the independent ones in order that new ideas, creative solutions, and critical responses to problems and issues can be made.

Logical Process Problems

Hirokawa compared groups working on a problem involving what equipment would be necessary for survival on the moon. After decisions were made by groups of students, he compared them with expert answers provided by the research section of the NASA

Manned Spaceflight Center. He then compared and analyzed the interactions of groups that arrived at the correct answers and the groups that did not. He determined that a group's failure can be attributed to a complex interplay among six factors:

1. *The group's misunderstanding of the problematic situation.* Poor choices were made because group members based their choices upon inaccurate or inappropriate premises regarding the nature of the problem.
2. *The group's overestimation of the positive benefits of alternative choices.* One persuasive member convinced his group to include a bottle of wine among its ten survival items because it could be used as a lighter fluid and helpful in starting fires.
3. *The nature of values accepted and utilized by the group as decisional premises.* Some groups made poor choices based upon beliefs about the "goodness" or "badness" of things. One group selected toilet paper as one of their ten survival items because of their value and belief that every effort must be made to maintain cleanliness and personal hygiene.
4. *The group's acceptance of inaccurate or invalid information.* An influential member of the group convinced the group to accept "flawed" information, as in the case of wine as a fire-starter.
5. *The group's rejection of accurate or valid information.*
6. *The persuasive influence of group members.* A persuasive sounding individual may override the logic of the other group members and lead them to poor choices.[11]

Figure 10.1 illustrates the interrelationships of the factors that lead to poor decisions. It must be recognized initially that it is hardly ever the case that a decision-making group can obtain *all* the detailed specific information that could be of some use to it in its deliberations. However, the point for our consideration here is the group that clearly lacks *sufficient* information.

One of the primary hallmarks of an efficient decision-making group is its ability to obtain adequate information; this involves both the recognition that current information is *insufficient* and the knowledge of ways a group may *become better informed.*

Individual members of groups are frequently unwilling to admit that they are relatively ignorant about certain aspects of a problem. Such admission can be embarrassing; it can appear to endanger their status in the eyes of other members of the group. Frequently a group member will assume that, because each person knows *some* problem aspect better than any other member, *collec-*

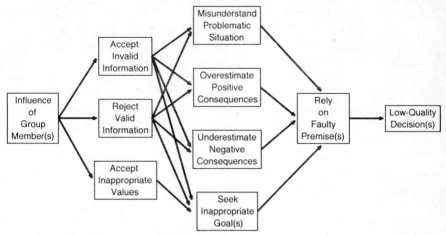

Figure 10.1 Interrelationship of causal factors in unsuccessful groups. (From Randy Hirokawa, "Group communication and problem-solving effectiveness: An investigation of group phases," *Human Communication Research* 9 No. 4, (1983), 291–305.

tively, information about *all* problem aspects is present in the group. This assumption should be checked carefully by the group, and certain impelling or constraining forces about which no one in the group has specific information should be investigated.

The group should experiment with ways of obtaining needed information. Some members, perhaps a committee, can "go take a look," observe firsthand the situation, or conditions, in question. Representatives from that situation may be asked to meet the group to present and discuss the information needed. Printed reports, surveys, and so on sometimes may be read and summarized by individual group members. In any event, the ability to recognize a lack of pertinent information and do something about it is a habit well worth cultivating by decision-making groups. No amount of erudite reasoning, fancy guessing, or interpersonal good feelings can substitute for pertinent information when a group is attempting to analyze a problem.

Data alone, however, are not enough. Reasonable inferences must be made. Gouran provided a case study of the Watergate cover-up and showed that even while possessing the right data to formulate the correct response, the group failed. Gouran explained:

> Of course, one has no basis for assuming that erroneous inferences necessarily lead to bad decisions. The point is that erroneous inferences—especially those that bear directly on the merits of a given choice—represent a source of influence predisposing individuals and groups toward particular choices. To the extent that inferences are inaccurate, the probability for choosing inappropriately is increased.[12]

PERSONALITY PROBLEMS

Each member of the group has needs to be fulfilled by the group. What is of major importance to one member may not be important to others. For example, a reticent member may hesitate to speak to associates if she or he has few ideas to offer. Other members may pull people into the conversation by asking their opinion or giving them special assignments that will make them expert in a given area.[13]

Withdrawal tendencies of group members also affect the group. One study discovered that as the number of members with withdrawal tendencies increased, satisfaction and cohesion of the group diminished. If one member withdraws, others may be likewise encouraged to do so.[14]

Self-esteem has also been studied as a dependent variable. Wilcox and Mitchell assigned members to groups with the task of selecting a member of the group to throw overboard in a hypothetical problem of overcrowding. They detected a significant reduction in self-esteem among those rejected.[15] Apparently an individual tends to assimilate others' perceptions of self; consequently, an act by others implying rejection reduces one's perception of self as valuable to the group. This in turn can affect how the individual subsequently interacts and contributes to performance of the group's tasks.

It is entirely logical as well as likely that different members of the same group will initially disagree on various aspects of a problem as they attempt to analyze it. Because of different experiences, value systems, and sources of information they will vary in their degree of recognition of the importance (or even existence) of certain impelling and constraining forces. Disagreement on the interpretation of relevant aspects of a problem is to be expected, tolerated, discussed, and eventually resolved by open and frank consideration of each others' viewpoints.

It may not be surprising, but it can be most distressing, when such honest *disagreement* is taken to mean *dislike* of one another. In a general way most people can accept disagreement by another person, particularly if it is thought to be temporary and possibly resolvable. Dislike, even if it is not an accurate perception of reality, is ordinarily distressing. It increases social distance and heightens suspicion; under these conditions the possibility of open discussion and resolution of disagreements is diminished.

The members of your group should constantly check with each other to identify carefully the possible expressions of personal dislike. These should be discussed openly and honestly, and a wide latitude should be provided for possible disagreement without an attendant assumption of dislike. On the other hand, it is psychologically unsound to assume that every group member *likes* every other group member and to assume that every individually directed snide remark is simply honest disagreement.

If personal dislike is present and identified as such, the involved members can be encouraged to seek ways of either overcoming it or keeping it from interfering with the rational process or problem analysis. However, the more disruptive situation arises when simple disagreement on substantive matters is *mistaken* for personal dislike.

Perceived dislike (actual or not) generates dislike; a vicious circle of dislike, hostility, and avoidance or aggression is set in motion. Rational analytical processes break down or are set aside, and problem solving gives way to defense of one's status or image. Such an occurrence is indeed too bad, but the frequency with which such events happen in groups is high. One of the authors of this book observed its occurrence seven times in one hour in the interaction of a class project group composed of ordinary, intelligent, well-meaning college students; in a follow-up debriefing, by listening to and discussing audiotapes, the class members agreed on the identification of the seven instances. In fact, they were somewhat shaken by their postevaluation of their own behavior.

We can think of no more significant a pitfall to be avoided in group problem analysis than that of interpreting honest disagreement as personal dislike. Disagreement can, of course, occur at any time during the deliberations of a problem-solving group, and it serves a valuable function. Disagreement may occur as group members initially meet and express their individual concerns about a problem area. It most often occurs (and is more easily accepted) when, later, alternative solutions are each considered and evaluated. As groups seek to analyze a specific, identifiable problem, members may insist that, if properly "identified," the problem can be viewed with only one correct interpretation. Expressing disagreement without disrupting personal relationships should be allowed and even encouraged. Personal dislike, when real, is distressing; an assumption of dislike, when not true, contains the essence of tragedy.

SUMMARY

We have focused attention on common obstacles to group effectiveness in order that they can be avoided or minimized when possible. In the procedures and processes of the group, efforts must be made to balance task considerations with personal feelings of the members. Conformity pressures and excessive cohesion can become barriers to group effectiveness.

Finally, we dealt with potential personality problems including the confusion of disagreement with dislike. Honest disagreement is vital to the success of the group as critical decisions are made, but when disagreements are perceived as dislike and elicit defensive behavior, not only is the decision-making process contravened, but considerable interpersonal difficulty results—all for no reason.

APPLICATIONS

10.1. Analyze one of the groups you have observed in terms of the major problems that limited the group's effectiveness.

10.2. Using instruments selected from Appendix A, determine how the group rated in cohesiveness.

10.3. From observations of the group with instruments shown in Appendix A, determine major areas in which the group could improve.

NOTES

1. T. W. Dougherty and R. D. Pritchard, "The measurement of role variables: Exploratory examination of a new approach," *Organizational Behavior and Human Decision Processes,* 35 (1985), 141–155.
2. B. M. Bass, *Stogdill's Handbook of Leadership.* New York: Free Press, 1981, p. 226.
3. G. A. Yukl, *Leadership in Organizations.* Englewood Cliffs, N.J.: Prentice-Hall, 1981, p. 238.
4. A. Zander, *Making Groups Effective.* San Francisco: Jossey-Bass, 1982, p. 160.
5. R. Y. Hirokawa, "Group communication and problem-solving effectiveness: An investigation of group phases," *Human Communication Research,* 9, No. 4, (1983), 291–305.
6. C. N. Parkinson, *Parkinson's Law.* Boston: Houghton Mifflin, 1957, p. 24.
7. I. L. Janis, *Victims of Groupthink.* Boston: Houghton Mifflin, 1972.
8. J. M. Innes, "Group performance," *Social Psychology,* ed. by G. Gardner. Sydney: Prentice-Hall, 1981, p. 173.
9. M. I. Flowers, "A laboratory test of some implications of Janis's groupthink hypothesis," *Journal of Personality and Social Psychology,* 35 (1977), 888–896.
10. B. Latané and S. Nida, "Social impact theory and group influence," in *Psychology of Group Influence,* ed. by P. B. Paulus. Hillsdale, N.J.: Lawrence Erlbaum, 1980.
11. R. Y. Hirokawa, "Why 'informed' groups fail to make high-quality decisions: An investigation of possible interaction-based explanations," paper presented at the annual meeting of the Speech Communication Association, Chicago, 1984.
12. D. S. Gouran, "Communicative influences on decisions to continue the Watergate coverup: The failure of collective judgment," paper presented at the annual meeting of the Speech Communication Association, Chicago, 1984.

13. M. W. Lustig and T. G. Grove, "Interaction analysis of small problem-solving groups containing reticent and non-reticent members," *Western Speech Communication,* 39 (1975), 155–164.

14. L. Leren and A. Goldberg, "The effects of socialization upon group behavior," *Speech Monographs,* 28 (1961), 60–64.

15. J. Wilcox and J. Mitchell, "Effects of group acceptance and rejection on self-esteem levels of individual group members in a task-oriented problem-solving group interaction," *Small Group Behavior,* 8, (1977), 169–178.

chapter *11*

Effective Group Decision Making

In the preceding chapters we have examined groups and the people in them from a number of perspectives. We have discussed the processes by which groups gather information from their members and arrive at decisions. Implicit in the discussions have been the factors that may facilitate or hinder group decision making. In this chapter we shall present some structures and strategies that have been shown to facilitate effective group interaction. The last portion of the chapter will serve as a general summary of the main ideas of this text.

STRATEGIES FOR EFFECTIVE DECISION MAKING

The effectiveness of any group obviously depends on the way in which decisions are made. Unfortunately, some groups have developed norms that inhibit discussion *about* the decision-making process itself. Recall for example, as cited in Chapter 5, that Berg discovered that logically connected arguments in 124 groups that he studied last only an average of 58 seconds.[1] The group members generally interjected into the discussions comments that were only remotely relevant to the issue being considered. Can the group improve by discussing its decision-making processes?

Janis and Mann have presented a theoretical framework for counseling groups on their understanding of the use of decision-making processes.[2] They discuss the role of the process analysis and recommend three strategies for groups to employ:

1. **Develop a balance sheet.** The balance sheet procedure was designed as a technique for fostering vigilant decision making. When a complex decision is at stake, a group should develop lists of positive and negative factors before making a final decision. This procedure was tested by Janis using Yale seniors facing career choices prior to graduation, by eliciting alternatives and probable outcomes (gains and losses). Typically, at the beginning of an interview, the students were asked to describe all of the alternatives they were considering and to specify the pros and cons for each. Then they were shown a balance sheet grid with empty cells as shown in Figure 11.1. They were asked to fill out a sheet for the most preferred alternatives, and asked to reexamine each cell on the balance sheet, trying to think of considerations not yet mentioned.

This procedure was also shown to be effective in a group situation involving a decision to remain physically active,[3] and in studies of occupational choice conducted in Germany.[4] The list should not be developed with the aim of proving whether a decision is good or bad. Rather, the group should simply try to generate as many ideas, pro and con, as possible.

2. **Role play the decision outcome.** Once a group decision appears to be a reasonable and preferred one, the group should envision the consequences by role playing the people affected by the decision. Janis and Mann have adapted this technique from emotional experiences in groups promoting personal change, for example, requiring heavy smokers to play roles of persons told by their physicians that they have lung cancer.[5] The technique requires a person to take the role of someone who learns vividly and dramatically the consequences of complacency.

Role playing may encourage the group to foster a more comprehensive appraisal of pros and cons by anticipating emotional as well as logical personal responses. The group may also be better prepared for dealing with negative feedback when the decision is implemented. Occasionally the group may feel that more information is needed before a final decision is made.

3. **Obtain decision counseling.** When a group has been in existence a long time, the ways of making decisions may be questioned. If the group feels that it has not always made the best possible decisions or finds the process difficult, an outside counselor might observe the group impartially and furnish

Alternative # _____

Gains	Losses
Material gains for self	Material losses for self
Material gains for others	Material losses for others
Gains in self-approval	Losses in self-approval
Approval by others	Disapproval by others

or

Alternative # _____

	Positive Anticipation +	Negative Anticipation −

1. Tangible gains +
   and losses −
   for self		

2. Tangible gains +
   and losses −
   for others		

3. Self-approval +
   or
   Self-disapproval −		

4. Social Approval +
   or
   Disapproval −		

Figure 11.1   The balance sheet grid. Alternative forms.

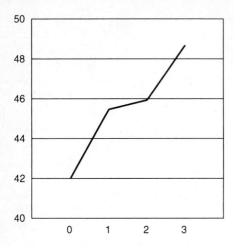

Figure 11.2 Relationship of strategy comments and group product. From J. R. Hackman and C. G. Morris, "Group tasks, group interaction process, and group performance effectiveness: A review and proposed integration," in *Advances in Experimental Social Psychology,* Vol. 8, ed. by L. Berkowitz. New York: Academic Press, 1975.

new insights. In Chapter 12 and Appendix A we show some ways of systematically observing and recording the actions of groups.

Since 1982 Mann and his colleagues at Flinders University in Australia have conducted workshops designed to help people make more effective decisions.[6] Based on the conflict theory cited in Chapter 10, the workshops focus on conflict theory and the major coping patterns. Participants also engage in role playing and the use of decisional balance sheets. A course for high school students known as "GOFER" has also been shown to improve the students' decision-making skills. "GOFER" is an acronym for the steps of *G*oals clarification, generation of *O*ptions, *F*act finding, consideration of *Ef*fects, *R*eview and implementation. These steps correspond to the format we presented in Chapter 6.

Sometimes the use of such strategies as those cited will facilitate the group. When group members plan strategy—when they explicitly discuss the way they will go about reaching a decision—the group's performance has been shown to improve. Hackman and Morris analyzed transcripts of 100 groups working on a variety of tasks.[7] The group products were judged independently on the basis of creativity. The research showed that the greater the amount of discussion of strategy, the higher the group's creativity. Figure 11.2 shows that as the number of comments increase, so does creativity. Let us now consider this phenomenon of creativity in greater detail.

LATERAL THINKING

Group reasoning and potential creativity are tied to the capacities of group members to draw inferences, as we saw in Chapter 5. Inferences frequently entail "cognitive shortcuts."[8] When they do, the

mind apparently functions to minimize any resistance to its efficiency through simplification, the use of familiar memory patterns,
the avoidance of alternative and persistent questioning, and the
imposition of selectivity. The type of thinking that these strategies
involve is what Edward de Bono refers to as "vertical" thought.[9] The
vertical mind organizes information through patterning systems.
Over time, habits of organization and approach will develop. These
habits form the basis for the individual's overall patterning system.
The attitudes that eventually evolve from these systems will act as
a general influence on the thinking processes of the individual.

The vertical mode of thinking is a system that works toward
closure and operates within a structure of perceived relevance. It is,
in fact, a shortcut, and therein lies the difficulty. Its efficiency *offers
a continuous series* of shortcuts to the organization of information.
New input is subjected to automatic analysis by existing experiential patterns. When such a powerful system is indiscriminately applied, frustration, misunderstanding, fantasy, myth, prejudice, in-
tolerance, and successive inferential errors may be the result.

For the most part, a vertical system functions effectively. There
are occasions, however, when a preponderance of vertical traits can
result in an imbalance. Under such circumstances, information is
quickly processed through low-resisteance paths. Perceived characteristics of inputs are then reduced and simplified to further aid in
categorical organization.

The vertical system heightens the probability that inappropriate inferences will occur. Further, such a probability appears to
exist, and may be amplified, in the group as well as in the individual.
Why questionable inferences should occur so often in a group setting has only recently come under investigation.[10] Perhaps the mere
volume of input encourages the vertical mode to operate in "high
gear" during group interaction. Perhaps the cumulative effect of
many individual vertical thinking systems creates a "false security"
in the reliability of such a system.

Fortunately, de Bono describes a complementary mode of
thought. The "lateral" mode is an attitude that moves in no predeter-
mined direction.[11] To function in a lateral way is to move through
and beyond existing borders. The most crucial facet of the lateral
attitude is this movement, and freedom of movement necessitates
an unrestricted fluidity. In the *true* lateral mode, there is no judgment, no logical analysis, only the continual acceptance and consequent generation of possibilities.

The optimal condition is the harmonious integration of vertical and lateral thinking. Lateral skill questions assumptions and
permits the generation and consideration of alternative perspectives, while vertical analysis provides a method of refinement and
systematic decision making. Existing analyses of individual and

group inferential errors, however, reveal a preponderance of vertical traits. It appears that, as cognitive shortcuts, inferences are too often welcomed in the vertical system, and too seldom criticized.

PROMOTING GROUP CREATIVITY

For the past 30 years researchers and theoreticians have attempted to develop techniques that promote greater creativity in groups. We shall consider four such approaches: lateral thinking, brainstorming, the Delphi Method, and quality circles.

Lateral Thinking

In his book *Lateral Thinking: Creativity Step by Step,* de Bono discusses the differences between vertical and lateral thinking.[12] If we were to lay these two modes side by side, an outline of his comparison might appear as follows:

Vertical	*Lateral*
1. Is selective	1. Is generative
a. Rightness matters	a. Richness matters
b. Excludes pathways	b. Opens up pathways
c. Selects most promising approach	c. Generates as many approaches as possible
2. Needs direction to move	2. Moves to find direction
a. Uses a definite approach	a. Moves for the sake of moving
b. Designs experiment to show effect	b. Designs experiment to provide opportunity to change one's ideas
c. Must move usefully	c. May play with ideas
3. Analytical	3. Provocative
4. Sequential: Each step arises from the preceding step	4. Nonsequential: One can jump ahead to a new point and fill in gaps afterward.
5. Needs correctness at every step	5. No need to be correct at every step
6. Uses the negative to block pathways	6. There is no negative
7. Concentrates and excludes the irrelevant	7. Welcomes chance intrusion
a. Selection by exclusion	a. Uses change from outside
b. Works within a frame of reference	b. No predetermined frame of reference required
c. Throws out what is not relevant	c. Irrelevant influences offer the chance of altering established patterns

8. Categories, classifications, and labels are fixed
  a. Needs consistency
  b. Needs rigid definitions
  c. Meaning has boundaries
	8. Categories, classifications and labels are not fixed
	  a. Classifications may change; used as signposts to help movements
	  b. Definitions are temporary classifications
	  c. Fluidity of meaning

9. Follows the most likely paths	9. Explores the least likely paths

10. Finite process
  a. One expects an answer
  b. Promises at least a minimum solution
	10. Probabilistic process
	  a. There may be no answer
	  b. Increases the chance of a maximum solution

De Bono further posits that when the optimum system is in operation, vertical and lateral thinking will function simultaneously. The *aim* of lateral thinking is to generate new ideas and approaches, but its *purpose* is to facilitate the analytic system. It is a necessity that the two modes function as complementary components of the thinking process. In this way lateral skill permits the generation and consideration of alternative perspectives, while vertical analysis provides a method of refinement and systematic decision making. Each mode functions to promote the maximum efficiency of the other.

Brainstorming

Brainstorming was developed by Alex Osborn 30 years ago for use in his advertising agency.[13] The technique employs four basic rules:

1. **Criticism is ruled out.** Adverse judgment of ideas must be withheld until later.
2. **"Free-wheeling" is welcomed.** The wilder the idea the better; it is easier to tame down than to think up.
3. **Quantity is wanted.** The greater the number of ideas, the more the likelihood of winners.
4. **Combination and improvement are sought.** In addition to contributing ideas of their own, participants should suggest how ideas of others can be turned into *better* ideas, or how two or more ideas can be joined into still another idea.

The primary objective is to free group members temporarily from inhibition, self-criticism, and criticism of others, in order to produce more imaginative alternative approaches to a specific problem. The problem should be carefully specified and all evaluation withheld. Somebody with secretarial ability should record *all* suggestions, and a spirit of fun and excitement should be encouraged. At a later session the group should evaluate the various suggestions produced.

After a large number of suggestions, sometimes as many as 100, have been presented, there is nearly always the need to clarify many of them. When they were first suggested, their potential value may have seemed obvious; on taking a second look, the intended meaning may be clouded. In some cases their relevance will need to be explored. This clarification process will need to be carried out when all group members are present. The original author of a suggestion will often be best equipped to explain its potential value; however, just because the brainstorming session is over, creative thinking should not be shut off. In many cases a suggested alternative can be modified, added to, or otherwise enhanced by a person other than its original author. Creative thinking, once started, should be encouraged and continued.

A number of informal experiments briefly described by Osborn support the view that the use of brainstorming in groups increases the production of valuable ideas. In addition, he reported many indications of its wide acceptance. Various other studies have shown that the use of brainstorming was superior to patterns in which critical evaluation was not delayed, in that the total number of ideas was greater and that, as the quantity of ideas was increased, the number of *valuable* ideas was increased proportionately.[14]

A field experiment in brainstorming was conducted by Balchan to test Osborn's technique using his directives.[15] She studied such variables as group size, the method of recording ideas, and the specific task upon productivity and member satisfaction. Both small groups (5 to 7 participants) and large groups (9 to 19) were tested using three different methods for recording the ideas presented: on a chalkboard with the list visible to the group, on a notepad by a designated secretary, and on a tape recorder. Two different tasks were assigned: One was "contrived," using the problem, "How many ways can you find to use a Pringle Potato Chip container?"; the other was "real" and formulated to generate alternative ideas to solve the problem identified by the group. The same leader was used in all the conditions of the experiment, and groups were given the same instructions and led through a training session using Osborn's suggestions for hitchhiking and idea creation. There were five significant findings:

1. Participants in small groups contributed a greater mean number of ideas per person than did participants in large groups.
2. Although all participants were satisfied with their involve-

ment and with their own participation, responses from the small groups indicated a greater satisfaction.

3. Participants in the board method indicated greater satisfaction with their productivity than did participants in the secretary or oral methods.

4. The real task was significantly more meaningful to participants than the contrived task.

5. All groups contributed more ideas in the first 5 minutes of the 15-minute brainstorming sessions.

This issue should not be confused with the question of whether brainstorming in groups produces more ideas or more valuable ideas than an equivalent number of persons working alone; on this particular question experimental findings are inconclusive.[16] However, there appears to be considerable evidence in support of the value of the brainstorming technique to a group working on a problem that requires a group decision. For such groups we advocate the use of brainstorming to uncover approaches that otherwise might be neglected.

The brainstorming technique should not be used until a problem has been well defined: Uninhibited creativity combined with ambiguity can produce a general sense of confusion. In addition, a group should recognize full well that uncovering a lot of good ideas does not eliminate the need to evaluate them later in order to select the best one. Careful evaluation of alternatives must always follow a brainstorming session.

It has been our experience that a 20- to 30-minute brainstorming session can be not only profitable to a problem-solving group but also a lot of fun. There is a sense of freedom from ordinary restraints, the challenge to think of something clever or new, the excitement of discovery, and the good-natured, temporary acceptance of apparently ridiculous suggestions. In many ways a brainstorming session can inadvertently satisfy a need to increase group cohesiveness at a particular time when a problem-solving group may be tempted to split into factions supporting pet solutions to a serious problem. The value of building group spirit at this particular time should not be overlooked.

No idea should be abandoned immediately just because it is apparently ridiculous; it should be given careful and serious consideration to realize its possible potential. For example, one of the authors helped a country club steering committee attack the problem of obtaining new members. One suggestion was to pay prospective members ten dollars to attend a free dinner. The committee, after some joking, came to see that a ten-dollar payment plus the cost of the meal totaled less than twenty dollars; the dues were more than $200; if one prospect in ten could thus be led to join the club, there would be an initial net income. For the better part of a year this approach was used as the primary instrument in a successful drive to increase the club's membership. To some "prospects" the suggestions seemed to make no sense; but on the other hand, what did they have to lose? Where else could they make ten dollars by eating a free meal?

The Delphi Method

The Delphi Method is simple in design. (1) Individual members are asked to state their opinions privately (independently) *in writing* regarding (a) the nature of a problem, (b) possible solutions to a selected problem, or (c) the potential value of a proposed solution. (2) The results are tabulated and shown to all members without identification of who owns what opinions. (3) Members who deviate from the majority (or most favored) opinion are asked to state anonymously and in writing their reasons for holding that position (unless they now wish to change their opinion). (4) After all members have read these statements, all are again asked to state their opinion *now,* independently and in writing. (5) These new results are tabulated and fed back to the members, together with concise summaries of the reasons provided by those who are still deviant. The call for a restatement of opinions with reasons for continued deviation may be repeated; this has been done by the Rand Corporation developers for as many as four or five times.[17]

The Delphi Method may be used by any group that wishes to avoid a direct confrontation by participants. It will be most useful when intuitive opinion must be substituted for factual data. There is experimental evidence that it can lead group members toward a consensus with less tension than is common in open confrontation; there is also evidence that the method is conducive to independent thought on the part of "experts."[18]

Although we recommend the use of the Delphi Method when only inexact data are available and "expert" opinion must be used, in no case should any opportunity to obtain precise information be neglected. We do not believe that judgment or opinion or tea leaves or divining rods are *ever* more desirable than facts obtained first-hand through careful observation. The Delphi Method can be most valuable to your group when you are dealing with a problem that, to your knowledge, has never before been solved anywhere.

Quality Circle

Quality circles had their origins in Japan in 1962, introduced by American quality control experts Deming and Juran.[19] More than 8 million Japanese workers have participated in quality circles, and a 1982 survey found more than 6,200 locations of activities within the United States.[20] A quality circle is a group of three to ten people from the same organization and work area who meet on a regular basis, usually an hour a week, to discuss and solve work-related problems. The objectives are to tap the creative problem-solving skills of the workers and to improve the quality of communication among workers.

Increased productivity and cost reductions have been measurable products of the programs. Other benefits cited have been improved attendance, better teamwork, enhanced technical knowledge, and improved attitudes toward management.[21]

Characteristically, an outside consultant serves as the facilitator to initiate such a program. Usually the first-line supervisors serve as leaders of the circles after receiving some training by the facilitator. Participation must be voluntary; after advertising the availability of the group, management agrees to support the program and attend meetings only upon invitation. The employees who choose to participate agree to attend and participate actively in all scheduled meetings and to be trained in quality circle techniques.

The first several weeks are devoted to training the quality circle members in participatory decision making. After a training period the group selects a name for itself, and agrees on a regular meeting time to discuss problems relating to the work area. The typical weekly agenda calls for opening remarks by the leader, the reading of the minutes of the previous meeting, suggested new topics, progress on existing projects, work assignments for next week's meeting, and the closing. The guidelines are always in effect and are agreed to by all members. Examples of such rules follow:

1. criticize ideas, not people;
2. the only stupid question is the one not asked;
3. everyone in the group is responsible for the group's progress and process; and
4. be open to the ideas of others.[22]

The types of issues that the circle will address are work quality, cost reduction, safety, work methods, tools and equipment, interorganizational communications, and processes and procedures. A quality circle does not deal with issues such as wages and salaries, hours of work, personalities, new product design, hiring, firing, and disciplinary decisions. Ideas for discussion topics can come from many sources; for example, circle members, managers, customers, or staff members; however, the selection is the circle's prerogative. Most circles can handle three to ten projects per year, depending on the complexity of the problems. If the circle requires outside information or assistance, the circle leader will contact the resource needed. Should the involvement of top management be needed to complete or approve a project, the circle will prepare a formal presentation. The circle also will make a presentation to top management periodically to review its progress.

You will note that the principles of the quality circles correspond with the general suggestions that we have made regarding all decision-making groups.

Stohl designed a study to investigate the relationship between quality circles and communication processes within an organization.[23] Her results suggest that the quality circles have positive consequences for cognitive processing, members' attitudes, members' perceptions of the communicative climate of the organization, and the overall effectiveness of the organization. While the meeting takes only an hour a week, the activities of the group carry over positively to other parts of the work day. Stohl states:

> The results indicate that quality circle programs provide structures and encourage communications that cut across the inherent divisions of an organization. To the degree that the quality circle process changes the relations among upper managers, middle managers, supervisors, and employees, the potential benefits are enhanced. Members of quality circles who occupy "linking" roles have better attitudes, know more about the company, share this information with other circle workers, and are less likely to drop out of the program.[24]

While more research is needed on the process itself, sufficient evidence exists to show the positive impact of quality circles. We anticipate that their use and value will be even more widespread.

SUMMARY

The success of any group attempting to reach the best possible decision depends on many factors. Extensive research efforts in the social sciences have given us abundant clues to the variables that are likely to have positive or negative impact upon a group's performance. Yet the complexity of human interaction still leaves a great deal to be discovered. In many ways, promoting effective group interaction remains as much an art as a science.

One of the consistent themes emerging from the research that we have cited has been the recurrent findings regarding the interlocking nature of task and maintenance behavior. We believe that this dual emphasis is requisite for the long-term success of a decision-making group. Both a sense of accomplishment in the decision made and a feeling of positive regard for self and coworkers are important if a group is to continue to function. Product and process are thus interdependent.

As a member of a group. you have a number of choices available to you. We have attempted to identify from the available research the consequences of some of the choices you will make. We hope that, from utilizing the principles we have cited and from receiving honest feedback from your colleagues, you will be able to contribute constructively to future group interactions.

APPLICATIONS

11.1. In your group, follow the suggestions made by Janis and Mann for helping groups understand the use of decision-making processes. Utilize the three strategies in your own group.

11.2. Analyze your group in terms of the principles presented for lateral thinking.

11.3. Select a simple problem and practice the techniques of brainstorming described in this chapter.

NOTES

1. D. M. Berg, "A descriptive analysis of the distribution and duration of themes discussed by task-oriented small groups," *Speech Monographs,* 34 (1967), 172–175.
2. I. L. Janis and L. Mann, "A theoretical framework for decision counseling," in *Counseling on Personal Decisions,* ed. by I. L. Janis. New Haven, Conn.: Yale University Press, 1982, pp. 47–72.
3. L. M. Wankel and C. Thompson, "Motivating people to be physically active: Self-persuasion vs. balanced decision making," *Journal of Applied Social Psychology,* 7 (1977), 332–340.
4. S. Jeromin and E. Kroh-Puschel, "Occupational choice: Information behavior in decision aids," in *Studies in Decision Making,* ed. by M. Irle. Berlin: de Gruyter, 1985, pp. 737–787.
5. I. L. Janis and L. Mann, "Effectiveness of emotional role-playing in modifying smoking habits and attitudes," *Journal of Experimental Research in Personality,* 1 (1965), 84–90.
6. L. Mann, "Decision making," in *Australian Psychology: Review of Research,* ed. by N. T. Feather. Sydney: Allen and Unwin, 1985, pp. 218–235.
7. J. R. Hackman and C. G. Morris, "Group tasks, group interaction process, and group performance effectiveness: A review and proposed integration," in *Advances in Experimental Social Psychology,* Vol. 8, ed. by L. Berkowitz. New York: Academic Press, 1975.
8. J. G. Stein and R. Tanter, *Rational Decision-Making: Israel's Security Choices, 1967.* Columbus, Ohio: Ohio State University Press, 1976, p. 76.
9. E. de Bono, *Lateral Thinking: Creativity Step by Step.* New York: Harper & Row, 1970.
10. See D. S. Gouran, "Communicative influences of inferential judgments in decision-making groups: A description analysis," paper presented at the American Forensic Association (Speech Communication Association conference on Argument, Alto, Utah, 1983).
11. de Bono, *Lateral Thinking,* pp. 39–40.
12. Ibid., pp. 39–45.

13. A. F. Osborn, *Applied Imagination.* New York: Scribner, 1957.

14. S. J. Parnes and A. Meadow, "Effects of brainstorming instructions on creative problem-solving by trained and untrained subjects," *Journal of Education and Psychology,* 50 (1959), 171–176; A. Meadow, S. J. Parnes, and H. Reese, "Influence of brainstorming instructions and problem sequence on a creative problem-solving test," *Journal of Applied Psychology,* 43 (1959), 413–416; J. K. Brilhart and L. M. Jochem, "Effects of different patterns on outcomes of problem-solving discussion," *Journal of Applied Psychology,* 48 (1964), 175–179.

15. E. M. Balchan, "Group brainstorming field study: Effect on size, recording method, and task, on productivity and participants' reactions," unpublished doctoral dissertation, University of Michigan, 1980.

16. See, for example, D. W. Taylor, P. C. Berry, and C. H. Block, "Does group participation when using brainstorming facilitate or inhibit creative thinking?" in *Problems in Social Psychology,* ed. by C. W. Backman and P. F. Secord. New York: McGraw-Hill, 1966, pp. 299–309.

17. O. Helmer, *Analysis of the Future: The Delphi Method, P-3558.* Santa Monica, Calif.: Rand, 1967.

18. See N. C. Dalkey and O. Helmer, *An Experimental Application of the Delphi Method to the Use of Experts, R17-727-PR.* Santa Monica, Calif.: Rand, 1962.

19. P. Thompson, *Quality Circles: How to Make Them Work in America.* New York: Amacom, 1982.

20. J. Searle, "Quality circles in United States industry," *Quality Circles Journal,* 5 (1982), 25–28.

21. H. B. Karp, "A look at quality circles," *The 1983 Annual for Facilitators, Trainers, and Consultants.* San Diego: University Associates, 1983, pp. 157–163.

22. Ibid., p. 161.

23. C. Stohl, "Quality circles and changing patterns of communication," *Organizational Communication, 1985 Communication Yearbook.* Beverly Hills: Sage, pp. 511–531.

24. Ibid., p. 528.

chapter 12

Improving Ability by Observing Other Groups

A well-respected myth often repeated in our culture is that we learn by doing. There is appropriate basis in fact if the myth is properly qualified or restricted: *We learn to do better if we make an attempt, evaluate this effort, and modify our consequent efforts in ways that increase our effectiveness.* One of the ways in which we can evaluate our efforts is to compare what we do with efforts made by others, paying special attention to the efforts of others that are effective.

In this chapter our primary objective is to help you improve your own ability to be an effective member of a decision-making group. We hope to do this by describing a way in which you can gain additional insight into the process of applying broad, general principles to specific situations. The procedure we advocate is to observe groups in real-life settings. These should be task groups—problem-solving or decision-making groups—as much as possible. Of particular interest to you should be the great discrepancy between the textbook ideal of group behavior and what is practiced by many poorly trained or inexperienced persons.

In our own teaching we routinely divide our classes into small groups of five to seven students, asking each group to observe an outside-of-class campus or community group in action. This means that our students must attend routine "business" meetings in which problems are discussed and decisions made. We tell our students that they should not just observe and leave; they must obligate themselves to report back to the observed group and help it as best they can to improve its problem-solving behavior. In this role as trainee *consultants* (unpaid, of course) they are not to claim that they are anything other than students, but as such they are to be as helpful as they know how to be. We carefully instruct them in the procedures outlined in the next section, cautioning them against trying to be helpful when help is not wanted.

OBSERVING AND CONSULTING WITH TASK GROUPS

This process involves three stages of interaction between the observing consultant group and the observed group: observation, feedback, and assisting in achieving change *if desired.*

> *Observation.* Together the consultants and the task group determine what task-group behavior should be observed; these should be in the group's natural setting and should involve work of major concern to the members. Together the group and the consultants decide on the types of data to be collected and the method of acquisition.
>
> *Feedback.* Data on the group behavior should be fed back to the group in a manner that allows a free choice of its use. The consultants should openly discuss any interpretation of these data with the group.
>
> *Assisting in Achieving.* The consultants and the group should reach an agreement upon those changes (or "improvements") that are desirable, and together they should discuss how these may be achieved. This process of goal setting and planning should allow free use of data and theory by the task group. The consultants should appropriately reflect those principles of group interaction that their training and experience can provide; the group members should be allowed to decide what behavioral changes can be achieved and will serve their needs. This stage is critical and is the most important of the three stages of the process.

The following procedure incorporates the essential principles that have been developed by consultants working with organizations to develop greater decision-making efficiency. (1) The focus is on the interaction process of the entire group, or organization, not on the efficiency of individuals. (2) Experiential learning techniques are emphasized. (3) Attention is given to real problems and events that happen in the group or organization. (4) Emphasis is placed on competence in interpersonal relations as well as on task skills. (5) Goals frequently include an increased competence in communicating, decision making, and problem solving.[1] In preparing our students to observe and work with groups on the campus or in the community we try to follow these general guidelines.[2]

INTERPRETING OBSERVED GROUP BEHAVIOR

It is not always easy to interpret observed behavior, even when the data gathered are fairly specific; frequently, it appears that more than one interpretation is reasonable. For this reason, after our student groups have observed and collected data on their out-of-class groups, we require them to present a report to the entire class and discuss their interpretations with their fellow students. We request that five items be covered in these reports:

1. A brief description of the nature (goals, membership, special regulations) of the group observed
2. Identification of some aspect of group problem-solving interaction that can be improved (occasionally our students observe a group that in their opinion does everything very well)
3. Evidence (data) to support item 2
4. Specific recommendations that are to be given to the group observed
5. Support from established authorities in the field or from published research that provides credibility for their recommendations (item 4)

While making their observations, gathering data, and thinking of the time they will report to the class, occasionally our students will say, "We looked for this or that and didn't find any problem. What do we do now?" Eventually, we have responded with a prepared list of items they might check out, one after the other; almost always there is some area that is less than perfect. A hidden virtue of using this list is that a student tends to gain familiarity and understanding regarding a number of problem-solving group behaviors. Although you, the reader, will probably recall having seen each of these items discussed in this text, the following list can be useful to you as a review of the essential principles we have presented in the previous pages.

The following is a list of group behaviors that may cause difficulty and possibly could be the basis for changes beneficial to the group.

If you observe the occurrence of one of the following, you should give enough detail so that the nature of the group, the task, or problem under consideration by the group, and the specific behavior of the group members can be understood.

Part I. Task-Oriented Behaviors

A. Lack of identification of group task or problem
 1. Lack of mutual concern—or lack of any concern
 2. Inability to overcome confusion regarding group task or problem
B. Inability to analyze a problem
 1. Failure to compare what *is* and what is *desired*
 2. Lack of information on *causes* of problem, that is, forces increasing need for a change from status quo
 3. Lack of information on *restraining* forces, that is, forces resisting desired change
 4. General lack of factual information regarding problem (too much reliance on unverified opinions, guesses, and suppositions)
C. Inability to evaluate proposals
 1. Lack of identification of possible solutions (inexperience in area, lack of creative thinking)
 2. Poor identification of criteria by which group could evaluate various proposals: (a) Does it meet problem as analyzed by group? (b) Any evidence it could really work? (c) Any serious disadvantages, for example, costly, or dangerous?
 3. Inability to agree on the best possible solution
D. Inability to implement group decision when reached
 1. Inability to sort and allocate relevant group resources
 2. Inability to agree on individual group members' responsibilities
 3. Inability to persuade others (outside the group) to give support, approval, assistance, and so forth

Part II. Interpersonal Behaviors

A. Interpersonal needs not met
 1. Personal needs for inclusion not met, poor spread of participation
 2. Severely competitive orientations—excessive need to dominate others
 3. Need not met for personal consideration, caring, or regard

B. Group member confusion on role functions
  1. Inability to agree on who can perform needed leadership functions
  2. Poor relationship between member's personality and role requirements
  3. Lack of consideration of one another's feelings
  4. Inappropriate or ineffective attempts to perform leadership functions
C. Difficulties caused by personal characteristics
  1. Lack of mutual attractiveness of group members
  2. Lack of cohesiveness of status or prestige of group
  3. Dysfunctional group norms; for example, tardiness, absenteeism, everyone talking at once, discourtesy, and so on
  4. Disagreement concerning individual's status or power (perhaps power struggle is evident)
  5. General apathy—poor motivation on part of members to be helpful to each other
  6. Size of group too large (or small)
D. Inability to handle or resolve conflict
  1. Inability to separate (a) honest disagreement on problem or on value of a possible solution from (b) interpersonal dislike
  2. Inability to handle cognitive dissonance; for example, inability to be comfortable with honest, reasonable disagreement on problem or task issues
  3. Inability to produce attitude congruence through communication

After the reports on the observed groups have been presented and discussed in class, we request that all students write their own reports. We do this because we know that writing for perusal and student evaluation by another person (in this case, the professor) can cause students to think through their ideas and experiences more carefully. In so doing the students reformulate and reconceptualize and so learn. In the preparation of these written reports we allow coauthorship, provided sufficient agreement can be reached by two or three students or even by an entire project group.

A MODEL OF REPORTING

In the following pages of this section we offer a student report as an illustration of the observing, evaluating, and interpreting processes we have been describing. This report was written by Lawrence B. Nadler, at the time a student in a course in problem-solving group discussion. The excerpts are here included with minor changes and the author's permission.[3]

A MODEL OF REPORTING

Final Project Report

(McCollum Hall Social Committee)

INTRODUCTION

This portion of the paper is designed to present an orientation to our purpose and methods for conducting our research on a decision-making group. The purpose of this study was to observe group dynamics in terms of task performance and interpersonal relations of group members.

The decision-making group we observed was the McCollum Hall Social Committee, a student group representing a residence hall at the University of Kansas. The Social Committee is responsible for all social events planned in the dormitory that require the utilization of hall facilities and the usage of allocated hall funds.

The group consisted of 30 members, with each individual representing a specific section and floor of the residence hall. The average attendance for group meetings was approximately 26 members. We perceived these individuals as highly self-motivated, involved participants in group functioning. We observed that four members contributed most of the communicative activity, with two members, Joanne and Nancy, participating the most in a dual-leadership situation.

In systematically observing the Social Committee, we employed various highly valid measuring instruments. A primary research tool we utilized was the R. F. Bales's scales. We used this instrument to evaluate the type of communication exhibited, both quantitatively and qualitatively, regarding 12 key areas defined by Bales. To analyze and evaluate leadership behavior on task and person dimensions, we utilized two questionnaires. The Halpin-Winer scales were employed to assess our perceptions of the two leaders, while the Sergiovanni, Metzcus, and Burden Task-Person scales were used to tap the leaders' self-perceptions on these same dimensions. As these scales have different endpoints, the Halpin-Winer scales were standardized to allow direct comparison with the Task-Person scales. To evaluate the personal needs of group members, we utilized the Self-Perception of Interaction Needs and Behavior (SPIN-B), in which group members described what they felt they expressed and what they wanted on the dimensions of interaction, control, and affection. Additionally, we employed the Interpersonal Perception Scales (IPS) to tap our perceptions of key group members on these dimensions. Further, direct comparisons between the SPIN-B and IPS were made. Finally, we used an original instrument, the Evaluation of Party Planning, to measure members' perceptions of the extent to which they had successfully accomplished their task. As the four weekly meetings we observed all involved the planning (and later evaluation) of a Halloween party, we asked members to evaluate the group's performance on ten elements relevant to this task. The factors evaluated were financial matters, arrangements concerning the band, dispensing of beer, admission procedures, the operations of floors' booths, party publicity, contests, decorations, cleanup arrangements, and the party overall. The members expressed the degree to which they perceived group efforts as being successful on a seven-point semantic differential–type scale.

The following sections will cover in depth our analysis of the McCollum Hall Social Committee.

SPIN-B AND IP SCALES*

We have performed various comparisons of the SPIN-B and IP scales. Giffin, following Schutz's work, designed the SPIN-B to measure the individual's expressed behavior toward others and the behavior he wants from other people in three areas of interpersonal needs: interaction, control, and affection. Schutz states that interaction concerns the entrance into association with others. Control is related to interactions involving influence and power, while affection entails the need to like others and to be liked by other people.

According to Schutz, satisfactory interpersonal relationships exist when the individual establishes a balance in each of these areas regarding the amount of behavior the person actively expresses versus the amount he desires to receive from other people (or, in regard to control, the extent to which he wants to control others).

The IPS was used to compare members' perceptions with the views of observers. Both the SPIN-B and IP scales provide five equally spaced (interval) response alternatives, ranging from very little to very much. We used these two scales to compare how four members of the McCollum Hall Social Committee viewed themselves and how we saw them. The four individuals we chose were the four members who engaged in the most interaction.

One observation we made was that the group members rated themselves high on all dimensions: On the five-point scale, all responses were "3" or above. We believe this might have occurred because of the large group size. If these four members, who contributed approximately 69 percent of total group interaction, compared their participation with the remaining group members, their self-perception would probably have been magnified because of the sharp contrast. Festinger's theory of social comparison supports this notion that individuals define their behaviors and beliefs on the basis of relevant others with whom they compare themselves.

Another observation we made is that in 9 cases out of 12 the four members' responses on expressed versus wanted interaction, control, and affection corresponded exactly. As Schutz notes, this pattern indicates satisfactory interpersonal relationships for these members. In general, we believe these four members were satisfied with their behavior. Another conclusion we drew is that our observations of the four members were consistently lower than the members' self-perceptions. Here, we noticed that although there were many differences, the group members basically seemed to elevate their perceptions in a consistent manner.

BALES'S SCALES

In the 1950s Robert R. Bales created the Bales Interaction Process Analysis (IPA). The purpose of this instrument, according to Bales, is to identify and record the nature (not the content) of each separate act in ongoing group interaction. An act is defined

*Author's note: See Appendix A for details of the instruments.

as a single simple sentence. Essentially, the IPA scales determine the quantity of communication in 12 different categories (see Charts A through D). The way IPA data are collected is by having one person observe a group member and record his or her communicative acts with a slash-mark. The data are later converted into percentages and compared to group norms on an individual and group basis.

The other analysis performed involves the Bales's Group Report. The group members complete scales that measure the same dimensions of interpersonal interaction in regard to how they perceive the group.

In utilizing these tools, our group observed the four most vocal group members and lumped the remaining individuals into a residual category. We chose to perform our observations in this manner because of the large group size. These four members were the two coleaders, the secretary, and a highly vocal individual.

According to Bales, the 12 categories can be broken into two overriding dimensions: task-related and maintenance-related behaviors. We rated the social committee as high on task information, in that the percent of communication in the task-related categories (gives and asks for information, suggestions, and opinions) exceeded the estimated norms. On the other hand, the maintenance-related categories were generally below the estimated norms. Here, it appears that the group does

Chart A BALES'S IPA—PERCENTAGE OF TOTAL OBSERVED
GROUP PARTICIPATION IN EACH IPA CATEGORY,
COMPARED WITH ESTIMATED NORMS

Category	Percent	Estimated Norms
Seems friendly	6.4	2.6– 4.8
Dramatizes	3.9	5.7– 7.4
Agrees	9.1	8.0–13.6
Gives suggestions	7.3	3.0– 7.0
Gives opinions	10.5	15.0–22.7
Gives information	37.6	20.7–31.2
Asks for information	17.5	4.0– 7.2
Asks for opinions	3.5	2.0– 3.9
Asks for suggestions	1.3	0.6– 1.4
Disagrees	1.2	3.1– 5.3
Shows tension	0.9	3.4– 6.0
Seems unfriendly	0.9	2.4– 4.4

Chart B PARTICIPANTS' SHARE
OF TOTAL OBSERVED
GROUP INTERACTION

Name	Percent
Joanne	20.5
Nancy	17.6
Bruce	15.8
Lori	14.8
Others	31.3
Total	100.0

Chart C   PERCENTAGE OF TOTAL OBSERVED GROUP PARTICIPATION IN EACH IPA CATEGORY FOR EACH GROUP MEMBER

Category	Percentage of Group Participation				
	Joanne	Nancy	Bruce	Lori	Others
Seems friendly	0.5	0.3	2.9	1.4	1.2
Dramatizes	1.0	0.3	0.6	1.4	0.6
Agrees	0.3	1.0	2.3	1.6	4.0
Gives suggestions	0.4	1.5	1.8	2.2	1.4
Gives opinions	0.9	1.3	1.9	3.3	3.0
Gives information	10.7	7.4	2.3	2.1	15.1
Asks for information	3.9	4.3	2.6	1.9	5.0
Asks for opinions	1.2	0.3	1.2	0.6	0.2
Asks for suggestions	0.8	0.1	0.1	0.3	0.1
Disagrees	0.4	0.0	0.1	0.0	0.6
Shows tension	0.3	0.3	0.1	0.0	0.3
Seems unfriendly	0.1	0.8	0.0	0.0	0.0
Total	20.5	17.6	15.9	14.8	31.5

Chart D   INDIVIDUAL IPA GROUP DATA COMPARED WITH ESTIMATED NORMS (ROUNDED TO NEAREST PERCENTAGE)

Category	Percent of Each Person's Total					
	Joanne	Nancy	Bruce	Lori	Others	Norms
Seems friendly	2.5	2.0	18.5	9.6	3.7	2.6– 4.8
Dramatizes	4.8	1.5	3.9	9.6	2.0	5.7– 7.4
Agrees	1.3	5.5	14.6	10.8	12.7	8.0–13.6
Gives suggestions	2.2	8.5	10.7	15.0	4.6	3.0– 7.0
Gives opinions	4.3	7.5	12.4	22.2	9.6	15.0–22.7
Gives information	52.4	42.2	14.6	14.4	48.0	20.7–31.2
Asks for information	19.0	24.1	16.3	12.6	15.8	4.0– 7.2
Asks for opinions	5.6	2.0	7.3	4.2	0.6	2.0– 3.9
Asks for suggestions	3.7	0.4	0.6	1.8	0.3	0.6– 1.4
Disagrees	2.2	0.0	0.6	0.0	2.0	3.1– 5.3
Shows tension	1.3	1.3	0.6	0.0	0.8	3.4– 6.0
Seems unfriendly	0.4	4.5	0.0	0.0	0.0	2.4– 4.4
Total	100.0	100.0	100.0	100.0	100.0	

not openly express disagreement, tension, and unfriendliness to the extent "prescribed" by Bales's estimated norms. From these data we concluded that the group is having difficulty expressing dissatisfaction or negative emotions. This statement is supported by two additional observations.

First, in looking at the Bales's Group Report, in terms of the individual breakdown of scores for the leaders, Joanne and Nancy rated the amount of disagreement as 3 and 2 respectively. These scores are on a five-point scale, with "1" meaning *never* and "5" being *very frequently*. Therefore, both leaders saw relatively little disagreement. On the other hand, Bruce and Lori saw high disagreement, as indicated by their scores of 4 and 5, respectively. From this pattern of results we concluded that some disagreement is occurring within the group but is being manifested as side comments behind the backs of the leaders. Here, the leaders do not pick up on the disagreement because of their relative isolation (i.e., sitting at the head table at the front of the room). The other members are sitting in the group body and thus are hearing (and also perhaps contributing to) some under-the-breath disagreement. Hence, we concluded that there is a lack of open expression of negative feelings.

Another observation supporting the possibility of hidden feelings of dissatisfaction is based upon the group discussion. One particular discussion was initiated by Nancy, one of the group leaders, when she discovered that people were criticizing the leaders behind their backs. She stressed that people should come directly to the leaders with complaints, instead of casting aspersions indirectly. Therefore, although her speech was given in the last of four weekly meetings we attended, she had become aware that dissatisfaction existed but was not being openly expressed.

At this point, a more specific consideration of certain categories is necessary. First, we observed that the actual amount of "gives information," 37.6 percent, deviates significantly from the upper bound, 31.2 percent, of the estimated norms. In looking at the leaders, 52.4 percent of Joanne's total communication was giving information, while 42.2 percent of Nancy's overall participation occurred in this category. Despite these high values, on the group report both leaders rated themselves low in this category. A possible explanation for this disparity may be that the leaders did not clearly communicate their feelings. Possibly, the leaders expressed details they viewed as opinions, while the other group members and the observers considered such statements as involving the transfer of information. Switching to the category "asks for information," a similar disparity was observed. Here, the group norms are 4.0 to 7.2 percent, yet we rated the group as exhibiting these communicative behaviors 17.5 percent of the time. A possible reason for the overabundance of asking for information may be that the group members did not contribute information very often of their own free will. This trend may be attributed to the leaders' not offering adequate opportunities for group members to speak. Instead, they merely solicited information when it was needed and generally received brief, yet concise, responses. This contention is supported by our ratings of the leaders' degree of control. We rated both Joanne and Nancy as over 4.00 on the five-point scale regarding control. Thus, perhaps both leaders are controlling not only the group in general but also the option of group members to supply information voluntarily as they see fit.

In considering the 12 categories overall, only 3 of the 12 involved percentages within the estimated norms. These were "agrees," "asks opinions," and "asks suggestions." Further, all of the "negative" categories ("dramatizes," "disagrees," "shows tension," and "seems unfriendly") were well below the estimated norms. We felt this pattern may have been due to the atmosphere the leaders created within the group. Specifically, meetings were highly structured and very businesslike. As a result, members were possibly afraid to disagree, express interpersonal tensions, or go against the majority opinion. We believe that more disagreement and expression of feelings would have reduced these tensions and perhaps enhanced group performance.

LEADERSHIP

Using the Halpin-Winer scales, our group assessed the two leaders, Joanne and Nancy, according to how well we believed they performed in regard to task and interpersonal behavior in their group. Also, we employed the Task-Person scales to tap the leaders' self-perceptions of their behavior concerning these dimensions. (See Charts E, F, and G.)

First, we discovered that Joanne felt her task- and person-oriented behavior were average in nature. In terms of the grid, this meant she felt she performed

Chart E   T/P SCALES AND HALPIN-WINER (OBSERVERS)

Based		Joanne		Nancy	
On	Dimension	T-P	H-W	T-P	H-W
20	Task	9	14.2	9	15.4
15	Person	7	10.5	8	8.7

Chart F   EVALUATION OF PARTY PLANNING

Dimension	Group Average
Finances	5.25
Band	4.44
Beer	5.13
Admission	3.44
Booths	3.19
Publicity	4.69
Contests	3.81
Decorations	5.50
Cleanup	4.20
Overall	4.81

1 = Very Unsuccessful
7 = Very Successful

Chart G   BALES'S GROUP REPORT

Category	Joanne	Nancy	Bruce	Lori	Others
Seems friendly	5	3	5	5	3.3
Dramatizes	3	3	3	5	2.6
Agrees	3	5	4	3	3.5
Gives suggestions	4	3	5	4	3.9
Gives opinions	4	4	5	5	3.9
Gives information	2	3	4	4	3.4
Asks for information	2	2	4	5	3.1
Asks for opinions	3	2	4	3	2.9
Asks for suggestions	4	3	4	4	3.2
Disagrees	3	2	4	5	3.4
Shows tension	3	3	3	1	2.6
Acts unfriendly	2	2	2	1	2.4

1 = Never
5 = Very frequently

adequately, though not spectacularly, regarding task and interpersonal behaviors. Nancy reported approximately the same pattern of perceptions concerning her leadership behavior. In comparing the leaders' self-perceptions to the collective observations of our group, we believed that Joanne was well above average on task performance and a little above average on maintenance behavior. We also perceived Nancy as being very high on task behavior, but we viewed her person-oriented actions as average. Both Joanne and Nancy emphasized the value of the group's performance to the rest of the residence hall. Further, we viewed Joanne as relatively open to suggestions from the group, as well as inducing participation. As noted earlier, these endeavors usually consisted of seeking needed information and elicited short, concise responses. Also, we felt Joanne did an excellent job of coordinating decision making regarding important matters. In short, she was well organized and always had a "game plan." Turning to Nancy, we noticed a condescending air about her. She was quite authoritative, but she did know what she was talking about. Further, she had good access to the resources needed for effective group functioning. Overall, there seemed to be a nice balance between the two leaders. There were no competitive incentives apparent between Joanne and Nancy, and we observed a mutual respect that was definitely beneficial in formulating and making decisions.

EVALUATION OF PARTY PLANNING

The Social Committee members also completed a questionnaire that asked them to assess the success of various aspects of their party planning efforts. Overall, the group perceived its efforts as slightly successful. They evaluated their work on decorations, finances, and alcoholic beverages as reasonably effective, yet considered their endeavors concerning admission procedures, floor booths, and contests as somewhat lacking. Cleanup arrangements, publicity attempts, and selection of a band were viewed as slightly successful. Overall, this questionnaire revealed both satisfaction and some degree of discontent with the group's efforts.

TASK STRENGTHS

Having described the functioning of the group, it is appropriate to turn to an evaluation of the group's performance on task- and person-oriented dimensions. (See Charts H and I.) An important aspect of the Social Committee's task performance entails the high degree of member motivation to fulfill the group's goals. Zander (1971) maintains that when members have a strong desire for group success and know that the group requires their best efforts, then the group's performance is likely to be better. Clearly, the large amount of volunteering for various tasks reflects the desire for group success and served to enhance the Social Committee's functioning. As Deutsch (1968) notes, greater productivity usually ensues when members are cooperative rather than competitive. The absence of a hidden agenda and the presence of shared goals seemed to assist task performance. Also, the group performed very efficiently considering its relatively large size. For instance, Leavitt and Mueller (1951) report that as group size increases, the degree of feed-

Chart H   SPIN-B: KEY MEMBERS

Category	Joanne	Nancy	Bruce	Lori
Interaction	5	5	4	5
Control	5	5	3	4
Affection	5	3	4	5
Interaction	5	5	4	5
Control	4	5	3	3
Affection	4	3	4	5

Chart I   I:P (OBSERVERS)

Category	Joanne	Nancy	Bruce	Lori
Interacts	4.50	3.67	2.67	3.67
Controls	4.17	4.17	1.83	3.00
Shows Affection	3.50	1.50	2.50	3.67

These are observer averages.

back generally decreases, yielding a loss of communication accuracy and heightened hostility. Further, studies by Carter (1951), Bales et al. (1951), and Bass and Norton (1951) indicate that increasing group size produces a communication élite whereby a few members dominate while remaining individuals participate much less frequently. While this difference in the relative amount of member contributions was observed, it did not seem to impede accomplishment of the group task. The group's functioning was also boosted by its possession of relevant task information. Here, the members seemed either to possess or to have access to all information requisite for task completion. Similarly, the group utilized its own assets as well as outside resources in an effective manner. For example, members were aware of dormitory regulations, had open channels of communication with advisors, and had contacts with various musical groups.

In regard to group meetings, a high degree of organization existed and communication consistently centered upon a preestablished agenda. The leaders were aware of group concerns and made certain that these matters were dealt with systematically. Further, the segmentation of problems into manageable units greatly aided group efforts in decision making. Proposals were given fair and thorough consideration, but little time was wasted, and the method of majority vote was successfully and efficiently employed. These efforts were facilitated by strong task leadership in that the group generally restricted its focus to relevant issues and moved smoothly toward desired outcomes. Finally, the high degree of task commitment was reflected in the steady attendance rate. Here, continuity of group affairs was nicely ensured from each meeting to subsequent meetings.

TASK WEAKNESSES

The majority of task deficiencies revolved around procedural matters. For instance, the meetings never started promptly, members would temporarily leave and then return, there was a preponderance of simultaneous talking, which was extremely distracting, and members frequently departed prior to the conclusion of meetings. As previously noted, the large group size produced a high degree of centrality. As Shaw (1954) reports, groups generally show more satisfaction with communication networks having less total centrality. Hence, the members may have felt they possessed little opportunity to participate, thus creating these slightly dysfunctional norms. However, our group unanimously concurred that these patterns of behavior did not seriously detract from task performance.

INTERPERSONAL STRENGTHS

According to Cartwright (1968, p. 91), "group cohesiveness refers to the degree to which the members of a group desire to remain in the group." Further, Back (1951) contends that group cohesiveness can be related to attraction of members to other members, the task itself, and/or perceived prestige gain. In regard to the Social Committee, the group appeared to be highly cohesive considering the relative absence of extrinsic rewards. We perceived the primary reason for the group's high cohesiveness as attributable to task attraction. The members seemed highly motivated to accomplish various task functions, and the close bonds that existed were predicated upon the shared perception that cooperative effort was necessary to achieve group goals. As Patton and Giffin (1978) succinctly assert, a cohesive group often develops when people with similar needs find similar reinforcements.

Other interpersonal strengths involved the openness of individuals to other members' ideas. Here, members interacted within a generally friendly, cooperative environment. Further, there was high clarity of role functions, with considerable latitude for individuals to define their roles as they chose. Basically, an important beneficial aspect of group functioning involved the flexibility afforded to group members.

INTERPERSONAL WEAKNESSES

Although the group exhibited little overt conflict, the results of the Evaluation of Party Planning questionnaire and the defensive speech given by one of the leaders concerning criticism suggest that some members were truly dissatisfied with some group functions and the group may not have been entirely aware of this situation. Also, as noted earlier, group cohesiveness was primarily based not on member attraction, but upon task attraction. As a result, some interpersonal tensions obviously existed within the group that were not usually voiced. Pepitone and Reichling (1955) suggest that members feel freer to express rather than suppress feelings of hostility when high group cohesiveness exists. Although the Social Committee seemed highly cohesive, the fact that this cohesiveness was based upon task (versus member) attraction may have inhibited members from expressing important feelings and perceptions. Further, this situation was intensified by the group leaders, who were not very person oriented. In summary, the task was performed quite well, but several members were unhappy with some aspects of group functioning.

RECOMMENDATIONS

As Bales (1951) observes, increasing group size produces greater dominance by a few members. Although group membership and centrality are inevitable accompaniments of a dormitory situation in which all floors desire representation, several measures can be adopted to improve group performance and member satisfaction. Floor representatives should be encouraged to contribute opinions and suggestions to a greater extent. Bales (1951) notes that group conflict can emerge from members neglecting other members' needs. Perhaps breaking into subcommittees that would report to the overall group on a weekly basis would lead to even greater member involvement and satisfy members' needs.

Another avenue for providing increased opportunity for participation entails creating an interpersonal environment conducive to airing complaints, frustrations, and criticisms. According to Zaleznik and Moment (1964), the optimum group norm would allow for the free expression of feelings. Here, the group should allow members a chance to openly express feelings of dissatisfaction. Additionally, this modification could be enhanced by the leaders' being more cognizant of members' interpersonal needs.

The final set of recommendations involves group norms concerning promptness, attentiveness, and "meandering." These behaviors, as previously described, seemed to communicate implicitly that members did not value other individuals' opinions. These disconfirming behaviors can be partially eradicated by members' being more sensitive to one another and by the group's seeking stricter adherence to more functional procedural norms.

Basically, the group performed quite well and was an effective decision-making unit. We believe that adopting these recommendations would further enhance the functioning of the McCollum Hall Social Committee.

NOTES

K. W. Back, "Influence through social communication," *Journal of Abnormal Social Psychology* 46 (1951), 9–23.

R. L. Bales, F. L. Strodtbeck, T. M. Mills, and M. E. Roseborough, "Channels of communication in small groups," *American Sociological Review* 16 (1951), 461–468.

B. M. Bass and M.F.T. Norton, "Group size and leaderless discussion," *Journal of Applied Psychology* 35 (1951), 397–400.

L. Carter, "The relation of categorizations and ratings in the observation of group behavior," *Human Relations* 3 (1951), 239–254.

D. Cartwright, "The nature of group cohesiveness," in *Group Dynamics,* ed. by D. Cartwright and H. Zander. New York: Harper & Row, 1968, pp. 165–181.

M. Deutsch, "The effects of cooperation and competition upon group process," in *Group Dynamics,* ed. by D. Cartwright and H. Zander. New York: Harper & Row, 1968, pp. 461–482.

H. J. Leavitt and R.A.H. Mueller, "Some effects of feedback on communication," *Human Relations* 4 (1951), 401–410.

B. R. Patton and K. Giffin, *Decision-Making Group Interaction.* New York: Harper & Row, 1978.

A. Pepitone and G. Reichling, "Group cohesiveness and the expression of hostility," *Human Relations* 8 (1955), 327–337.

M. E. Shaw, "Some effects of problem complexity upon problem solution efficiency in different communication nets," *Journal of Experimental Social Psychology* 48 (1954), 211–217.

A. Zaleznik and D. Moment, *The Dynamics of Interpersonal Behavior.* New York: Wiley, 1964.

A. Zander, *Motives and Goals in Groups.* New York: Academic Press, 1971.

APPLYING INSIGHTS TO YOUR OWN BEHAVIOR

It is important that your observations of other groups contribute to the evaluation of your own behavior. In fact, the primary point of this chapter has been to provide a way of enhancing your learning and improving your own performance, even though at times it may have seemed to you that we were presenting guidelines or classroom procedures to be used by your instructor.

As you observe others, you may find yourself saying, "I do that, too—and I wish I didn't!" You must remember that it is always easier to see such things and even to say such things than it is actually to accomplish these personal changes. Changes in one's behavior ordinarily require these conditions (at least): (1) specific knowledge of the new (to you) behavior you would like to adopt, (2) a strong desire to carry out the new behavior, and (3) the assistance of another person who will show patience (not critical impatience) and give you feedback on his or her perception of the degree to which you have demonstrated the new behavior. If these conditions are present, and these new behaviors are actually within your range of capabilities, then experimental attempts to change can be successful. It is important to remember that practice does not make perfect if you are practicing an inefficient way of behaving. Practice (without change) simply makes for permanence: permanently inefficient behavior, if such is the behavior practiced. Our students have used their project groups somewhat as a laboratory in which they can, in an exploratory fashion, attempt new behaviors in a search for individual self-improvement. By "project groups" we mean the in-class student groups who worked together to observe and critique out-of-class real-life groups. Sometimes members of these student groups have shared an experience like the following: "You know, when I saw a member of the city council behaving the way I caught myself doing in our own group, I made up my mind I just shouldn't be that way anymore!" It seems clear to us that the observation of others, the interpretation of the effects of various behaviors, and the comparison of these observations with one's own performance are important steps in attempting to improve one's own behavior.

SUMMARY

In this chapter we have emphasized the point that individuals can gain insight into and understanding of their own behavior by observing the task-oriented techniques and interpersonal relations exhibited by members of other groups. We have described procedures of observing, analyzing, and interpreting such behavior—procedures that our own students have generally found useful to them in gaining personal insight and understanding. In this section we reviewed the concepts covered in this book, suggesting sources of difficulty in groups which individuals might wish to attempt improvement.

APPLICATIONS

12.1. Evaluate the report presented in this chapter. Are the inferences reasonable, based upon the data presented?

12.2. Select an outside group that would be agreeable to your investigation and analysis. Decide as a team on the instruments from Appendix A that would be useful for such an examination.

12.3. Following the outline provided in this chapter, formulate an approach and methodology for observing the outside group and preparing a detailed report.

NOTES

1. Cf. C. Argyris, *Interpersonal Competence and Organizations.* Homewood, Ill.: Dorsey-Irwin, 1962. W. G. Bennis, *Changing Organizations.* New York: McGraw-Hill, 1966. R. R. Blake and J. S. Mouton, *Grid Organization Development.* Houston: Gulf, 1968.

2. For further suggestions for observing and consulting with community development groups, see S. Tubbs and K. Giffin, *The Role of the Communication Specialist in Community Development.* Lawrence, Kan.: The Communication Research Center, the University of Kansas, 1969.

3. L. B. Nadler (Ph.D., 1983, The University of Kansas) is currently Associate Professor of Communication at Miami University (Ohio).

APPENDIXES

We conclude this text with two resources that we hope prove useful. Appendix A contains a number of questionnaires and observational guides for gathering data about a group. As you participate in a group or observe a group in action, these instruments can add to your understanding of the group process.

Appendix B is a research report prepared by three communication scholars analyzing the decision making involved in the *Challenger* disaster. The article is an excellent illustration of how group process can be analyzed and criticized.

Appendix *A*

Evaluating Group Performance

Casual observation of the behavior of your group can give tentative answers to the question, "How well are we doing in our decision-making behavior?" As you participate with the other members you can note the degree of competence you show in identifying mutual concerns, examining impelling and constraining forces, evaluating various proposals, and so on. However, assessment of group performance by casual observation may neglect some important considerations; in addition, your casual observations are likely to be colored by your own personal feelings, needs, and biases. The way to improve these observations is to work from a prepared list and obtain observations that may be checked for reliability by other members of your group.

In this appendix we will present questionnaires and other instruments that have been developed for looking closely at group process and individual member attitudes and behaviors. By using these instruments you can become more sensitive not only to the total process of group interaction but also to how individual contributions combine to determine the relative success or failure in reaching decisions. The first set of instruments are the self-report type, which allows you to learn more about yourself by responding to specific questions. After that set, we will present structured guides for gathering data by observing a group in action.

SELF-REPORTS OF NEEDS, PERCEPTIONS, AND ORIENTATIONS

Individual group members' views of themselves can be a useful source of information. Self-reports can also be collected on

177

how other group members are seen and the reports can be compared.

FIRO-B is a subjective questionnaire designed to measure the individual's expressed behavior toward others and behavior he or she wants from others in the three areas of interpersonal need. It has, therefore, six scales: *expressed inclusion, wanted inclusion, expressed control, wanted control, expressed affection,* and *wanted affection.* This instrument (questionnaire) is published by Consulting Psychologists Press and may be obtained at nominal cost.[1]

We have used FIRO-B to help our students assess their own and each others' interpersonal needs. As we did this, our students requested some means of assessing the degree to which they were meeting each others' needs. In response to this request we developed the Interpersonal Perception Scale (IPS), a rating scale modeled after FIRO-B and employing the same three basic dimensions. The IPS can be used to compare one's self-perceptions with the perceptions of others and can serve as a check on the degree to which an individual's interpersonal needs are recognized by the other members of her or his group.

Interpersonal Perception Scale (IPS)

The questions listed below refer to the group interaction experience in which you have just participated. The other members of the group will be interested in knowing how you perceive them, and you will be interested in knowing how they perceive you. Please answer the questions as carefully and as honestly as possible.

Read the questions and answer them regarding the member of the group whose name is on this sheet. Answer each item according to this scale:

Very Little	Little	Average	Much	Very Much
1	2	3	4	5

1. To what extent does this person *interact with others?*
   Circle your response: 1 2 3 4 5
2. To what extent does this person *control or influence others?*
   Circle your response: 1 2 3 4 5
3. To what extent does this person *show warmth or affection toward others?*
   Circle your response: 1 2 3 4 5

The major effect of having our students use FIRO-B with the IPS in their decision-making project groups has been to call attention to the nature of the interpersonal needs of each other; this has helped them to gain insight into the importance of these needs. Usually our students then make special efforts to meet these needs; this consideration of the interpersonal needs of others often has produced results that were satisfactory to the individuals involved.

The T/P Questionnaire*

Several scales have also been developed for self-evaluation in terms of the two major dimensions of any group-task orientation and maintenance concerns. The first of two such scales we include is labeled T/P (for Task/Person).[2]

Name_____   Group_____

The following items describe aspects of group member behavior. Respond to each item according to the way you would be most likely to act if you were in a problem-solving group. Circle whether you would be likely to behave in the described way always *(A)*, frequently *(F)*, occasionally *(O)*, seldom *(S)*, or never *(N)*.

If I were a member of a problem-solving group:

A F O S N   1. I would be very likely to act as the spokesman of the group.

A F O S N   2. I would encourage overtime work.

A F O S N   3. I would allow members complete freedom in their work.

A F O S N   4. I would encourage the use of uniform procedures.

A F O S N   5. I would permit the others to use their own judgment in solving problems.

A F O S N   6. I would stress being ahead of competing groups.

A F O S N   7. I would speak as a representative of the group.

A F O S N   8. I would encourage members toward greater effort.

A F O S N   9. I would try out my ideas in the group.

A F O S N   10. I would let the others do their work the way they think best.

A F O S N   11. I would be working hard for personal recognition.

A F O S N   12. I would be able to tolerate postponement and uncertainty.

A F O S N   13. I would speak for the group when visitors were present.

A F O S N   14. I would keep the work moving at a rapid pace.

A F O S N   15. I would help to identify a task and let the others go to it.

*Reprinted by permission from J. W. Pfeiffer and J. E. Jones, *Structured Experiences for Human Relations Training.* Iowa City, Iowa: University Associates Press, 1969, pp. 9–10.

(*Continued*)

A	F	O	S	N	16. I would settle conflicts when they occur in the group.
A	F	O	S	N	17. I would be likely to get swamped by details.
A	F	O	S	N	18. I would represent the group at outside meetings.
A	F	O	S	N	19. I would be reluctant to allow the others freedom of action.
A	F	O	S	N	20. I would decide what should be done and how it should be done.
A	F	O	S	N	21. I would push for better results.
A	F	O	S	N	22. I would let other members have some authority.
A	F	O	S	N	23. Things would usually turn out as I predicted.
A	F	O	S	N	24. I would allow the others a high degree of initiative.
A	F	O	S	N	25. I would try to assign group members to particular tasks.
A	F	O	S	N	26. I would be willing to make changes.
A	F	O	S	N	27. I would ask the others to work harder.
A	F	O	S	N	28. I would trust the group members to exercise good judgment.
A	F	O	S	N	29. I would try to schedule work to be done.
A	F	O	S	N	30. I would refuse to explain my actions when questioned.
A	F	O	S	N	31. I would persuade others that my ideas are to their advantage.
A	F	O	S	N	32. I would permit the group to set its own pace.
A	F	O	S	N	33. I would urge the group to beat its previous record.
A	F	O	S	N	34. I would act without consulting the group.
A	F	O	S	N	35. I would ask that group members follow standard rules and regulations.

The T/P Scale can be scored as follows:

A. Circle the *item letter* for items 1, 4, 7, 13, 16, 17, 18, 19, 20, 23, 29, 30, 31, 34, and 35.

B. Put an *X in front of only those circled item numbers* for items to which you responded *S* (seldom) or *N* (never).

C. Put an *X in front of items whose numbers were not circled*, only when you responded to such items with *A* (always) or *F* (frequently).

D. Circle any *X* that you have put *in front of any of the following item numbers:* 3, 5, 8, 10, 12, 15, 17, 19, 22, 24, 26, 28, 30, 32, and 34.

E. Count the circled *X*s. This is your Person Orientation (P) Score.

F. Count the uncircled *X*s. This is your Task Orientation (T) Score.

An individual's T and P scores are then plotted on the T/P Grid and are interpreted in terms of the descriptive elements given in the appropriate cell (see Figure A.1).

Name   Group

Locating oneself on the grid:

To locate yourself on the grid below, find your score on the Person dimension (P) on the horizontal axis of the graph. Next, start up the column above your P score to the cell that corresponds to your Task score (T). Place an *X* in the cell that represents your two scores.

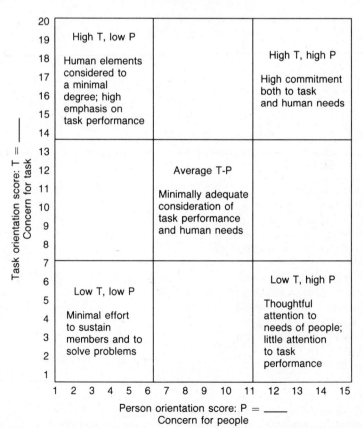

Figure A.1 The Task/Person Grid. (From J. W. Pfeiffer and J. E. Jones, *Structured Experiences for Human Relations Training.* Iowa City, Iowa: University Associates Press, 1969, p. 10).

The Team Orientation and Behavior Inventory (TOBI)*

A second instrument for looking at the same dimensions is the *Team Orientation and Behavior Inventory.*[3]

Instructions: Taking this instrument will help you to learn more about your attitudes toward teams and work groups as well as your behaviors in such groups. There are no right or wrong answers. You will learn more about yourself if you respond to each item as candidly as possible. Do not spend too much time deciding on an answer; use your first reaction. Circle one of the numbers next to each statement to indicate the degree to which that statement is true for you (or the degree to which that statement is descriptive of you).

	Strongly disagree (very unlike me)	Disagree (unlike me)	Slightly disagree (somewhat unlike me)	Neither agree nor disagree (neither like nor unlike me)	Slightly agree (somewhat like me)	Agree (like me)	Strongly agree (very like me)
	1	2	3	4	5	6	7
1. I am often at a loss when attempting to reach a compromise among members of my group.	1	2	3	4	5	6	7
2. I am effective in ensuring that relevant data are used to make decisions in my group.	1	2	3	4	5	6	7
3. I find it difficult to summarize ideas expressed by members of the team.	1	2	3	4	5	6	7
4. I believe that the existence of positive feelings among team members is critical to the team's efforts.	1	2	3	4	5	6	7

*Reproduced from *The 1983 Annual for Facilitators, Trainers, and Consultants.* Leonard D. Goodstein and J. William Pfeiffer, editors. San Diego, Calif.: University Associates, 1983.

	Strongly disagree (very unlike me)	Disagree (unlike me)	Slightly disagree (somewhat unlike me)	Neither agree nor disagree (neither like nor unlike me)	Slightly agree (somewhat like me)	Agree (like me)	Strongly agree (very like me)
(Continued)	1	2	3	4	5	6	7
5. It often is important in my group to summarize the ideas and issues that are raised.	1	2	3	4	5	6	7
6. I think that, to be effective, the members of a team must be aware of what is occurring in the group.	1	2	3	4	5	6	7
7. I am able to convey my interest in and support for the other members of my team.	1	2	3	4	5	6	7
8. In my opinion, it is very important that team members be sources of support and encouragement for one another.	1	2	3	4	5	6	7
9. I am effective in establishing an agenda and in reminding the other members of it.	1	2	3	4	5	6	7
10. I am particularly adept in observing the behaviors of other members.	1	2	3	4	5	6	7
11. When the group becomes bogged down, it often is helpful if someone clarifies his or her goal or purpose.	1	2	3	4	5	6	7
12. I frequently keep the group focused on the task at hand.	1	2	3	4	5	6	7
13. I think that testing for members' commitment is one of the most important components of group decision making.	1	2	3	4	5	6	7

	Strongly disagree (very unlike me)	Disagree (unlike me)	Slightly disagree (somewhat unlike me)	Neither agree nor disagree (neither like nor unlike me)	Slightly agree (somewhat like me)	Agree (like me)	Strongly agree (very like me)
(*Continued*)	1	2	3	4	5	6	7
14. In my opinion, summarizing what has occurred in the group usually is unnecessary.	1	2	3	4	5	6	7
15. One of the things that I contribute to the team is my ability to support and encourage others.	1	2	3	4	5	6	7
16. I think that examining the assumptions that underlie the group's decisions is not necessary in terms of the group's functioning.	1	2	3	4	5	6	7
17. It is difficult for me to assess how well our team is doing.	1	2	3	4	5	6	7
18. In my opinion, work groups are most productive if they restrict their discussions to task-related items.	1	2	3	4	5	6	7
19. I believe that for the team to regularly evaluate and critique its work is a waste of time.	1	2	3	4	5	6	7
20. In my opinion, it is very important that team members agree, before they begin to work, on the procedural rules to be followed.	1	2	3	4	5	6	7
21. I think that, to be effective, a group member simultaneously must participate in the group and be aware of emerging group processes.	1	2	3	4	5	6	7

	Strongly disagree (very unlike me)	Disagree (unlike me)	Slightly disagree (somewhat unlike me)	Neither agree nor disagree (neither like nor unlike me)	Slightly agree (somewhat like me)	Agree (like me)	Strongly agree (very like me)
(Continued)	1	2	3	4	5	6	7
22. It is really difficult for me to articulate where I think other members stand on issues.	1	2	3	4	5	6	7
23. I am effective in helping to ensure that all members of the group have an opportunity to express their opinions before a final decision is made.	1	2	3	4	5	6	7
24. I believe that one's feelings about how well the group is working are best kept to oneself.	1	2	3	4	5	6	7
25. I am skillful in helping other group members to share their feelings about what is happening.	1	2	3	4	5	6	7
26. I usually am able to help the group to examine the feasibility of a proposal.	1	2	3	4	5	6	7
27. I believe that it is a waste of time to settle differences of opinion in the group.	1	2	3	4	5	6	7
28. I often am unaware of existing group dynamics.	1	2	3	4	5	6	7
29. I do not think that the participation of all members is important as long as final agreement is achieved.	1	2	3	4	5	6	7
30. I am skillful in organizing groups and teams to work effectively.	1	2	3	4	5	6	7

	Strongly disagree (very unlike me)	Disagree (unlike me)	Slightly disagree (somewhat unlike me)	Neither agree nor disagree (neither like nor unlike me)	Slightly agree (somewhat like me)	Agree (like me)	Strongly agree (very like me)
(Continued)	1	2	3	4	5	6	7
31. I feel that, to be effective, group members must openly share their feelings about how well the group is doing.	1	2	3	4	5	6	7
32. In my judgment, sharing feelings about how the group is doing is a waste of members' time.	1	2	3	4	5	6	7
33. When the group gets off the subject, I usually remind the other members of the task.	1	2	3	4	5	6	7
34. One of the things that I do well is to solicit facts and opinions from the group members.	1	2	3	4	5	6	7
35. Ascertaining the other members' points of view is something that I do particularly well.	1	2	3	4	5	6	7
36. I think that it is important that my group stick to its agenda.	1	2	3	4	5	6	7
37. In my opinion, an inability to clear up confusion among members can cause a team to fail.	1	2	3	4	5	6	7
38. I feel that it is important to elicit the opinions of all members of the team.	1	2	3	4	5	6	7
39. It is not easy for me to summarize the opinions of the other members of the team.	1	2	3	4	5	6	7
40. A contribution that I make to the group is to help the other members to build on one another's ideas.	1	2	3	4	5	6	7

	Strongly disagree (very unlike me)	Disagree (unlike me)	Slightly disagree (somewhat unlike me)	Neither agree nor disagree (neither like nor unlike me)	Slightly agree (somewhat like me)	Agree (like me)	Strongly agree (very like me)
(Continued)	1	2	3	4	5	6	7
41. I believe that the group can waste time in an excessive attempt to organize itself.	1	2	3	4	5	6	7
42. I believe that it is very important to reach a compromise when differences cannot be resolved in the group.	1	2	3	4	5	6	7
43. I am effective in helping to reach constructive settlements of disagreements among group members.	1	2	3	4	5	6	7
44. I am effective in establishing orderly procedures by which the team can work.	1	2	3	4	5	6	7
45. I think that effective teamwork results only if the team remains focused on the task at hand.	1	2	3	4	5	6	7
46. I am particularly effective in helping my group to evaluate the quality of its work.	1	2	3	4	5	6	7
47. In my opinion, it is important that the team establish methods by which it can evaluate the quality of its work.	1	2	3	4	5	6	7
48. I find it easy to express ideas and information to the other members of my group.	1	2	3	4	5	6	7
49. In my judgment, searching for ideas and opinions is one of the criteria of an effective team.	1	2	3	4	5	6	7

	Strongly disagree (very unlike me)	Disagree (unlike me)	Slightly disagree (somewhat unlike me)	Neither agree nor disagree (neither like nor unlike me)	Slightly agree (somewhat like me)	Agree (like me)	Strongly agree (very like me)
(Continued)	1	2	3	4	5	6	7
50. I believe that it is critical to settle disagreements among group members constructively.	1	2	3	4	5	6	7
51. I believe that it is important that members of the team understand one another's points of view.	1	2	3	4	5	6	7
52. I am adept in making sure that reticent members have an opportunity to speak during group meetings.	1	2	3	4	5	6	7
53. I think that the synergy that occurs among group members is one of the most important components of group problem solving.	1	2	3	4	5	6	7
54. I rarely volunteer to state how I feel about the group while it is meeting.	1	2	3	4	5	6	7
55. When my group wanders from the task at hand, it is difficult for me to interrupt the members and attempt to refocus them.	1	2	3	4	5	6	7
56. I am able to restate clearly the ideas that are expressed in my group.	1	2	3	4	5	6	7

The scores may then be transferred onto this scoring sheet:

| TASK ORIENTATION | | | | MAINTENANCE ORIENTATION | | | |
| Values | | Skills | | Values | | Skills | |
Item Number	Your Score	Item Number	Your Score	Item Number	Your Score	Item Number	Your Score
5.	—	3.	—*	4.	—	1.	—*
11.	—	9.	—	6.	—	2.	—
14.	—*	12.	—	8.	—	7.	—
18.	—	17.	—*	13.	—	10.	—
19.	—*	30.	—	16.	—*	15.	—
20.	—	33.	—	21.	—	22.	—*
32.	—*	34.	—	24.	—*	23.	—
36.	—	39.	—*	27.	—*	25.	—
38.	—	40.	—	29.	—*	26.	—
41.	—*	44.	—	31.	—	28.	—*
45.	—	46.	—	37.	—	35.	—
47.	—	48.	—	42.	—	43.	—
49.	—	55.	—*	50.	—	52.	—
53.	—	56.	—	51.	—	54.	—*
Total	—	Total	—	Total	—	Total	—

*Reverse score item. Change your score as follows:

1 = 7	3 = 5	5 = 3	7 = 1
2 = 6	4 = 4	6 = 2	

The TOBI total scores can then be plotted on the graph shown in Figure A.2. First, find the point where the scores intersect; for example, if the task-values score is 40 and the maintenance-value score is 35, find where 40 on the vertical axis and 35 on the horizontal axis intersect and mark that spot. Do the same with the task-skills and maintenance-skills scores. The two points can now be compared. Are they more or less on the same level? These scores can also be compared between individuals in the group to find which members are most committed to task and which to people. Perceptions of others can also be checked.

The Halpin-Winer Questionnaire

*The next self-report instrument was developed to measure leadership behavior on the same dimensions of task and maintenance.

*A. W. Halpin and J. Winer, "A factorial study of the leader behavior descriptions," in *Leader Behavior: Its Description and Measurement,* ed. by R. M. Stogdill and A. E. Coons. Columbus, Ohio: Bureau of Business Research, The Ohio State University, 1957, pp. 39–51. The questionnaire is reproduced here with the permission of the publisher.

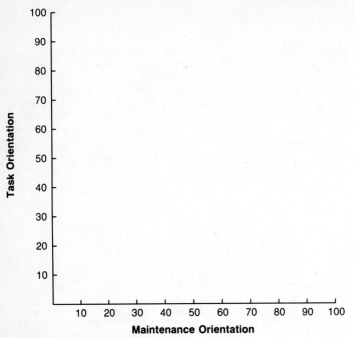

Figure A.2 Plotting TOBI scores.

This scale includes 15 items on task behavior (called "initiation of group structure") and 15 on maintenance behavior (called "consideration of others"). All group members can be rated, even though some have never been regarded as the group leader.

You are to judge the behavior of a specified person against a series of descriptive scales. Please make your judgments on the basis of what the following concepts mean to you. Circle whether this person always (*A*), frequently (*F*), occasionally (*O*), seldom (*S*), or never (*N*) behaves in the manner described in each item.

For example, if you believe that the person being rated *frequently* speaks without thinking, you would circle the F in the following:

A F O S N   1. This person speaks without thinking.

Please circle only one evaluative code letter for each item.

A F O S N   1. S/he makes her/his attitudes clear to the group.

A F O S N   2. S/he does personal favors for group members.

A F O S N   3. S/he tries out new ideas in the group.

A F O S N   4. S/he tries to "rule with an iron hand."

A F O S N   5. S/he does little things to make it pleasant to be member of the group.

A F O S N   6. S/he criticizes poor work.

(*Continued*)

A	F	O	S	N	7. S/he speaks in a manner not to be questioned.
A	F	O	S	N	8. S/he is easy to understand.
A	F	O	S	N	9. S/he works without a plan.
A	F	O	S	N	10. S/he asks that members perform particular tasks.
A	F	O	S	N	11. S/he asks that members follow standard procedures.
A	F	O	S	N	12. S/he finds time to listen to other members.
A	F	O	S	N	13. S/he sees to it that members are working up to capacity.
A	F	O	S	N	14. S/he maintains definite standards of performance.
A	F	O	S	N	15. S/he keeps to herself/himself.
A	F	O	S	N	16. S/he looks out for the personal welfare of individual members.
A	F	O	S	N	17. S/he refuses to explain her/his actions.
A	F	O	S	N	18. S/he acts without consulting the group.
A	F	O	S	N	19. S/he is slow to accept new ideas.
A	F	O	S	N	20. S/he tries to see that the work of members is coordinated.
A	F	O	S	N	21. S/he treats all members as her/his equal.
A	F	O	S	N	22. S/he is willing to make changes.
A	F	O	S	N	23. S/he makes members feel at ease when talking with her/him.
A	F	O	S	N	24. S/he is friendly and approachable.
A	F	O	S	N	25. S/he tries to put suggestions made by the group into operation.
A	F	O	S	N	26. S/he emphasizes the meeting of deadlines.
A	F	O	S	N	27. S/he encourages the use of certain uniform procedures.
A	F	O	S	N	28. S/he gets group approval on important matters before going ahead.
A	F	O	S	N	29. S/he makes sure her/his part in the group is understood by members.
A	F	O	S	N	30. S/he lets members know what s/he expects of them.

Although all scales start with "always" on the left end, an "always" response may be scored high or low; that is, some items are worded "positively" and some "negatively." The way each item is scored and those items that contribute to one or the other factor are explained in the scoring key given in Table A.1. For example, a response of *A* to item 1 is scored as "5"; conversely, a response of *A* to item 9 is scored as "1."

Table A.1   SCORING KEY FOR THE HALPIN-WINER SCALES

Initiation of structure						Consideration of others				

Scores on the following items are summed for the factor of *initiation of structure;* the scores for each item are tallied in the following way:

Scores on the following items are summed for the factor of *consideration;* the scores for each item are tallied in the following way:

1.	A=5,	F=4,	O=3,	S=2,	N=1	2.	A=5,	F=4,	O=3,	S=2,	N=1
3.	A=5,	F=4,	O=3,	S=2,	N=1	5.	A=5,	F=4,	O=3,	S=2,	N=1
4.	A=5,	F=4,	O=3,	S=2,	N=1	8.	A=5,	F=4,	O=3,	S=2,	N=1
6.	A=5,	F=4,	O=3,	S=2,	N=1	12.	A=5,	F=4,	O=3,	S=2,	N=1
7.	A=5,	F=4,	O=3,	S=2,	N=1	15.	A=1,	F=2,	O=3,	S=4,	N=5
9.	A=1,	F=2,	O=3,	S=4,	N=5	16.	A=5,	F=4,	O=3,	S=2,	N=1
10.	A=5,	F=4,	O=3,	S=2,	N=1	17.	A=1,	F=2,	O=3,	S=4,	N=5
11.	A=5,	F=4,	O=3,	S=2,	N=1	18.	A=1,	F=2,	O=3,	S=4,	N=5
13.	A=5,	F=4,	O=3,	S=2,	N=1	19.	A=1,	F=2,	O=3,	S=4,	N=5
14.	A=5,	F=4,	O=3,	S=2,	N=1	21.	A=5,	F=4,	O=3,	S=2,	N=1
20.	A=5,	F=4,	O=3,	S=2,	N=1	22.	A=5,	F=4,	O=3,	S=2,	N=1
26.	A=5,	F=4,	O=3,	S=2,	N=1	23.	A=5,	F=4,	O=3,	S=2,	N=1
27.	A=5,	F=4,	O=3,	S=2,	N=1	24.	A=5,	F=4,	O=3,	S=2,	N=1
29.	A=5,	F=4,	O=3,	S=2,	N=1	25.	A=5,	F=4,	O=3,	S=2,	N=1
30.	A=5,	F=4,	O=3,	S=2,	N=1	28.	A=5,	F=4,	O=3,	S=2,	N=1

Source: R. M. Stogdill and A. E. Coons, eds., *Leader Behavior: Its Description and Measurement.* Columbus, Ohio: Bureau of Business Research, The Ohio State University, 1957, pp. 47–48.

The Halpin-Winer scales have received citations by numerous scholars and are widely recognized as a useful research instrument.[4] Our students have found them most useful as a basis for comparing their self-perceptions with the perceptions of their fellow members regarding their task and interpersonal behavior. Although they were originally designed to measure the behavior of group "leaders," we presume that any member of a group may from time to time exhibit behavior that helps or "leads" the group and that the measurement of such behavior for *any* member is a useful approach to an evaluation of the group's effectiveness.

OBSERVATIONAL APPROACHES TO THE STUDY OF GROUPS

Observers who have been trained in what to look for and how to categorize various behaviors can add to our knowledge of group performances. We shall consider two approaches that are readily available and can be used effectively without considerable special training.

The first approach attempts to chart the flow of communication in a group through the use of sociometric techniques.[5] While ideally you would get everyone in the group to state her or his first and second choice of people with whom they most readily communicate within the group, you can get the behavioral equivalents of such statements of choice through observation. The analysis involves three steps:

1. Identify by observational tallying the communication links between the people in the group. Who is addressed by name and given nonverbal attention by each member of the group? Also note people who are blocked out or interrupted. For each member of the group, determine whom they talk to most and second most often and whether they exhibit patterns of dislike toward anyone.

2. Construct a matrix to record your observations. Put the names of the members in two rows, horizontally and vertically. Record across in rows under the appropriate name whom that individual chooses, identifying the first choice with an asterisk and the second with a plus sign. Note dislikes as a minus sign. Record the totals in the columns, awarding two points for a first choice and one point for a second choice. "Stars" are the people chosen most often, while "isolates" are people not chosen. See Figure A.3 for an example of a 16-person group.

Choosers		A	B	C	D	E	F	G	H	I	J	K	L	M	N	O	P
St.	Agnes												+		*		
Is.	Bridget				−	*							+				
	Chuck							+							−	*	
	Don											*	+				
St.	Elaine								+	*							
Is.	Fred										+				−		*
?St.	George												+		*		
	Henry	+												*			
	Iris							*							+		
	Janet			*		*		−					+				
	Ken	+															
	Lionel	*								+							
	Maurice	+				*											
	Norma	*	−							+							
?St.	Otto		+					*									
	Peter		*													+	
Total choices received		5	2	1		3		3	1	2	1	2	3	3	2	2	1
Total points received		7	3	2		6		5	1	2	2	3	3	4	3	5	2
Total dislikes			−1	−1				−1							−2		
		St.	Is.			St.	Is.	?St.							?St.		

Key:

St. = star
?St. = possibly a star
Is. = isolate
* = first choice;　+ = second choice;　− = dislike

(A first choice is worth *two* points; a second choice gets *one* point; a dislike gets a *minus* point.)

Figure A.3 Hypothetical sociomatrix.

3. Begin construction of your sociogram. Place the stars in the center of a sheet of paper, representing each by a small circle with the person's initials inside it. Represent the star's first and second choices by arrows pointing at the persons chosen (another initial inside a circle). First choices are represented by arrows with solid shafts and second choices by arrows on dotted lines. Next put in the choices of the persons chosen by the stars. Try to observe sociometric distance as follows: Two persons linked by mutual first choices will be closest, followed by mutual second choices, unreciprocated choices, and finally dislikes. Indicate dislikes with lag arrows. Note the semi-isolates (pairs who chose each other, but whose other choices are not reciprocated) and isolates (who are chosen by no one). Figure A.4 reflects the data in Figure A.3. A fine line has been placed around clusters of people representing an "island." To be in an island, a person has to choose someone in it and be chosen by someone in it (not necessarily the same person).[6]

From sociograms the potential for cohesiveness and the patterns of information flow can be noted. Many factors may influence the models, such as responses to newcomers, expertise on a given topic, and patterns of leadership. The examples in the figures are likely to be more complicated than is the case in most groups ob-

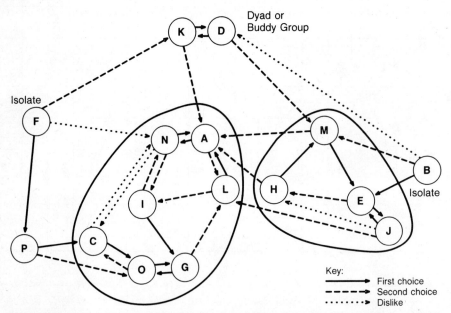

Figure A.4   Sociogram. From R. F. Bales and S. P. Cohen, *SYMLOG: A System for the Multiple Level Observation of Groups,* New York: The Free Press, 1979, p. 21.

served. The group shown is a large one with interaction problems illustrated.

The second approach to observing groups, developed by Robert Bales, has been widely used.[7] Bales and his associates developed a set of categories designed to provide a system for classifying the actions of group participants. The purpose of the *Interaction Process Analysis* was to identify and record the *nature,* not the *content,* of each separate communication act in a group.

The basic unit of measurement was an "act" or any verbal or nonverbal message detected by the observer. These verbal statements or nonverbal messages were then tabulated according to 12 categories, described briefly as follows[8]:

1. *Seems friendly.* Any act showing hospitality, being neighborly, expressing sympathy or similarity of feeling; indications of being attracted; demonstrations of affection; urging of unity, or harmony; expressing desire for cooperation or solidarity; showing a protective or nurturing attitude; praising, rewarding, approving, or encouraging others; sustaining or reassuring a person having difficulty; complimenting or congratulating; exchanging, trading, or lending objects (for example, cigarettes, or matches); confiding in another; expressing gratitude or appreciation; surrendering or giving in to another (for example, when interrupted); friendly submission so that another can go ahead; confessions of ignorance; acts of apology; grinning with pleasure; smiling directly at another. This category should be used whenever an act primarily appears to convey good feeling toward another person.[9]

2. *Dramatizes.* Any act that emphasizes hidden meaning or emotional implications or is especially self-revealing about a person. Most frequently these are jokes or stories with a double meaning. They may take the form of an anecdote about a particular person in which emotional feelings are expressed, or they may be symbolic actions: shrugs or bodily and facial expressions portraying great amazement, surprise, fear, or anger. More than one meaning is nearly always implicit in dramatizations as here defined; for example, a posturing, a facial expression, a remark, or all three together may imply (a) "He certainly thinks he is something!" and (b) "I don't agree." The personal tone of this dramatic bit, coupled with the overtones of partially hidden emotional feelings, are typical of acts scored in this category.[10] According to Bales, "The joke is a very common form of dramatization in group interaction. The joker expects, although perhaps not always too clearly, to produce a shock of recognition of the hidden meaning, to provoke a laugh, a

sudden release or display of tension."[11] Bales goes on to suggest that the concept the joker offers is loaded and that whoever laughs admits "the hidden truth."[12] The essential quality of this category is that of some special, personal, partially hidden meaning subtly exposed in a way that is emotionally releasing even though risky; thus one ordinary hallmark of such acts is that they seem to have two meanings, one dangerous to expose and the other somewhat amusing on the surface.[13] Behavior such as this may seem to you to be dangerous or better avoided; however, Bales makes this evaluative comment: "In terms of psychological services performed, and general importance in the group as well as individual life, these activities are not task-oriented, but they are nevertheless serious psychological business."[14]

3. *Agrees.* Any act that shows accord, concurrence, or assent about facts, inferences, or hypotheses: "I think you are right," "That's true," "Yes, that's it." Nonverbal agreement may involve nodding the head, showing special interest, or giving significant visible attention to what is being said. Another variation may be overtly expressing comprehension or understanding: "Oh, now I get it."

4. *Gives suggestions.* Any act that takes the lead in the task direction. This category includes routine control of communication and directing the attention of the group to task problems when they have been agreed on by the group. Thus, mentioning a problem to be discussed, pointing out the relevance of a remark, calling a meeting to order, referring to the agenda, and opening a new phase of activity are all scored as "Gives Suggestions," if they are routine, agreed-on moves and if they are brought forth in a way that implies the acceptability of dissent if anyone so desires.[15] Bales gives this definition: "In general, direct attempts to guide or counsel, or prepare the other for some activity, to prevail upon him, to persuade him, exhort him, urge, enjoin, or inspire him to some action, by dependence upon authority or ascendance rather than by logical inference are called *giving suggestions.*"[16] Such suggestions usually propose ways of modifying the problem situation, the group, certain members, or the norms.

5. *Gives opinions.* Any act that involves a moral obligation, offers a major belief or value, or indicates adherence to a policy or guiding principle. Such acts should be serious but not personal, sincere but objective. If such an act is not serious or is insincere, you should score it in category 2, "Dramatizes." Category 5, "Gives Opinions," includes expressions of understanding or insight besides those of value judgments: "I believe I see your point" or "I think we should

recognize our obligation to . . ." or "I feel we are on the right track." "Gives opinions" should be distinguished from Category 6, "Gives information," primarily on the basis of its use of inference or value judgment.[17]

6. *Gives information.* Any act reporting factual (not necessarily true) or potentially verifiable (testable) observations or experiences. Bales gives this instruction: "Any statement too vague in principle to be tested is not classified as giving information, but, usually, as giving opinion."[18] Common cases of giving information are reports on problem situations confronting the group: "The legislature has not yet acted on that bill" or "We have three days left" or "I contacted the city council, and they can meet with us on Tuesday."[19]

7. *Asks for information.* Any act that requests a factual report. Bales's definition includes requests for a "descriptive, objective type of answer, an answer based on experience, observation, or empirical research."[20] The questions making requests are not always direct, but sometimes indirect: "I have forgotten whom we appointed." You should include in this category only requests for simple factual answers; if an inference, an evaluation, or the expression of a feeling is requested, such should be tabulated as category 8, "Asks for Opinions."[21]

8. *Asks for opinions.* Any act that seeks an inferential interpretation, a statement involving belief or values, a value judgment, or a report of one's understanding or insight. It may include a request for diagnosis of a situation or a reaction to an idea. A warning should be given here regarding questions like "Do you know what I mean?" and "Do you see?" These are examples of attempts to elicit agreement and should be identified as persuasive effort, properly tabulated in category 4, "Gives Suggestions."[22] Another problem you may encounter occurs when an elected chairperson or leader, serving the group according to the commission she or he has received, struggles to fathom and comply with the group's wishes. In such a case the chairperson might ask for an opinion on the manner: "Would you like to have a committee work on that?" However, a chairperson asking, "What should we do about increasing our membership?" is seeking suggestions regarding ways of solving a group problem, and this kind of question should be identified as belonging in category 9, "Asks for Suggestions."[23]

9. *Asks for suggestions.* Any act that requests guidance in the problem-solving process, is neutral in emotional tone, and attempts to turn the initiative over to another. Such requests sometimes indicate a feeling of confusion, or uncertainty.[24] To fit this category properly the request should be

"open ended," without the implication of any specific answer: "What do you think we should do about that?" If, on the other hand, the question is asked in such a way that a specific answer is implied, it should be coded in category 4, "Gives Suggestions." An example of a veiled suggestion is "I wonder if there are any other ways of getting information from the legislature?" This seems to imply there *are* other ways and suggests they be considered.[25]

10. *Disagrees.* Any *initial* act in a sequence that rejects others' statements of information, opinion, or suggestion. It is a reaction to others' action as defined by Bales: "The negative feeling conveyed is attached to the content of what the others have said, not to them as a person. And the negative feeling must not be very strong, or the act will seem unfriendly."[26] (It would, in such a case, be scored in category 12, "Seems Unfriendly.") Statements that follow the initial rejection of another's position, such as arguments, rebuttals, and questions, are not scored as disagreement; rather, they are scored in other categories. Examples of acts scored in this category are "I don't think so" and "I don't think that's right."[27]

11. *Shows tension.* Any act that exhibits conflict between submission and nonconformity yet does not clearly show negative feeling toward another person.[28] Bales gives this general definition: "Signs of anxious emotionality [that] indicate a conflict between acting and withholding action. Minor outbreaks of reactive anxiety may first be mentioned, such as appearing startled, disconcerted, alarmed, dismayed, perturbed, or concerned."[29] Other behavior suggested by Bales is hesitation, speechlessness, trembling, flushing, gulping, and licking of the lips.[30] Of special import in this category is laughter. On the surface laughter may seem to indicate a reduction of tension, and it may in part serve that purpose. In fact, however, it appears to be more dependable as a sign of tension rather than as a sign of its reduction.[31] We are not speaking here of friendly smiles in a relaxed atmosphere of interpersonal warmth; rather, we are identifying embarrassed or tense laughter. Bales gives this explanation: "Laughter seems to be a sudden escape into motor discharge of conflicted emotional states that can no longer be contained."[32] An additional behavior to be included in this category is any embarrassed reaction to disapproval, such as the appearance of being chagrined, chastised, or mortified.[33]

12. *Seems unfriendly.* Any act that is personally negative; it is not content oriented, which would be classified as "Disagrees" when negative, but is oriented toward another per-

son. It includes very slight signs of negative feeling, arbitrary attempts to subjugate another, uninvited attempts to "settle" an argument, to judge another's behavior, to override, interrupt, deflate, deprecate, disparage, or ridicule.[34] Also included are attempts to "show off," embarrass a generally accepted authority, or inordinately make a nuisance of oneself.[35] In general, Bales suggests that this category be used to identify all overt acts that seem to the observer to be in any way both negative and personal.[36]

Over the years the *Interaction Process Analysis* provided a reliable system that was widely used by both researchers and students of group communication. Three types of analysis were typical:

1. A calculation of the total group interaction of each participant. This tabulation of the gross number of communication acts gave some insight into dominance behaviors and the balance of participation.

Name	Percent
Joe	10.3
Mike	7.2
Bill	42.8
Mary	28.3
Jill	11.4
Total	100.0

2. The percentage of group interaction recorded in each of the 12 categories Bales listed estimated norms for the categories as follows:

Category	Estimated norms*
1. Seems friendly	2.6– 4.8
2. Dramatizes	5.7– 7.4
3. Agrees	8.0–13.6
4. Gives suggestions	3.0– 7.0
5. Gives opinions	15.0–22.7
6. Gives information	20.7–31.2
7. Asks for information	4.0– 7.2
8. Asks for opinions	2.0– 3.9
9. Asks for suggestions	0.6– 1.4
10. Disagrees	3.1– 5.3
11. Shows tension	3.4– 6.0
12. Seems unfriendly	2.4– 4.4

*Taken from R. F. Bales, *Personality and Interpersonal Behavior.* New York: Holt, Rinehart and Winston, 1970, p. 92. Bales estimated these norms by a process of inference described on pp. 482–486 of his book. Adapted and reprinted by permission of Holt, Rinehart and Winston, Inc.

These norms are merely guidelines but can provide some basis for interpreting the behavior of a group.

The data for categories 4 to 9 are primarily task oriented, while the data for the other six are related to maintenance behaviors. A group may be seen as "overly personal" if an excessive number of the contributions are found in categories 1 to 3.

3. The percentage of each member's contributions in the 12 categories (Table A.2). The analysis provides insight into the characteristic role of each group participant.

Table A.2   PERCENTAGE OF TOTAL OBSERVED GROUP PARTICIPATION IN EACH IPA CATEGORY FOR EACH GROUP MEMBER

	Percentage of Group Participation				
Category	Joe	Mike	Bill	Mary	Jill
1. Seems friendly	—	0.9	1.2	0.2	1.2
2. Dramatizes	3.4	1.3	—	—	2.3
3. Agrees	—	0.4	11.4	5.5	1.2
4. Gives suggestions	—	—	2.6	1.2	—
5. Gives opinions	3.4	—	13.0	8.1	—
6. Gives information	—	—	6.2	2.1	—
7. Asks for information	—	—	7.1	3.2	—
8. Asks for opinions	—	1.2	0.1	8.0	3.2
9. Asks for suggestions	—	—	1.2	—	1.1
10. Disagrees	1.0	—	—	—	—
11. Shows tension	2.0	3.4	—	—	2.4
12. Seems unfriendly	0.5	—	—	—	—
Total	10.3	7.2	42.8	28.3	11.4

In the hypothetical group shown in Table A.2, Joe fails to participate in the task-oriented categories (4, 6, 7, 8, and 9). Bill and Mary probably are spending too much of the group's time talking to each other.

In the late 1970s Bales and his associates formulated a new system for analyzing groups by an adjective-rating scale. They use the acronym SYMLOG (*Sy*stem for the *M*ultiple *L*evel *O*bservations of *G*roups).[37] While the total system is longer and rather complicated, it is flexible enough to permit reduction to a relatively simple study of a single person or a single group. The basis for such study is the SYMLOG Adjective Rating Form (see Table A.3), which can be used to describe the behaviors of a person observed in an interactive situation.[38] The observer can then tabulate and analyze the ratings without need of complicated statistics or a computer. The initials preceding each category refer to the multiple-level aspect of the analysis. Visualize a cube, providing a three-dimensional per-

Table A.3   THE SYMLOG ADJECTIVE RATING FORM

Your name _____ Group_____
Name of person described _____

		Circle the best choice for each item:				
		(0)	**(1)**	**(2)**	**(3)**	**(4)**
U	active, dominant, talks a lot	never	rarely	sometimes	often	always
UP	extroverted, outgoing, positive	never	rarely	sometimes	often	always
UPF	a purposeful democratic task leader	never	rarely	sometimes	often	always
UF	an assertive businesslike manager	never	rarely	sometimes	often	always
UNF	authoritarian, controlling, disapproving	never	rarely	sometimes	often	always
UN	domineering, tough minded, powerful	never	rarely	sometimes	often	always
UNB	provocative, egocentric, shows off	never	rarely	sometimes	often	always
UB	jokes around, expressive, dramatic	never	rarely	sometimes	often	always
UPB	entertaining, sociable, smiling, warm	never	rarely	sometimes	often	always
P	friendly, equalitarian	never	rarely	sometimes	often	always
PF	works cooperatively with others	never	rarely	sometimes	often	always
F	analytical, task oriented, problem solving	never	rarely	sometimes	often	always
NF	legalistic, has to be right	never	rarely	sometimes	often	always
N	unfriendly, negativistic	never	rarely	sometimes	often	always
NB	irritable, cynical, won't cooperate	never	rarely	sometimes	often	always
B	shows feelings and emotions	never	rarely	sometimes	often	always
PB	affectionate, likable, fun to be with	never	rarely	sometimes	often	always
DP	looks up to others, appreciative, trustful	never	rarely	sometimes	often	always

Table A.3 (*Continued*)

		Circle the best choice for each item:				
		(0)	**(1)**	**(2)**	**(3)**	**(4)**
DPF	gentle, willing to accept responsibility	never	rarely	sometimes	often	always
DF	obedient, works submissively	never	rarely	sometimes	often	always
DNF	self-punishing, works too hard	never	rarely	sometimes	often	always
DN	depressed, sad, resentful, rejecting	never	rarely	sometimes	often	always
DNB	alienated, quits, withdraws	never	rarely	sometimes	often	always
DB	afraid to try, doubts own ability	never	rarely	sometimes	often	always
DPB	quiet, happy just to be with others	never	rarely	sometimes	often	always
D	passive, introverted, says little	never	rarely	sometimes	often	always

spective. The three dimensions correspond to the qualities that can be inferred from an interpersonal communicative behavior:

1. Dominant vs. submissive (height)
2. Friendly vs. unfriendly (width)
3. Instrumentally controlled [task] vs. emotionally controlled (depth)

Each dimension should be thought of as having two ends viewed as opposites with a zero point in the middle. Figure A.5 provides Bales's view of the three-dimensional space we need to visualize. The letters refer to the direction the item is geared to measure. *U* and *D* refer to *U*pward and *D*ownward, referring to the degree of dominance-submission. *P* and *N* refer to the *P*ositive and *N*egative, corresponding to friendly-unfriendly, and *F* and *B* refer to *F*orward and *B*ackward, relating to degree of instrumental control or of emotional expressiveness. The directional codes each have three points, with the center point (labeled AVE by Bales) determined to be neutral and omitted when descriptions are called for.

The three central dimensions and the personality types were

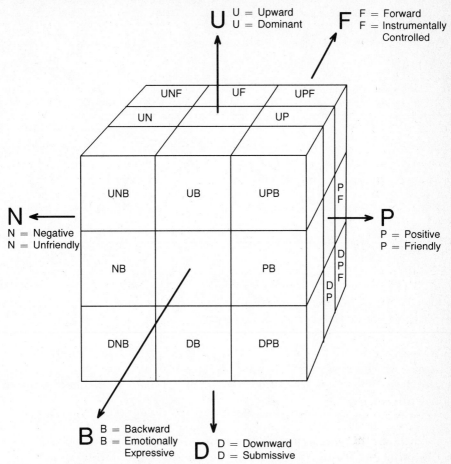

Figure A.5   The SYMLOG three-dimensional space, showing classes of directions or locations, defined by logical combinations of the six named reference directions. (This cube is seen from an outside point. The directions are named from a reference point at the intersection of the three dimensions, looking forward.)

introduced and described in Chapter 2. Table A.3 contains 26 descriptive categories, omitting the center point on all these indices.

Refer back now to the SYMLOG Adjective Rating Form (Table A.3). A person who is often entertaining, sociable, smiling, and warm is characterized as UPB, that is upward, positive, backward. Translated, this label suggests degrees of dominance, friendliness, and emotion (as related to maintenance behaviors). Go over the categories and the labels until you understand the logic involved.

Bales has also presented an observational format for the use of SYMLOG. He suggests that the observer draw a diagram of the meeting space with names or designations given each participant (called *ACTOR*). Thus members can be identified quickly. On the observations sheet (see Figure A.6), the observer records a series of

Observer _____ Group _____ Date _____ Page _____

Draw a diagram of the physical location of group members on a separate page.

Time	Who Acts	Toward Whom	ACT/ NON	Direction	Ordinary Description of Behavior or IMAGE	PRO/ CON	Direction	Image Level

Figure A.6   The SYMLOG interaction scoring form.

messages, usually at a rate of one per minute.[39] Following the code name for the observer (such as initials), the label for the group, and the date (as 6-22-88), the elements of the message have been defined as follows:

Time. A two-digit number representing the minute from the beginning of the hour period in which the session occurs. For example, if a session is scheduled at 9:00 A.M., the time 9:10 A.M. is designated by the two-digit number *10.* If the scheduled time of the beginning of the meetings is 9:00 A.M., then the time 10:01 A.M. is designated by the number *61,* and so on consecutively for succeeding min- utes. A digital clock is necessary to obtain sufficient accu- racy to coordinate the observations of more than one ob- server. (Without a digital clock, observers tend to round to the nearest five-minute mark.) Accuracy by minute, and proper sequencing within the minute, are important in comparing the observations of different observers, and for proper recall of actual events.

Who Acts (ACTOR). A short code name representing the name of the group member who is making the communi- cation and whose behavior is being observed. The same names are used as the names for the persons as observers. (Each group member indicates the abbreviation he or she would like to use; the instructor checks for duplications and issues the list of standard abbreviations, with full names attached.) It is necessary to avoid use of the same code name for two different persons, of course.

Toward Whom (RECEIVER). The other person (or the group as a whole) to whom the ACTOR is talking or toward whom the ACTOR is acting. The group as a whole may be indicated as the RECEIVER with the use of the abbreviation GRP, if this seems most appropriate. The name of the specific person, as designated by the code name (see above), is ordinarily used. If the communication is addressed to some person outside the group (rare) the abbreviation OTH may be used.

ACT or NON. The classification of the communication at the behavioral level, either as ACT (an overt act toward the other intended to carry a communicated content) or as NON (an unintended nonverbal sign of emotion, feeling, or attitude given off previous to or during the actor's overt intended communication, or instead of overt communication, as shown in facial expression, tone of voice, bodily movement, position, or posture). The same piece of behavior may be described by two messages, one at the ACT level and one at the NON level, if the directions are different. If the directions are the same, the message at the ACT level suffices.

Direction of ACT or NON. The directional classification of either ACT or NON (whichever has been specified) in terms of 26 directions (or 27 if AVE is counted). The direction describes the behavior qualitively. The direction of the behavior at the ACT or NON level is *independent* of the direction of any element contained in an IMAGE. The direction of ACT or NON describes the ACTOR's attitude toward the RECEIVER (as seen by the RECEIVER).

Ordinary Description of Behavior or IMAGE. A few words in ordinary English, the ACTOR's words if feasible, or a paraphrase, to tell the reader the content the observer is selecting as an IMAGE. (The *global* classification of the IMAGE selected is given in the last column, and the direction of the specific element in the IMAGE is given in the next-to-last column.) If the behavior classified at the ACT or NON level carries no IMAGE beyond itself, the space headed "Ordinary Description of Behavior or IMAGE" is used to describe in ordinary language what the ACT or the nonverbal behavior sign was. The ordinary language description of the behavior or IMAGE is critically important in feedback, since members always want to be able to recognize what it was that the observer was scoring, and they cannot tell otherwise.

PRO or CON. One of these two codes, or a question mark, is written to indicate whether the ACTOR appears to be in favor of (PRO) or against (CON) the directional element of the IMAGE selected for attention. Value judgments PRO or CON are treated as independent of the direction of the element of the IMAGE. They are "higher-order" positive or negative judgments of the directional elements. Thus, the ACTOR may express a PRO value judgment about an element that may be ACT N, or, vice versa, the actor may express a CON value judgment about an ACT P element. A PRO or CON statement is usually more or less equivalent to a proposal for a group norm—a suggestion as to what value judgments others should also make.

Direction of the Element of the IMAGE. An element selected from a global IMAGE is described by the directional term that seems best to express the meaning it has for the ACTOR. Sometimes this is apparent from context, tone of voice, and so forth, sometimes not. Often the meaning is similar for the ACTOR and for the other group members. If one supposes the ACTOR gives an IMAGE a particular meaning, not the same as other group members give it, the meaning for the ACTOR is the one chosen. The direction of the element, in other words, is the direction ACTOR seems to assign to the element.

IMAGE Level. The observer may well have a list of the six levels as a reminder of the various classes of IMAGES: SEL, OTH, GRP, SIT, SOC, and FAN. Images are assumed to have different psychological qualities according to these general classes. Brief definitions are given below.

> *SEL.* Images of the SELF, that is, the self of the ACTOR, as visualized by the ACTOR. The term SEL is written in the message, and the reader determines who is meant by looking to see who is given as the ACTOR. An image of the SELF is given by a remark that indicates a characterization of the SELF or some element of it by references to own behavior, thoughts, feelings, or by the use of adjectives or trait names. When a situational, societal, or fantasy image is presented that the ACTOR seems to accept, or claim, as a part of the SELF-IMAGE, the IMAGE is classified as SEL. Thus, "I come from an upper-class family" would probably be scored PRO U in SEL.

OTH. Images of particular members of the immediately interacting group, *other* than the ACTOR. The term OTH is not written in the message. Rather, the *abbreviated name* of the group member meant is given. The OTH in question may be the same as the RECEIVER of the ACT or it may not. An image of an OTHER is given by a remark that indicates a characterization of that other person, or some aspect or element of the person; by references to behavior, thoughts, or feelings of the OTHER; or by the use of adjectives or trait names. Images of nongroup members are classified as either in the *situation,* in *society,* or in *fantasy.* However, when the ACTOR uses images from the situation, society, or fantasy in order indirectly to characterize some person in the group, the IMAGE is classified as OTHER and the name of the person is given. Thus, "John says he comes from an upperclass family," would probably be scored (PRO or CON)? U in JOHN.

GRP. Images of the present interacting GROUP, considered as a collectivity, that is, as constituting a higher-order entity. The GROUP in this sense can be described in somewhat the same terms as a person, that is, by references to characteristic or normative behavior, thoughts, feelings, or by the use of adjectives or trait names describing some particular aspects of or element in the GROUP. Note that "GROUP" is an IMAGE and that images exist in the minds of the individual actors. When the ACTOR uses images from the situation, society, or fantasy in order indirectly to characterize the GROUP, the IMAGE is classified as GRP. Thus, "We may as well give up. We don't have any power in this situation," would probably be scored PRO D in GRP.

SIT. Images of objects or aspects of the SITUATION immediately external to the interacting membership group and constituting its immediate environment. Includes the task or tasks, if any, but also all of the freedoms, possibilities, and psychologically significant features of the immediate environment for provoking or supporting any kind of behavior, thoughts, or feelings. The SITUATION, the immediate environment, is described in terms of these meanings it has for the members—the images they construct of it, rather than in the observer's terms. References to persons outside the membership group, but who interact to some degree with it (for example the observers), may be classified as images of the SITUATION. For example, "Those observers, sitting in judgment, make me nervous," would probably be scored CON UNF in SIT.

SOC. Images of the SOCIETY within which the GROUP and its immediate SITUATION exist. Elements of the society in this global sense may be publicly known persons, groups, occupations, social classes, institutions, or any element of the society as defined and referred to by the ACTOR. The directional description of an element is often the meaning that it has for the majority of society, but if the ACTOR's definition of it seems to be different, the ACTOR's meaning is taken. Images of elements in SOCIETY are often vague, abstract, stereotyped, ideological, and prejudicial, and the direction assigned depends upon the ACTOR's attitude. Images of other societies and international relations are included in SOC. Thus, "The international situation is a mess" might be scored CON UNB in SOC.

FAN. Images that seem to arise in the imaginal processes or the FANTASY of the ACTOR, or seem to have a strong emotional meaning for the ACTOR though based upon actual experience. Classification of an image as FAN does not imply it has no factual basis—it means that its present significance for the ACTOR is given by its fantasy-arousing potential. The ACTOR may not think of the image as one from fantasy; the ACTOR may think of it as purely factual. In case of conflict as to whether to classify an IMAGE in FAN or in some other class, the FAN classification is preferred. The use of the term FANTASY in SYM-LOG is much broader than in ordinary definition. Any report of doings of the ACTOR in contexts other than the group are scored as FAN, because they are assumed to function as arousers of fantasy in other group members, who have no direct access to the outside life of the ACTOR.[40]

Let's consider an example of how a message might be coded. Suppose that early in the meeting that started at 10:05 A.M., Sharon comments, "You know, this group really seems friendly." The message might be recorded as

07 SHAR GRP ACT UP a really friendly group PRO UP GRP

The 07 indicated the message transpired at seven minutes after the hour. SHAR is the abbreviation for *Sharon,* and GRP suggests the message was addressed to the group as a whole. ACT means that the message was verbal rather than nonverbal and overtly shows the actor's attitudes and feelings. UP means upward: positive, suggested dominant, friendly directions.

The final three elements in the observer's notes refer to the kind of IMAGE presented in the *content* of the message, as distinguished from the interpretation given the *behavior.* Sharon has projected an image of what the group appears to be or might be. This image can then be discussed, reinforced, or modified. This image is something that exists in the mind of one individual and is shared with the group. By evaluating the message as PRO, a value judgment has been applied by the observer in terms of group norms.

Three levels of observations can thus be recorded: (1) the behavior level, (2) the level of images presented, and (3) the level of value judgment.

Much of the power of such observations depends upon aggregations of information from other observers that can serve either to reinforce or to cancel out perceptions. While the individual judgments are obviously subjective, the compilations of data can provide some degree of objectivity. As Bales observes:

> One can recapture the memory of the individual act, locate it on the sound record, compare the observations of different observers, and examine it at its various levels of meaning. One can analyze it "in depth" as usual in the "clinical" approach. But, in addition, one may obtain statistical information about the frequency with which observers have picked up similar aspects of behavior. The present method thus integrates a "statistical" with a "naturalistic" approach, and its use may be turned in either direction, as needed.[41]

In a recent study Victor D. Wall, Jr., and Gloria J. Balanes have used SYMLOG to predict the quality of a group's outcome, the amount of conflict experiences, the manner in which conflict is managed, and the amount of satisfaction reported by group members.[42]

SUMMARY

Group performance may be systematiclly evaluated by the use of self-reports for the members of the group or process observations by trained observers. We have presented instruments with varying degrees of sophistication that should prove helpful in analyzing group behavior. It should be emphasized that much of the data gathered will be subjective and possibly limited in dependability; however, the data can be useful in promoting dialogue about the ways a group might wish to make improvements.

NOTES

1. *FIRO-B.* Write to Consulting Psychologists Press, Inc., 577 College Avenue, Palo Alto, CA 94306.
2. T. J. Sergiovanni, R. Metzcus, and L. Burden, "Toward a particularistic approach to leadership style: Some findings," *American Educational Research Journal,* 6 (1960), 62–79.
3. L. D. Goodstein, P. Cooke, and J. Goodstein, "The team orientation and behavior inventory (TOBI)," *The 1983 Annual for Facilitators, Trainers, and Consultants.* San Diego, Calif.: University Associates, 1983, pp. 108–114.
4. See, for example, *Group Dynamics,* 3rd ed., ed. by D. Cartright and A. Zander. New York: Harper & Row, 1968, p. 307. L. Petrullo, "Introduction," in *Leadership and Interpersonal Behavior,* ed. by L. Petrullo and B. M. Bass. New York: Holt, Rinehart & Winston, 1961, p. xvi. D. Krech, R. S. Crutchfield, and E. L. Ballachey, *Individual in Society.* New York: McGraw-Hill, 1962, pp. 432–433. A. P. Hare, *Handbook of Small Group Research.* New York: Free Press, 1962, pp. 326–327.
5. The term was originally used by J. L. Moreno, "Sociometry and the cultural order," *Sociometry,* 6, (1943), 299–344.
6. T. Carney and B. Carney, *Organizational Communications.* Toronto: Holt, Rinehart, and Winston of Canada Ltd., 1981.
7. R. F. Bales, *Personality and Interpersonal Behavior.* New York: Holt, Rinehart & Winston, 1970.
8. Ibid., pp. 471–491. For many years we have had our students use the categories as defined by Bales in his earlier book (R. F. Bales, *Interaction Process Analysis, A Method for the Study of Small Groups,* Reading, Mass.: Addison-Wesley, 1950). The set of definitions included here has been used and viewed by many of our students as an improved set of categories.
9. Ibid., pp. 100–105.
10. Ibid., pp. 105–108.
11. Ibid., pp. 108.
12. Ibid.
13. Ibid., p. 477.
14. Ibid., p. 108.
15. Ibid., pp. 109–112.
16. Ibid., p. 111.
17. Ibid., pp. 112–116.
18. Ibid., p. 117.
19. Ibid., pp. 116–119.
20. Ibid., p. 119.
21. Ibid., pp. 119–120
22. Ibid., p. 121.

23. Cf. ibid., p. 121.
24. Ibid., p. 121.
25. Ibid., pp. 121–122.
26. Ibid., p. 123.
27. Ibid., pp. 123–124.
28. Ibid., p. 124.
29. Ibid.
30. Ibid.
31. Ibid., p. 125.
32. Ibid.
33. Ibid., pp. 124–127.
34. Ibid., pp. 127–129.
35. Ibid., pp. 129–132.
36. Ibid., p. 127.
37. R. F. Bales and S. P. Cohen, *SYMLOG: A System for the Multiple Level Observation of Groups.* New York: Free Press, 1979.
38. Ibid., p. 21.
39. Ibid., p. 164.
40. Ibid., pp. 171–174.
41. Ibid., p. 175.
42. V. D. Wall, Jr., and G. J. Balanes, "The SYMLOG dimensions and small group conflict," *Central State Speech Journal,* 37, No. 2 (Summer 1986), 61–78.

Appendix *B*

A Critical Analysis of Factors Related to Decisional Processes Involved in the *Challenger* Disaster

DENNIS S. GOURAN, RANDY Y. HIROKAWA AND AMY E. MARTZ

On January 28, 1986, Mission 51-L of the highly successful American Space Shuttle Program tragically ended 73 seconds into launch. One of several missions involving civilian personnel, the flight of *Challenger* was to symbolize the inseparability of space exploration and the future of education.[1] Instead, millions of people sat witness to a tragedy that was to become the most significant setback in the history of the United States space program and one that would quickly attract the label, "The *Challenger* Disaster."

Within days of the fateful launch, President Reagan appointed a commission, headed by former Secretary of State and Attorney General William P. Rogers, to determine the causes of the accident, to provide recommendations aimed at preventing "any recurrence of the failure related to this accident," and "to the extent possible to reduce other risks in future flights."[2] Between February 3 and June 6, 1986, the release date of the final report, the Commission conducted an extensive investigation. Its inquiry produced the finding that the primary cause of the accident was a mechanical failure in

Reprinted with permission from *The Central States Speech Journal*, Fall 1986, 37/3, 119–135. *Dennis S. Gouran is Professor and Head of Speech Communication at The Pennsylvania State University. Randy Y. Hirokawa is Associate Professor of Communication Studies at The University of Iowa. Amy E. Martz is a Ph.D. candidate in Speech Communication at The Pennsylvania State University.*

one of the joints of the right solid rocket booster, in which an O-ring malfunctioned (40). Had the possibility of such an occurrence been previously undetected, the accident, while no less tragic, might well be viewed in a different light—perhaps, as the unfortunate result of an anomaly that no one could reasonably have anticipated. Instead, the Commission discovered that what proved to be the cause of the accident had been, in some quarters, a continuing concern, especially in the several months immediately prior to Mission 51-L. Members of the Commission, therefore, appropriately concluded that there was a contributing cause—"flaws in the decision-making process" (82)—and that the accident was "rooted in history" (120).

According to testimony gathered by the Commission, the O-rings on the solid rocket booster had been designated C1 since December of 1982 (84). Such a classification stands for "Criticality" and suggests "a failure point—without back-up—that could cause a loss of life or vehicle if the component fails" (84). During the four years in which this important component of the solid rocket booster retained the "Criticality" rating of 1, no successful remedial action was taken to eliminate the potential threat it posed.

Throughout previous missions, the component had functioned as designed even though there was evidence of erosion of the seal from escaping gas that could conceivably prevent the O-ring from sealing properly. Consequently, there appeared to be no pressing need to assign high priority to a safer design. In July of 1985, however, erosion of a secondary O-ring in the nozzel joint of Flight 51-B suggested that a primary seal had failed. As a result, potential failure of O-rings in the solid rocket booster became a launch constraint—one that was subsequently waived in seven consecutive flights, including 51-F through 51-L. In the specific case of 51-L, moreover, engineers at Morton Thiokol, manufacturer of the solid rocket booster, recommended on January 27 against launch due to a lack of knowledge concerning the sealing capacity of O-rings at temperatures below 53 degrees Fahrenheit (84–86). Despite this history and the recommendation not to launch, the flight proceeded and ended with its now well-publicized consequences.

In light of these facts, the Commission concluded that the decisional process was seriously flawed and that it was disturbed by what seemed to be "a propensity at Marshall [The Marshall Space Flight Center[3]] to contain potentially serious problems and to resolve them internally rather than communicate them forward" (104). The Commission also concluded that management at Morton Thiokol apparently reversed its initial recommendation against launch "contrary to the views of its engineers in order to accommodate a major customer [presumably, the Marshall Space Flight Center]" (104).

To be sure, the conclusions reached by the Commission capture

the more general actions leading to a highly questionable and re-
grettable decision, but in reducing the explanation to such broad
statements, these conclusions neither reveal the complexity of the
process nor identify all of the relevant factors involved. A careful
examination of the testimony of figures appearing before the Commission suggests a number of influences that in combination provide a much clearer understanding of the climate in which informed judgment ostensibly was either precluded or sacrificed to
the interests of expediency by intelligent, experienced, and seem-
ingly safety-conscious decision makers. The purpose of this essay is
to identify these influences and to examine their apparent impact
on the unfolding of the decision to launch the *Challenger* space
shuttle.

THE SHUTTLE LAUNCH PROCESS

A decision to launch in NASA's Space Shuttle Program is the culmination of a series of reviews and recommendations occurring at four
levels and involving many individuals and groups. The agency con-
ducts its business from three locations: the Kennedy Space Center
in central Florida, the Johnson Space Center in Houston, Texas, and
the Marshall Space Flight Center in Huntsville, Alabama. Launches
take place at the Kennedy Space Center, while responsibility for
mission control resides at the Johnson Space Center. The Marshall
Space Flight Center is concerned with matters of design of the space
transportation system and general flight readiness. Different contractors report directly or indirectly to managers at the three centers. In terms of their role in launch decisions, contractors are classified as Level IV. Prior to a scheduled launch, a contractor's
representatives confer with managers at the respective center to
which the firm is contractually obligated. These representatives
certify flight readiness of the components in the space transportation system for which they are responsible. Level III managers, all
of whom are employed by NASA, consolidate information from individual contractors along with their own assessments and prepare
a recommendation to personnel at Level II. Level II managers conduct a preflight readiness review and recommend to those at Level
I—the flight management team, in particular—whether or not there
are problems warranting delay or termination of a scheduled
launch. Level I managers are responsible for the final flight readiness review and inform the mission management team whether a
launch may proceed.

The decision hierarchy involved in space shuttle launches is
structured in such a way that Level I has final authority to determine launch readiness. In principle, its review is the last safeguard
in a deliberately complicated sequence designed to prevent risk to

the crew and craft. Those at Level I could well decide not to proceed even if all previous assessments of flight readiness are favorable. They are presumably constrained against launching, however, if any assessment from a lower level is unfavorable. In this sense, even a Level IV manager can prevent a launch by asserting that the components in the system for which his or her contractor is responsible are not in an acceptable state of readiness and that he or she, therefore, recommends against continuation of the mission.

FAILURE OF THE PROCESS

Given a decision structure that seems to have such possibilities for preventing unwise and potentially unsafe launching of a space shuttle, and given the fact that managers representing Morton Thiokol had initially opposed proceeding with *Challenger,* how is it that the system failed? The Commission's reconstruction of the events occurring between the afternoon of January 27 and the launch on January 28 reveals a scenario in which Level IV managers reversed their original recommendation and those at Level III apparently felt it unnecessary to communicate upward the fact that there had been a reversal, or even that Thiokol engineers were concerned about the effects of temperature on the O-rings in the solid rocket boosters. Neither action alone, or in combination, however, is necessarily indicative of a "flawed" decisional process. If the actions were warranted, then their mere occurrence does not justify indicting the process.

More illuminating are the social and psychological factors, as manifest in the reported communicative behavior of parties associated with these actions. These factors, we submit, clearly show that the actions mentioned were inappropriate and conspired to reduce the likelihood of an appropriate decision. Among the influences most evident in the testimony of witnesses appearing before the Rogers Commission were: (1) perceived pressure to produce a desired recommendation and concurrence with it among some of those initially opposed to the launch, (2) an apparent unwillingness by several parties to violate perceived role boundaries, (3) questionable patterns of reasoning by key managers, (4) an ambiguous and misleading use of language that minimized the perception of risk, and (5) a frequent failure to ask important questions relevant to the final decision.

Perceived Pressure

By January 27, the *Challenger* launch had already been postponed three times and scrubbed once (17). Understandably, such a history and the prospect of continued delay would create a general atmosphere of impatience, with serious implications for maintaining the ambitious schedule that NASA had established for the shuttle program. Impatience undoubtedly was exacerbated by news commentators' observations, such as Dan Rather's "Yet another costly, red-faces-all-around space-shuttle launch delay," and ABC *World News Tonight*'s "Once again a flawless liftoff proved to be too much of a challenge for *Challenger*" (cited by Hickey 3). Despite such uninformed comments, up to January 27, responsible officials at Levels I and II had avoided taking unnecessary risks. The scrubbing of the mission on the morning of January 27 prompted an immediate discussion among launch-related personnel at these levels about the prospects for the next day, even though weather conditions were expected to be very poor. Those conditions notwithstanding, the mission was rescheduled for the next day.

By early afternoon, engineers at Morton Thiokol had begun developing concern about the temperature predicted for January 28, and especially about the absence of data concerning how the solid rocket booster field joints might be affected. This led to a teleconference in which officials at Thiokol and the engineers conversed with their representatives at the Kennedy Space Center and Level III representatives of the Marshall Space Flight Center located both at Kennedy and headquarters in Huntsville, Alabama. In the teleconference, which started at approximately 5:45 P.M., EST, managers at Morton Thiokol recommended that the launch be delayed until noon or later on January 28. This suggestion resulted in the scheduling of another teleconference that took place about three hours later. Having discussed the matter with their engineering staff, Thiokol managers recommended that the launch not occur unless the temperature were 53 degrees F or higher. The two managers involved at this point were Robert K. Lund and Joe C. Kilminster. George B. Hardy, Deputy Director of Science and Engineering, who was participating from Marshall headquarters, said he was "appalled" by the recommendation, or at least by the analysis of data on which it was based.

NASA officials, including Hardy, Lawrence Mulloy, and Stanley Reinartz, continued to challenge the recommendation. This prompted Kilminster to request time for Thiokol managers and engineers to caucus. By 11:00 P.M., the teleconference resumed, and Kilminster now indicated that discussion with engineering led management to agree that the data were inconclusive, that the primary O-ring had a considerable tolerance for erosion, and that even if it failed to seal, the secondary ring would. Kilminster was asked to put the recommendation in writing and to "fax" it both for the Kennedy and Marshall Centers.[4]

In their testimony to the Commission, both managers and engineers at Thiokol reported feeling pressured to change their recommendation. For instance, Brian Russell from the Solid Rocket Motor Office indicated that several statements made in the teleconference and during the caucus he took as signs of pressure. One was the statement by Hardy that he was "appalled," another was a caustic query about whether NASA was expected to wait until April to launch, and a third was an allegation by Lawrence Mulloy, the person in charge of Marshall's Solid Rocket Booster Program, that Thiokol engineers were being illogical in their choice of an acceptable temperature.[5] Russell characterized the perceived pressure as a "distinct feeling that we were in the position of having to prove that it [the launch] was unsafe instead of the other way around, which was a totally new experience" (*Official Transcript* 1487). The feeling was also reported by Robert Lund, Thiokol's Vice President for Engineering and one of the four officials who reversed his and Kilminster's original recommendation: "We had to prove to them that we weren't ready, and so we got ourselves into the thought process that we were trying to find some way to prove to them it wouldn't work, and we were unable to do that" (1456–57). Similar observations were offered by Roger Boisjoly (1421–22), a member of the Seal Task Force, and Allen J. McDonald, Thiokol's manager for the Space Booster Project (1303–04). McDonald was present at the Kennedy Space Center and persisted in his opposition even after his colleagues at Thiokol reversed themselves. The perception of external pressure from Level III eventually led to a state in which the Thiokol managers succumbed to a self-induced pressure. Robert Lund, for example, was reportedly told by Jerald Mason, Senior Vice President, Wasatch Operations, to "take off his engineering hat and put on his management hat" (1383).

Level III managers testified that there was no pressure being placed on Morton Thiokol for a change in recommendation. According to George Hardy, "I was fully prepared, and so stated . . . that I would accept a recommendation of Thiokol, or the opposite of that, I would not go against the recommendation of Thiokol" (1621). As Commission Chairman Rogers pointed out, however, the manner in which Hardy had registered has initial reaction, his persistent disagreement with the engineering analysis, and Mulloy's reference to whether he was expected to delay the launch until April surely contributed to the feeling that there was strong disagreement with the recommendation not to launch (1622).

Whether external pressure existed or not, the perception that it did apparently constituted a powerful stimulus for Thiokol managers to feel obliged to reverse their recommendation. They did so in the absence of any acknowledged expressions of support and despite the fact that they had previously been apprised of the potential seriousness of an O-ring failure in a July 31, 1985, memorandum from Roger Boisjoly, in which he indicated that unless the problem were attended to, there could be "a catastrophe of the highest order" (1406).

The change in position is consistent with what one could expect from a substantial literature on susceptibility to social influence and responses to opposition displayed by those not in positions of control. Possibly anticipating the loss of future contracts with NASA, Thiokol managers interpreted disagreement with their company's engineering analysis, whether correctly or not, as one of those situations in which a change agent leaves the target with little or no choice. In addition, once this perception had crystalized, reluctance to support the decision was greeted with the compliance-gaining strategy that Jerald Mason displayed in urging Robert Lund to start thinking as an administrator rather than as an engineer. Continued opposition from those lacking decisional authority—most notably, Roger Boisjoly and Arnold Thompson, a supervisor in the Rocket Motor Cases Division—was without effect.[6]

A more defensive reaction to opposition by Allen McDonald was shown by Level III managers following the teleconference. Concerned that previous testing of the solid rocket booster O-rings had qualified them only to a low temperature of 40 degrees F, McDonald testified that "I told them that I sure wouldn't want to be the person who had to stand in front of a board of inquiry to explain why we launched this outside of the qualification of the solid rocket motor or any shuttle system. When I made that statement, no one commented on that" (1295). Pressing further, McDonald indicated that the combination of the potential O-ring problem, the icing on the launch pad, and the likelihood that high wind velocity would jeopardize recovery of the solid rocket boosters from the Atlantic, he reportedly was informed that these additional matters were not his concern (1296–97). He testified being assured, however, that his concern about the O-ring would be passed on to responsible officials at Level II. As events developed, the problem was not mentioned in the subsequent communication to those at Level II.

Rigid Observation of Role Boundaries

The presence of perceived pressure among the managers and engineers at Level IV, in and of itself, does not fully account for Morton Thiokol's reversal of its initial recommendation. Since individuals involved were not reluctant to give their views when asked, it is difficult to believe that cessation of opposition was exclusively a response based on any fear of reprisal. This motive may have been stronger in the case of some Level IV managers, although Kilminster and Lund denied harboring any such fears (1498). In any event, the engineers had little to be concerned about in this respect. They had initiated the discussion in the first place. It may have been that they simply reached the point where further argument seemed pointless. A more compelling and generally applicable explanation lies in the rigidity with which roles in a hierarchically arranged decision structure are often enacted. At least, in this specific case, there is considerable evidence of a reluctance to cross role boundaries.

Roger Boisjoly, possibly the most vocal of the engineers at Morton Thiokol, indicated such reluctance in his statement to the Commission that "I had my say, and I never take any management right to take the input of an engineer and then make a decision based upon that input, and I truly believe that" (1421). Brian Russell, another of the Thiokol engineers, said, "It was a management decision at the vice presidents' level, and they had heard all they could hear, and I felt there was nothing more to say . . ." (1487). Ben Powers, an engineer at Marshall, agreed with Thiokol's engineering staff. When asked if he had reported that to his superior, George Hardy, Powers responded, "No sir, I report to Mr. John McArty" (1946). Unfortunately, McArty was not a person who could affect the launch decision.

A much more explicit illustration of the unwillingness to violate role boundaries surfaced in the testimony of William Lucas, Director of the Marshall Space Flight Center. Although Lucas was not involved in the teleconference, Lawrence Mulloy and Stanley Reinartz, Shuttle Projects Office Manager, apprised him before the teleconference and the following morning that concern had been expressed about weather conditions, but not specifically about the possible effect of temperature on the functioning of the O-rings. When asked why he did not report the concern to Level II, however generally it had been conveyed to him, Lucas's response was, "That is not the reporting channel" (1877). Reinartz, whose reporting channel was directly to Level II, and to Arnold Aldrich, in particular, failed to give any indication of the controversy that had earlier occurred to Level II managers because in his judgment the issue "had been satisfactorily dispositioned" (1678).

Several individuals at Levels III and II admitted in their testimony that, had they known of the opposition of the Thiokol engineers following the caucus, or even among personnel at Marshall, they would not have recommended or supported launching *Challenger.* George Hardy was particularly emphatic on this point in the February 26 hearing (1630). Stanley Reinartz asked everyone participating in the teleconference if there were any disagreement with the Thiokol managers' revised recommendation (1666). Since none was expressed, as far as Marshall Space Flight Center officials were concerned, the matter was closed.

The engineers at Thiokol had had a final chance to register opposition, but they apparently felt at this point that it was not their place to do so. Even Allen McDonald, who continued arguing with Marshall officials after the teleconference, confessed not carrying his concerns forward to Level II because the responsibility belonged to Level III managers (1310). He did not even ask whether the concern had been conveyed when at a later point he visited Cecil Houston's office where Marshall managers were engaged in a teleconference with Arnold Aldrich, the Level II official responsible for preflight readiness reviews (1298–99). NASA's policy, according to Aldrich, requires that "critical" concerns be brought to the attention of Level II and Level I (2538–41). Since the established reporting channel is from IV to III to II to I, however, McDonald believed the relaying of his arguments to be a Level III responsibility and assumed that they had been conveyed.

As the preceding review makes clear, a number of participants found themselves in a conflict situation insofar as their proper roles were concerned. The conflict stemmed from the discrepancy between what these individuals felt needed to be done and the belief that their particular positions prevented them from exceeding the limits of their authority. To the extent that a person believes he or she has no right to cross boundaries, conflict is likely to be resolved precisely in the manner represented by the preceding examples. Were the individuals involved less "morally oriented" (to use Gross, Mason, and McEachern's terminology), the resolution of conflict more than likely would have been based on a perception of costs and related sanctions. Since none indicated that he feared punishment or even expected it, propriety appears to have been the standard by which role conflicts were managed.

Deutsch and Krauss have also noted that "the more rigorously roles are defined, the more stringently are their prescriptions enforced, and the more difficult it is for a person to resolve the conflict by deviating from them" (178). This seems to be an apt description of what occurred in the several cases cited. The mode of conflict resolution chosen was as one would expect from the stringency of role definitions in a complex decision structure. Whether stringency of role prescriptions or the moral orientation of the actors provides the better explanation cannot be determined without additional evidence. Whatever the case, the testimony of individuals who may have been able to prevent the launch clearly suggests an almost unwavering observance of perceived role requirements that ultimately prevented important information from reaching others responsible for the final decision.

Questionable Reasoning

Despite the fact that several people at both Levels IV and III either succumbed to perceived pressure or displayed a reluctance to exceed their authority, enough information was available to Level III, II, and I managers to cast serious doubt on the wisdom of proceeding with the launch. Not only were those at Level III aware of concerns about the solid rocket booster field joints, they had been apprised by ice team member Charles Stevenson of a separate concern about icing and its possible damage to the tank (*Official Transcript* 1712). In addition, North American Rockwell officials had independently expressed the feeling to Level II managers that the shuttle could be damaged. Martin Cioffoletti testified that at approximately 9:00 A.M. on January 28 he informed Arnold Alrich, head of the Mission Management Team, that he could not assure flight safety (1804–05). Similar accounts were offered by Robert Glaysher and Rocco Petrone (1806–07). Since Rockwell is the designer and builder of the shuttle, such concerns presumably would carry weight, but in this instance obviously did not. Although the heavy icing proved not to be a cause of the accident, the feeling that it posed a substantial threat to flight safety was strong enough to warrant delay, if not cancellation, of the launch.

With considerable doubt being expressed about the desirability of launching for at least three different reasons, one wonders why the mission was not halted at some level. Surely, enough of those in positions of authority were aware of enough of the concerns to reconsider the wisdom of proceeding. On the surface, it appears as if key figures simply ignored the information they were receiving. A closer examination of their behavior, however, suggests that the difficulty may not have been so much a matter of ignoring information, but more a matter of discounting its importance. This tendency was abetted by inferential shortcomings that several individuals displayed. In some instances, critical decision-makers' logical deficiencies involved inferences about what others were thinking. In other cases, the problem arose in the interpretation of information about the shuttle system. Regardless of the focus, questionable judgment contributed to seeing problems as less serious than they were considered by those recommending delay. Several specific examples serve to illustrate the point.

Following the caucus at Morton Thiokol, Stanley Reinartz, as previously mentioned, asked all of those involved in the teleconference if there were any disagreement with the revised recommendation to launch. Hearing none, he concluded that everyone now supported the recommendation. Had such strong opposition not been expressed prior to the caucus, inferring agreement from the absence of disagreement might be quite reasonable. Under the circumstances of the preceding three hours, however, such a conclusion would appear to be doubtful at best.

The inference drawn by Reinartz is perhaps more easily excused than a similar one made by Jerald Mason. Reinartz was not party to the discussion when during the teleconference Thiokol went off net to caucus, but Mason was one of the participants. The engineers had unanimously opposed launching prior to the caucus, and in the discussion no one indicated that he had changed his position. Yet when asked by Chairman Rogers if anyone changed his mind, Mason replied, "Well, I would say then that I would have to look at my list here. Based upon the conversation that we had there, I felt that Mr. McBath and Kapp were supportive. And Mr. Brinton, who was at Marshall, it is harder to judge, because he didn't have a lot to say. What we were faced with was that the outspoken individuals—and the rest participated to a lesser degree. But I believe that we are familiar enough with the people and their manner to be able to judge their feelings, and we heard what they had to say" (1363–64). In fact, none of Thiokol's engineers admitted to a change of heart, but clearly, the four managers who reversed the original recommendation made no effort to find out.

Still another instance of inferring what others were thinking involved Robert Lund. At first, he was reluctant to alter his position but, when asked to take off his engineering hat, did change. As we pointed out earlier, this reversal, in part, seemed to be a response to internal pressure, but, as Lund testified, it was also a result of his having inferred that Marshall would probably overrule Thiokol whether he changed or not. When Rogers suggested that NASA (Level III managers at Marshall) had indicated that they would not fly without a written report saying that Thiokol approved the launch, Lund's response was, "I didn't know NASA would accept that" (1476). Since NASA had never in its history launched over the objection of a contractor, the more appropriate inference in this case was that a negative recommendation would be respected. Yet, Lund acted in accordance with the less probable outcome. This particular inferential shortcoming has been noted in a large body of research on social judgment in which people tend to ignore baseline data in calculating probabilities (Nisbett and Ross). The work of Tversky and Kahneman is especially relevant in this regard.

As a final illustration of the tendency to draw unwarranted inferences about the contents of others' thoughts, Arnold Aldrich made clear that he concluded from Rockwell representatives' comments that "they did not intend to ask me not to launch" (*Official Transcript* 1843). Even though those very same individuals testified that they had recommended against launching, Aldrich reasoned that because past interactions with Rockwell personnel had not resulted in negative recommendations, the current concern was insufficiently indicative of a reluctance to proceed. As we shall point out later, the manner in which Rockwell officials expressed their opposition may have facilitated Aldrich's erroneous conclusion. On the other hand, it is curious that the absence of a supportive recom-

mendation could so easily be taken as a sign of the lack of opposition. Again, the reasoning process seems to have been that one can
accurately infer what another is thinking from what he or she fails
to say.

In addition to questionable inferences about what was transpir-
ing in the minds of others, critical ones relating to the assessment
of relevant technical data were in evidence. For instance, in accus-
ing Thiokol engineers of being illogical, Lawrence Mulloy displayed
the very quality he was indicting. Specifically, Thiokol had recommended that the launch not occur at a temperature less than 53
degrees F because they had no experience with the possible effect
of lower temperatures on O-ring erosion and the related escape of
dangerous gases. Mulloy found this to be illogical because, he argued, past launches had occurred at different temperatures in
which erosion and blow-by of the primary seal had occurred, and
there was no correlation of temperature with either the likelihood
or amount of blow-by (1529–30). Why the absence of a systematic
correlation within the available data base would justify taking a
risk outside the data base, however, is not intuitively obvious. The
fact that there was evidence of blow-by at all should have been the
immediate concern, not the magnitude of the correlation of its presence and amount with a range of temperatures. But even if this were
not the main issue, Mulloy's reasoning leaves much to be desired.
His position is rather like arguing that if there is no correlation
between academic success and GRE scores above 1000, then anyone
with a score of less than 1000 could justifiably be admitted to a
graduate program because he or she is just as likely to succeed
academically as to fail.

The non sequitur in both examples should be apparent, and as
Rogers so clearly pointed out in the case of Mulloy's analysis, data
were no more supportive of a decision to launch than one not to
launch: "But they [documents assessing the O-ring problem] don't
say the worst conditions would be acceptable. In other words, they
don't say if the weather was even worse, it [the risk of launching]
would be accepted . . ." (2668). If Mulloy were so concerned about
logic, he might have concentrated more on the consequences of
failure than on the absence of a correlation between temperature
and O-ring erosion. Given the possible costs of being wrong under
the circumstances surrounding the discussion, logic would seem to
demand a cautious rather than risky decision.

George Hardy exhibited a similar line of reasoning to that of
his colleague Lawrence Mulloy. Since the data involving the effects
of temperature on the likelihood of O-ring blow-by were inconclusive, in his thinking, there was stronger justification for launching
than not launching (1590). When it was suggested that NASA had
been informed that blow-by of the primary seal could have catas-

trophic consequences, Hardy's response was that that possibility was also "true of every other flight we have had" (1590). His reasoning seemed to be that because past risk taking had not led to a catastrophic result, such a result was not likely to occur in the future even under conditions of unknown risk.[7] The probability of a possible event, of course, is not reduced by virtue of its not having occurred. Moreover, even an unlikely event over the range of situations in which it can occur may have a relatively high probability of occurring at least once. For example, if the probability of a one on the roll of a die is 0.167, in six successive tosses, the probability of a one's occurring at least once is $1 - 0.833$. In other words, the probability of at least one occurrence is a function of the joint probability of the number's successive nonoccurrence, or in this particular situation approximately 0.67.

From the perspective of utility theory, deciding to proceed with a launch outside a data base that permits one to calculate the relative probability of success and failure (in this case, the proper functioning of the O-rings) was irrational. A logical and, hence, preferred choice is one that has the greatest expected utility after both relative costs and benefits of the alternatives have been taken into consideration. Expected utility is a multiplicative function of the likelihood of a possible outcome and its value or importance (Arkes and Hammond 4–7). Regardless of the value of a successful launch, in the absence of an adequate basis for determining its likelihood, the expected utility of a decision not to launch would, logically speaking, have to be presumed greater.

Possibly the most serious logical deficiency directly affecting Level IV and III managers' tendency to discount the concerns of Thiokol's engineers had to do with their interpretation of the Criticality classification of 1 that had been assigned to the O-ring joint seals. As we indicated earlier, a Criticality rating of 1 is assigned if a component in failing to function properly could cause failure of the entire system. Although this particular component had carried the classification since 1982, it was routinely waived as a launch constraint. This waiver appears to have been the result of Thiokol managers' treating the classification as if it were C1R, that is, as part of a redundant system, in which failure of the primary seal would be offset by proper functioning of the secondary seal. Previous testing had shown that up to a point the system had this kind of redundancy. According to Jerald Mason, "the charts that we had said that if you seat in 160 milliseconds that . . . during the first 160 milliseconds the joint is closed enough that the secondary O-ring actually provides redundancy" (1348).

To have redundancy under some conditions, however, does not warrant the conclusion that a system is redundant. In fact, to the extent that any probability of failure in the backup exists, a system by definition is not redundant. As Commissioner Ride suggested, "[I]t sounds to me like you're trying to exercise some kind of engineering judgment on whether you can consider this a 1R or a 1, and I just don't think that the system allows that. I think that once something is classified as Criticality 1, that sets a red flag in everyone's mind that that is an extremely dangerous situation" (1349). There is an obvious circularity in the reasoning displayed by Mason and others who found reason to minimize the significance of the C1 rating. The thinking was that if the system worked under certain conditions, there would be no problem. Therefore, it was acceptable to treat the classification as if it were actually C1R on the assumption that such conditions would exist. This assumption persisted even though the original cause for concern among engineers had been prompted by the discovery of erosion of a secondary O-ring in an earlier flight. This suggested not only that the primary seal had failed but that the secondary seal could also fail if the amount of erosion were great enough.

As a final illustration of the kind of questionable reasoning some of the individuals involved in the decision to launch *Challenger* displayed is a curious inconsistency in Lawrence Mulloy's thinking. On the one hand, he argued with Thiokol engineers that temperature was not on his list of launch constraint criteria; therefore, no established basis existed for considering temperature in determining whether or not to recommend launch (1537–41). On the other hand, a classification of C1 did constitute a launch constraint that he routinely waived. His behavior suggests the line of reasoning that if a launch constraint would prevent a flight that is otherwise recommended, under certain conditions, one can overlook the constraint. However, if the recommendation is unfavorable, its appropriateness can be justified only on the grounds of nonconformity with previously approved criteria. In other words, if the disposition to launch is unfavorable, one goes by the book.[8] If it is favorable, one has greater freedom to deviate from established constraints. This kind of inconsistency seems to be at the base of the alleged shifting presumption in launch decisions that several individuals characterized as having to prove that it is unsafe to fly rather than proving that it is safe.

Questionable reasoning per se does not inevitably lead to improper decisions. It certainly increases their likelihood, however, under circumstances in which such thinking influences the resolution of issues central to a decision. Gouran has discussed this relationship in some detail ("Inferential Errors"), but for purposes of illustration, consider a situation in which one is trying to decide whether to replace a defective headlight at the point of discovery or to wait until later when he or she has more time, and making the replacement will be less of an inconvenience. If the person, in question, were to infer that "I probably won't be driving much at night or any place where I am likely to be stopped by the police" he or she might easily decide to wait, only later to be on the receiving end of a ticket or, perhaps worse, involved in an accident. The inference, while reasonable from the point of view of the person making it, nonetheless, would prove to have been in error.

The type of thinking in which questionable or erroneous inferences influence decisional choices has been documented in both case studies and laboratory research. Gouran, for instance, analyzed the transcripts of conversations between Richard Nixon and others involved in the Watergate coverup and found that decisions to prolong it were consistently accompanied by erroneous predictive inferences ("Communicative Influences"). Irving Janis reported evidence of faulty predictions in such historical incidents as the Japanese attack of Pearl Harbor, the crossing of the 38th parallel in the Korean conflict, the Bay of Pigs invasion, and the escalation of United States involvement in Vietnam. Finally, Hirokawa and Pace determined that ineffective decision-making groups in laboratory settings showed relatively little propensity to examine unwarranted and questionable inferences compared to effective groups.

The examples of reasoning we have been discussing have one thing in common. Each shows insufficient attention to the costs of being wrong. A more thorough consideration of the alternatives would entail asking whether the costs of being wrong in one's inferences are worth the risk relative to the value of being right. In the *Challenger* episode, the costs of being wrong were "catastrophic," as against the only apparent gains in being correct of getting back on schedule and avoiding monetary costs to which further delay might lead. Persons reasoning well, we can presume, would have been more sensitive to the implications of the alternative courses of action available to them if the inferences justifying each proved to be in error.

Ambiguous and Misleading Use of Language

As one reads the transcripts of the Rogers Commission hearings, a style of language that may have contributed to officials displaying the sorts of inferential inadequacies noted becomes increasingly conspicuous. If reports of the interactions among those involved are accurate, then one can conclude that several parties who may have been able to exert greater influence not to launch failed to do so partly because of the ambiguous way in which they both voiced concerns and responded to questions about them.

Fearing that ice might damage the shuttle, Rockwell representatives testified to the Commission that they were opposed to the launch. Yet in reporting their concerns to Arnold Aldrich, no one went so far as to say, "We recommend that you do not launch." Instead, they claimed making such statements as, "we do not have the data base from which to draw any conclusions for this particular situation," "we did not have a sufficient data base to absolutely assure that nothing would strike the vehicle," and "Rockwell cannot assure that it is safe to fly" (*Official Transcript* 1803–06). Saying that one cannot assure that an event will not occur can be as easily construed as meaning the event is unlikely as it can be construed to mean that the event is likely. In fact, the first construal is more probable, as in the case of one's saying, "I cannot be sure that I will not be hit by a car crossing the street." In making this sort of observation, one presumes that one will not be hit. In Rockwell's case, a more direct expression of concern would have been, "We think it is unsafe to launch, and we are recommending that NASA not proceed." Such a direct statement would be extremely difficult for anyone to misinterpret or misunderstand. Chairman Rogers underscored this point in his statement to Arnold Aldrich that NASA's decision-making process was curious for the absence of clear stands among consultative personnel (1940–41).

Another example of the impact of the ambiguous use of language on judgment was revealed in the recommendation that Joe Kilminster sent from Thiokol headquarters to Lawrence Mulloy at the Marshall Space Flight Center. Although the recommended action is clear, the document also contained the statement, "TEMPERATURE DATA NOT CONCLUSIVE ON PREDICTING PRIMARY O-RING BLOW-BY" (*Report* 90). The statement does not indicate the sense in which data were inconclusive or what inconclusiveness might imply about the cautions appropriate to launching. The document further expressed the belief that if the primary O-ring did not seal, the secondary seal would. But there was no explanation of the degree of confidence with which this prediction was made. The categorical nature of the prediction seems oddly contradictory in light of the characterization of the relevant data as "inconclusive."

Lawrence Mulloy took this statement, along with other information, to conclude that there was a high probability of redundancy. Yet, when asked by Commissioner Walker what a "high probability" in this case meant, Mulloy responded, "I don't know. I can't quantify that" (*Official Transcript* 2677). *Probability* is an inexact term unless accompanied by a specific value. In the absence of such a value, Mulloy seemed to take the expression, "high probability," to mean virtual certainty.

Further illustrating the ambiguous use of language is a brief discussion involving William Lucas, Director of the Marshall Space Flight Center. Although not in the reporting chain, Lucas was in-

formed by Stanley Reinartz of Thiokol engineers' concern about the
weather on January 27. He asked to be kept informed. When Lucas
asked Reinartz about the teleconference later on January 28, he was
reportedly told that the engineering staff had "a concern about the
weather, that that had been discussed very thoroughly by the Thiokol people and by the Marshall Space Flight Center, and it had
been concluded agreeably that there was no problem, that he [Rei-
nartz] had a recommendation by Thiokol to launch and our most
knowledgeable people and engineering talent agreed with that"
(1876–77).

If this is an accurate reconstruction, and apparently it is since
Reinartz did not contradict it, one can appreciate the lack of follow-
up by the Director. Due to the omission of specific details, Reinartz's
report, while technically accurate, is also quite misleading. Specifically, it places the focus on general weather conditions, not on the
fact that certain individuals were particularly concerned about the
effect of temperature on the performance of the O-rings. Nor does
the statement provide any indication that Thiokol's original recommendation was not to launch. This is not to say that Reinartz acted
deliberately to mislead. In terms of the impact of the statement,
however, his intentions are beside the point.

The effects of the ambiguous use of language have long been
an object of interest among popular writers (e.g., Newman), general
semanticists (e.g., Chase; Hayakawa), linguists (e.g., Neisser), and
communication theorists (e.g., Berlo; Brown) alike.[9] But it does not
require a theory or voluminous body of research for one to appreciate the simple fact that the more vague and indirect the language
an individual employs, the greater the range of meanings he or she
can evoke. The preceding illustrations suggest that the ambiguous
and sometimes misleading manner in which some people involved
in the *Challenger* case expressed themselves influenced not only the
understanding of those in positions to postpone or terminate the
launch but also their judgment of the wisdom of doing so. Rockwell
officials especially were guilty of expressing opposition in a way
that portrayed their concerns as being far less serious than they
actually were.

Since Level II officials were apparently predisposed to proceed
with the launch, statements suggesting that one could not be certain
that it was safe could easily be assimilated in the manner in which
Sherif, Sherif, and Nebergall's work on social judgment suggests. In
other words, ambiguous language may facilitate one's perceiving
another's position as closer to one's own that it, in fact, is. Ambiguous language can also facilitate the sort of selective perception that
Janis and Mann have noted in various cases of flawed decision making.

Failure to Ask Important Relevant Questions

Although the four factors discussed to this point can help us to understand what, in retrospect, were glaring deficiencies in the decision-making process and which the Rogers Commission identified as the contributing cause of the *Challenger* accident, completing the picture is evidence of the failure of key figures at Levels III, II, and I to ask important questions prior to and during the period in which the decision to launch was forming. The O-ring problem, for instance, did not arise on January 27 for the first time. As we previously indicated, this solid rocket booster component had had a classification of Criticality 1 for several years. L. Michael Weeks, Deputy Associate Administrator for Space Flight at NASA, admitted, moreover, the problem had been noted in every monthly report reviewed at Level I for the past two years (2861ff). Weeks further testified that in August of 1985 he had raised the question with George Hardy at Marshall about the lack of progress. According to Weeks, "Mr. Hardy allayed my concerns" (2861). That his questioning was less than sufficient is suggested in his subsequent confession that, "Maybe I wasn't tough enough . . ." (2862).

Another curious failure to raise questions occurred when the teleconference on January 27 resumed following the caucus of Thiokol personnel. Management at Thiokol had reversed its position on the launch, but no one at Kennedy or the Marshall Space Flight Center asked why or whether the new recommendation had the endorsement of all concerned. Marshall officials testified that they would not have recommended launch if they knew that Thiokol's engineers were still opposed, but they did not make the effort to poll them. Reinartz simply asked if there were any disagreements. Hearing none, as we previously indicated, he assumed consensus and accepted Kilminster's statement that his people had decided the data concerning the O-ring were inconclusive.

As we also earlier pointed out, Allen McDonald, who continued to oppose launch after the teleconference had concluded, did not ask if Lawrence Mulloy had conveyed his concern about the O-rings in his teleconference with Arnold Aldrich. He merely presumed that the concern had been reviewed (1310). Similarly, Jerald Mason found it unnecessary to ask the engineers at the end of the caucus if they remained opposed because, as he claimed, he felt he knew his people well enough to judge what they were thinking (1364). The energy required to verify the suspicions in these two cases would have been minimal, and yet for some reason, the parties involved chose not to take such a simple precautionary measure.

When representatives from Rockwell were expressing their concerns to Level II in the ambiguous manner earlier described, no one raised the obvious question of whether Rockwell was recom-

mending "go" or "no go." Commissioner Kutyna asked Rocco Petrone whether this specific question was raised on the morning of
January 28. Although Petrone responded that Rockwell's earlier report suggested that it was unsafe to fly, insofar as the meeting at
Kennedy was concerned, he could not be sure because he was not
present (1807). Nowhere in the testimony of the Rockwell representatives who were present is there evidence of any NASA official's
having asked the question. The question was not raised, despite the
fact that Aldrich testified that he would never have launched over
a definite "no go" from Rockwell. Apparently, neither he nor other
Level II personnel found it necessary to ask if that was the recommendation (1858).

The failure to ask important questions and its consequences for
effective decision making has been discussed by Hirokawa and
Scheerhorn, and in the present case, their conclusions clearly apply.
Why the individuals in examples cited failed to raise important and
obvious questions, however, is a matter of conjecture. In some instances, the questions may simply not have occurred to them. In
others, there may have been a reluctance to ask a question based on
the individual's sense of propriety. In still others, the person in a
position to raise the question may have anticipated receiving a response he would prefer not to have. The absence of significant questioning at appropriate junctures could have induced a state of plu-
ralistic ignorance—that is, a condition in which several people
acquiesce in an action as a result of perceiving that most, if not all,
others involved favor the actions when, in fact, most may be opposed
(Shaw 444–45). On the other hand, Kruglanski has argued that the
problem in the *Challenger* incident was that most of those involved
were committed to launching. Under these circumstances, the absence of questioning would prevent discovering that there were
good reasons for not proceeding. As Kruglanski suggests, "People
are more likely to stick with a decision . . . if they don't have access
to evidence that the judgment could be incorrect" (48). Questioning
might well have given the committed persons such evidence. Whatever the cause, the absence of questions related to matters affecting
the final decision to launch contributed to a perception at the highest level of the decision hierarchy that the process of review warranted proceeding. In fact, it did not, and the tragedy that followed
will long serve as a painful reminder of how critical the failure to
verify one's interpretations of others' comments by means of such
questions can be.

CONCLUSIONS

NASA had in place a decision structure and related process of review in the Space Shuttle Program that from all appearances pos-

sessed the necessary safeguards for preventing the accident occurring in the case of Mission 51-L. The remarkable series of successes
in the program had reinforced the public's perception of a fail-safe
system and obscured the fact that undesirable risks had been taken
almost from the outset. These successes also presumably contributed to NASA officials' willingness to continue taking risks and
the allegedly shifting presumption of needing to prove that flights
were unsafe rather than safe. The investigation prompted by the
Challenger disaster revealed that persistent problems had not been
satisfactorily addressed and that even previously successful flights
had probably been ill advised. This is clearly the position of Roger
Boisjoly in his recent suit against Morton Thiokol (see Lewis). The
finality of this judgment, however, is perhaps best left to those with
appropriate expertise.

The purpose of this inquiry has been to assess the human factors that seem to have rendered ineffective a decisional process
that, in principle, should have led to a different course of action.
Our analysis has revealed that no matter how carefully crafted a
decision structure may appear in terms of the sequence of analysis
and choice to which it commits decision makers, its effective utilization is still reliant on the social, psychological, and communicative environment in which responsible parties function. In the
case of *Challenger,* there is substantial evidence that influences
from these three domains played an instrumental role in contributing to a choice that, in their absence, most likely would not
have been made. Numerous opportunities to prevent the launch
presented themselves in the 20 hours that preceded, but on each
occasion, one or more of the influences we have identified surfaced
and reduced the chances for altering the collision course upon
which NASA had set itself. A simple act of disagreement by a possibly over self-confident Level III official was to undermine the respect which NASA had achieved and which it must now struggle
to regain (Biddle).

NOTES

1. Among the seven crew members was an elementary public school
   teacher named Christa McAuliffe, whose involvement ostensibly
   was tied to a concern with the need to stimulate public interest
   and, more specifically, to develop appreciation among school-
   aged children for the potential of scientific achievement. Much
   concern had been expressed in recent years about the compara-
   tive lag in the scientific and technical education of American
   children.
2. From Chairman Rogers' letter at the beginning of the *Report of
   the Presidential Commission on the Space Shuttle Challenger
   Disaster* (v). The Commission was created in accordance with

Executive Order 12546 on February 3, 1986, and, in addition to Chairman Rogers, consisted of Neil A. Armstrong, David C. Acheson, Eugene E. Covert, Richard P. Feynman, Robert B. Hotz, Donald J. Kutyna, Sally K. Ride, Robert W. Rummel, Joseph F. Sutter, Arthur B. C. Walker, Jr., Albert D. Wheelon, and Charles E. Yeager. Each of these individuals was selected because of his or her scientific and technical expertise or previous association with the National Aeronautics and Space Administration.

3. Managers at the Marshall Space Flight Center are involved in determining flight readiness in terms of the space shuttle engine, solid rocket booster, and external tank. Flight readiness is assessed on the basis of direct input from contractors and Marshall's own engineering staff. In the case of the solid rocket booster, the contractor is Morton Thiokol. Although contractors are at the fourth level in NASA's launch decision structure, presumably, a negative recommendation will be observed by managers at higher levels of decisional authority.

4. This summary is derived from the chronology presented in the *Report of the Presidential Commission* 104–10.

5. See the testimony of Brian Russell (*Official Transcript* 1484–86). Among other things, Mulloy had argued that if the previous evidence of erosion had occurred at temperatures higher than 53 degrees F, then it was illogical to set a lower temperature.

6. Research on pressure for uniformity and compliance with authority is consistent with these occurrences and has been summarized by Marvin E. Shaw. Stanley Milgram has also shown significant tendency among experimental subjects toward compliance with authority in his extensive program of research on that phenomenon. The communicative behavior of those allegedly exerting pressure is very much like that reported in Stanley Schacter's classic study of conformity. Finally, the behavior aimed at producing concurrence is very similar to that reported in several historical case studies reviewed by Irving Janis.

7. Even more telling of this kind of thinking perhaps is Commissioner Sutter's questioning of Jerald Mason concerning why, if there was a problem above 53 degrees F, Thiokol managers concluded that it would be safe below that temperature (*Official Transcript* 1380). The point here is that if safety were a concern based on a problem within a known temperature range, it probably should have been even more of a concern outside that range. Thiokol managers, however, did not reason that way.

8. It may be noteworthy that Jesse Moore and Arnold Aldrich both later testified that launch constraint criteria could be changed at launch (*Official Transcript* 1910–20). In other words, NASA officials have the power to impose new constraints right up to launch if such action appears to be necessary.

9. The National Council of Teachers of English even has a group committed to combatting what they refer to as "Doublespeak" among government officials and other public personae (see Dietrich). In fact, this organization gave a "doublespeak" award to NASA in late 1986.

WORKS CITED

Arkes, Hall R., and Kenneth R. Hammond, eds. *Judgment and Decision Making.* Cambridge: Cambridge UP, 1986.

Berlo, David K. *The Process of Communication.* New York: Holt, 1960.

Biddle, Wayne. "NASA: What's Needed to Put It on Its Feet." *Discover* Jan. 1987:30–49.

Brown, Roger. *Words and Things.* New York: Free Press, 1958.

Chase, Stuart. *The Tyranny of Words.* New York: Harcourt, 1938.

Deutsch, Morton, and Robert M. Krauss. *Theories in Social Psychology.* New York: Basic Books, 1965.

Dietrich, Daniel. *Teaching about Doublespeak.* Urbana: NCTE, 1976.

Gouran, Dennis S. "Communicative Influences on Decisions Related to the Watergate Coverup: The Failure of Collective Judgment." *Central States Speech Journal* 34 (1984):260–68.

———. "Inferential Errors, Interaction, and Group Decision-Making." *Communication and Group Decision-Making.* Ed. Randy Y. Hirokawa and Marshall Scott Poole. Beverly Hills: Sage, 1986:93–112.

Gross, Neal C., Ward S. Mason, and Alexander W. McEachern. *Explorations in Role Analysis: Studies of the School Superintendency Role.* New York: Wiley, 1957.

Hayakawa, S. I. *Language in Thought and Action.* 2nd ed. New York: Harcourt, 1963.

Hickey, Neil. "The Challenger Tragedy: It Exposed TV's Failures—as Well as NASA's." *TV Guide* 24 Jan. 1987:2–11.

Hirokawa, Randy Y., and Roger Pace. "A Descriptive Investigation of the Possible Communication-Based Reasons for Effective and Ineffective Group Decision-Making." *Communication Monographs* 50 (1983):363–79.

Hirokawa, Randy Y., and Dirk R. Scheerhorn. "Communication in Faulty Group Decision-Making." *Communication and Group Decision-Making.* Ed. Randy Y. Hirokawa and Marshall Scott Poole. Beverly Hills: Sage, 1986:63–80.

Janis, Irving L. *Groupthink.* 2nd ed. Boston: Houghton, 1972.

Janis, Irving L., and Leon Mann. *Decision Making.* New York: Free Press, 1977.

Kruglanski, Arie W. "Freeze-think and the Challenger." *Psychology Today* Aug. 1986:48+.

Lewis, Nancy. "Engineer Sues Thiokol for 'Criminal Homicides'." *Washington Post* 29 Jan. 1987:A15.

Milgram, Stanley, *Obedience to Authority.* New York: Harper Colophon, 1975.

Neisser, Ulrich. *Cognition and Reality.* San Francisco: Freeman, 1976.

Newman, Edwin. *Strictly Speaking.* New York: Warner Books, 1975.

Nisbett, Robert, and Lee Ross. *Human Inference: Strategies and Shortcomings of Social Judgment.* Englewood Cliffs: Prentice, 1980.

Official Transcript Proceedings Before Presidential Commission on Space Shuttle Challenger Accident. Washington, D.C.: Alderson Reporting, 1986.

Report of the Presidential Commission on the Space Shuttle Challenger Disaster. Washington: GPO, 1986.

Schacter, Stanley. "Deviation, Rejection, and Communication." *Journal of Abnormal and Social Psychology* 46 (1951):190–207.

Shaw, Marvin E. *Group Dynamics: The Psychology of Small Group Behavior.* 3rd ed. New York: McGraw, 1981.

Sherif, Carolyn W., Muzafer Sherif, and Roger E. Nebergall. *Attitude and Attitude Change: The Social Judgment-Involvement Approach.* Philadelphia: Saunders, 1956.

Tversky, Amos, and Daniel Kahneman. "Judgment Under Uncertainty: Heuristics and Biases." *Science* 185 (1974):1124–31.

Index

Activity tracks, 61
Aquino, C., 92
Ardrey, R., 32
Asch, S., 51–52, 104, 135
Attitude, 29, 37–41
Attribution, 35–36
Axelrod, R., 126–127

Balance sheet, 144
Balchan, E. M., 150
Bales, R. F., 3, 6, 34, 48, 58, 99, 112, 163–167, 171, 195–209
Barnard, C., 94
Bass, B. M., 87–88, 100–101
Bavelas, A., 5, 23–24
Bay of Pigs. *See* Cuban missile crisis
Belief systems, 14–15
Benne, K. D., 99
Berg, D., 59, 143
Biases, 38
Blake, R., 95–96
Blanchard, K. H., 96–97
Bradford, L. P., 97–99
Bradley, P. H., 113

Brainstorming, 149–152
Burleson, B., 25–26

Cartwright, D., 108, 170
Challenger, 1, 53, 175, 235, 213–235
Choice shifts, 53–54
Churchill, W., 91
Cissna, K. N., 62
Closed-mindedness, 38
Cohen, S. P., 34
Cohesiveness, 106–109
Committee, 2, 4, 9
Communication, 3–4, 7–8, 11–27
    within the group, 11–27
    nets, 23, 25
    nonverbal, 21–23
    patterns, 23–26
Competition, 5
Conflict, 117–128
    definition, 117–118
    between groups, 123–126
    within the group, 119–123
    and interdependence, 117–119

Conflict (*Continued*)
  types: distributive and
    integrative, 120–121
Conformity, 51–53, 135
Contingency model of leadership,
  92–94
Contingency theory of group
  development, 61–62
Cooperation, 5, 48–49, 126–128
Coser, L., 121
Cost and rewards. *See* Exchange
  theories
Creativity
  brainstorming, 149–152
  Delphi method, 152
  modes of decision making,
    148–154
  ways of handling conflict, 119
Credibility, 15–16
Crowell, L., 58
Cuban missile crisis, 9, 134

Davis, J. H., 37–38, 110
DeBono, E., 147–149
Deception, 21
Decision counseling, 144–146
Decision implementation, 81–85
Defensive behavior, 49–51
Delphi method, 152
Deutsch, M., 5, 48, 49, 125–126
Development sequence. *See*
  Phases in group development
Dewey, J., 58

Exchange theories of interaction,
  40–41
Experimental methodology, 5

Facial expressions, 22
Fallacies. *See* Reasoning
Feedback, 59, 158
Festinger, L., 105
Fiedler, F. E., 92–94
FIRO (fundamental interpersonal
  relations orientations). *See*
  Needs
Force-field analysis, 73–74

Galanes, G. J., 209
Gender makeup of group, 112–113
Gergen, K. J., 40, 127

Gergen, M. M., 40, 127
Gestures, 22
Gibb, C. A., 112
Gibb, J., 20, 50, 51, 90–91
Goals, 2, 4, 127–128
Gouran, D. S., 137–138, 213–235
Group
  definition, 3
  development, 58–61
  observation, 157–173
  size, 5, 111–112
"Groupthink," 109, 134–135

Hackman, J. R., 110, 146
Halpin-Winer Scales, 162,
  167–168, 189–192
Haney, W., 50
Hastorf, A., 91
Hersey, P., 96–97
Hirokawa, R. Y., 135–137, 213–235
Homans, G. C., 3, 40
Horney, K., 39–40

Independence, 51–53, 82
Inferences, 135–138, 146–147,
  226–227
Intentions, 13–14
Interaction process analysis,
  163–168, 195–200
Interdependence, 4, 117–119
Interpersonal perception scales,
  162, 178–179
Interpersonal response traits, 39–40

Janis, I. L., 122–123, 134–135,
  143–146
Job diagnostic survey, 110

Kabanoff, B., 121–122
Kelley, H. H., 40, 108
Kemp, S. G., 119
Ketrow, S., 96
Kiesler, C. A., 105
Kiesler, S. B., 105

Laboratory method, 6
Lafferty, J. C., 113
Language, 227–231
  connotative meanings, 13
  denotative meanings, 12–13
  misleading, 227–231

Latane, B., 135
Lateral thinking, 146–148
Leadership
  behaviors, 99–100
  characteristics, 88–89
  functions, 94–96
  group-centered, 97–99
  styles, 89–91
Leathers, D., 59
Leavitt, H. J., 24
Lewin, K., 5, 6, 73
Lippitt, R., 89
Listening, 16–21
  for decisions, 18–20
  with empathy, 20–21
  for information, 17
L.P.C. Scale, 92–94

Maintenance behaviors, 45–46
Managerial grid, 95–96
Mann, L., 122–123, 143–146
Martz, A. E., 213–235
Maslow, A., 30–31, 72
Mayer, M. E., 54
Message, 11–14
Minimax strategy, 41
Mitchell, J., 138
Modes of thinking, 146–149
  lateral, 147–148
  vertical, 148–149
Morris, C. G., 110, 146
Motivations, 30–32
Motives, 15

Nadler, L. B., 161–172
NASA (National Aeronautics and
  Space Administration), 1–2, 9,
  53, 135–136, 213–235
National training laboratories,
  120
Needs, 70–72
  FIRO (fundamental
    interpersonal relations
    orientations), 33
  hierarchy of basic human
    needs, 30–32, 72
  innate, 32
  self-reports, 177–192
Nets, 23–25
Newcomb, T., 3
Nida, S., 135

Nonverbal communication, 21–23
Norms, 4, 103–106
  definition, 104
  emergence, 105–106
  sanctions, 106
Norton, R., 14

Orientations, 29–43, 177–192
Observational approaches to the
    study of groups, 158–161,
    192–209
Osborn, A., 149–151

Parkinson, C. N., 133
Perceptions of others, 35–38,
    51–55, 177–179
Personality
  central dimensions, 34
  problems in group, 138–139
Phases in group development,
    59–63, 69–86
Pond, A. W., 113
Poole, M. S., 61
Prediction, 63–66
Prisoner's dilemma, 48, 49, 119,
    126
Probability, 63–65
Problem analysis, 72–81
  evaluation of solutions, 80–81
  forces, 73–74
  goal setting, 77–78
  identification, 69–72
  information gathering, 78–80
  and logical reasoning, 221–227
  problem analysis, 75
  problem intensity, 75–78
  scope, 73
Procedural problems, 131–133
  evaluating proposals, 133
  problem analysis, 132–133
  rule conflicts and procedures,
    131–132
Process problems, 133–137
  cohesion, 134–135
  conformity pressures, 135
  logical process problems,
    135–137
Project groups, 172–173

Quality circles, 152–154

Rapoport, A., 126–127
Raven, B., 117
Reagan, R., 213
Reasoning
  deductions, 64–65
  fallacies, 18–19, 136–137,
    221–226
  generalizations, 64–65
  induction, 64–65
  syllogism, 65–66
Richards, I. A., 11
Rogers, C., 21
Rogers, W., 1
Rokeach, M., 38
Role playing, 144

Scales
  Halpin-Winer, 162–168, 189–192
  interpersonal perception, 162,
    178–179
  interaction process analysis
    (IPA), 163–166
  Spin-B, 163, 169
  task-person, 179–181
Schachter, S., 108
Schiedel, T. M., 58
Schultz, B., 96–97
Schutz, W., 33, 34
Self-esteem, 138
Self-oriented behavior, 45–48
Self-reports, 177–192
Shaw, M. E., 24, 170
Sheats, P., 99
Sherif, C. W., 123, 127
Sherif, M., 123, 127
Shuttle launch process, 215–
  231
Slater, P. E., 112
Social Contract, The, 32

Social exchange. *See* Exchange
  theories
Sociometric techniques, 192–194
Steiner, I. D., 109–110
Stogdill, R. M., 4, 87
Stohl, C., 154
Stokes, J. P., 107–108
Strodtbeck, F. L., 58
Superordinate goals, 127–128
Supportive behavior, 49–50
Survival problems, 13
System for multiple level
  observation of groups
  (Symlog), 200–209
  adjective rating form, 201–202
  dimensions of Symlog model,
  203

Task, 109–111
Task behaviors, 45–46, 160,
  168–170
Team orientation and behavior
  inventory (TOBI), 182–189
T-groups, 6
Thibaut, J. W., 40, 108
T/P (task/person) questionnaire,
  167–170, 179–181
Trust, 48–51
Tuckman, B. W., 59
Types of work, 109–110

Venable, C., 3

Wall, V. D., Jr., 209
Watergate cover-up, 137
White, R., 89
Wilcox, J., 138

Zander, A., 62, 112, 132